R̲e̲ ̲ ̲'ɔnal social work

of related interest

Partnerships in Social Care
A Handbook for Developing Effective Services
Keith Fletcher
ISBN 1 84310 380 X

Collaboration in Social Work Practice
Edited by Jenny Weinstein, Colin Whittington and Tony Leiba
ISBN 1 84310 092 4

Social Work and Disadvantage
Addressing the Roots of Stigma Through Association
Edited by Peter Burke and Jonathan Parker
ISBN 1 84310 364 8

Social Capital and Mental Health
Edited by Kwame McKenzie and Trudy Harpham
Foreword by Richard Wilkinson
ISBN 1 84310 355 9

Fabio Folgheraiter

Relational social work
toward networking and societal practices

Foreword by Professor Ann Davis

Translated from Italian
by Adrian Belton

First published in the United Kingdom in 2004
by Jessica Kingsley Publishers
116 Pentonville Road
London N1 9JB, UK
and
400 Market Street, Suite 400
Philadelphia, PA 19106, USA

www.jkp.com

Copyright © Fabio Folgheraiter 2004
Printed digitally since 2006

Library of Congress Cataloging in Publication Data
Folgheraiter, Fabio.
[Teoria e metodologia del servizio sociale. English]
Relational social work : toward networking and societal practices / Fabio Folgheraiter ; foreword by
Ann Davis ; translated from Italian by Adrian Belton.
p. cm.
Includes bibliographical references and index.
ISBN 1-84310-191-2 (pbk.)
1. Social service--Philosophy. 2. Social service--Practice. 3. Social service--Citizen participation.
4. Social service--Teamwork. 5. Communication in social work. I. Title.
HV40.F615 2004
361.3'01--dc22

2003027952

British Library Cataloguing in Publication Data
A CIP catalogue record for this book is available from the British Library

ISBN-13: 978 1 84310 191 8
ISBN-10: 1 84310 191 2

2

Contents

Foreword
to the English edition

Social work is concerned with achieving negotiated change in the lives of people who face difficulties. Most people who receive social work services are members of disadvantaged, stigmatised and socially excluded groups. In working with these marginalized citizens, social workers actively engage with the social- seeking ways to enable individuals, their families and communities to interact productively with the society in which they live. In doing this they deliver moral, cultural and social messages about the position and value of service users in the societies in which they live.

Social work requires a knowledge base that critically addresses private troubles and public issues. Conceptual frameworks that explain the insecurity, pain and confusion that individuals experience in their private lives as well as those that explore and acknowledge the diverse legal, political, cultural and social contexts in which individuals live. Whilst social work has an international presence it takes distinct national forms. Its interventions are shaped and reflect state welfare, social movements, civil society and academic and professional discourses. These interrelated factors in driving the direction of social work theory and practice contribute to its rich diversity within and across nation states.

Social work has from its nineteenth century origins worked to effect change locally, nationally and globally. Social work was part of the welfare structures imposed by colonising European nation states. At the same time social work innovators and pioneers chose to meet and exchange ideas and practice wisdom with their peers from other countries. These traditions of international exchange have provided a rich resource for social work as an academic discipline in building theory and practice systematically and critically. In the twenty first century debates about the ways in which globalisation is impacting on the different and distinct national traditions that shape exchanges between social workers and citizens are contributing to this resource.

It was on a European social work exchange that I first met the author of this book. Teaching social work students and practitioners at Trento University in the Spring of 2002, we found ourselves discovering similarity and difference in the ways in which social work is understood, practiced and researched in Italy and England. What I learnt from our exchanges not only stimulated my interest in the Italian approach to social work theory and practice, it led me to reflect on the directions we are currently taking in social work in Britain. In extending these reflections by reading this book I deepened my understanding of the style, direction and dominant discourses in British and Italian social work.

Fabio Folgheraiter takes as his starting point the relational hub of what currently constitutes the practice and theory of social work and social care. From this position he develops an approach to building theoretically informed, socially relevant and individually transforming practice. His concern is to both understand and engage the expertise and commitment of those who comprise the networks of individuals in difficulties. In carefully considering what such networks have to offer to the practice and theorising of social work he engages with the critical issues of power and the social competence as they inform and shape the negotiated interventions of social workers in the lives of those who face social exclusion and stigma.

Fabio Folgheraiter argues that to be effective social work needs to pay close attention to the ways in which individuals understand their needs as well as the ways in which they meet them through their networks. In pursuing this approach he demonstrates the importance of practitioners tuning into the worlds in which service users live their lives. He demonstrates that by making these connections social workers open up the possibility of releasing the energies and potential of networks within civil society to effect positive change. This approach necessarily involves a repositioning of social work in relation to the state and civil society. It also promotes a view that those who become service users have an active part to play in building therapeutic responses to their problems.

This book offers intellectual perspectives that will assist British practitioners and academics to think about the impact that the increasingly procedural and legalised climate in which social work has been confined over the past decade has had on their practice and understandings. The richness of the case material the author draws on reaffirms the importance of making the service user central to thought and action in social work. Because of this it raises critical questions about the scope and direction of current debates in Britain, in particular evidence based interventions and the measurement of outcomes. At the same time it has much to offer to current debates on partnership with service users, their families and communities.

In making a contribution to the international social work literature this book reaffirms the importance to social work theory and practice of recognising, across our differences, common concerns with social change, social ideas and social movements.

Birmingham, June 2003 Professor Ann Davis

Introduction to
the English edition

This book is based on a broader and more systematic work published in Italy in 1998 with the title *Theory and Methodology of Social Work: The Networking Perspective*. It has been conceived for students attending university courses in social work and partly reflects the distinctive nature of personal social services and social care in Italy.

Italy has a traditional welfare state apparatus that is 'good enough', but not to the extent that it could ever claim to be exhaustive. Alongside the considerable development of statutory community services in the traditional areas of community care and child protection, the past two decades have seen a perhaps unparalleled development of a non-profit Third Sector endowed with substantial decision-making and operational autonomy from the state, although it depends on the latter financially. The 'social cooperative' movement has more than 4000 cooperative enterprises for solidarity purposes scattered across the country, and voluntary organizations are also well represented. User and carer movements have developed a variety of community initiatives, ranging from socio-cultural awareness campaigns to the creation of organizations for the autonomous delivery (or in some cases jointly with 'friendly professionals') of personal social services, conventional as well as innovative. The '*market*' dimension of social care has remained generally limited, and it has never been promoted by national legislation of neoliberalist thrust, as has happened in other European countries. Only in recent years has debate begun on care quasi-markets, and it is only in the north of the country that we can see a rapid evolution of markets in social care. Throughout the country, however, the traditional family base is still quite solid, so that informal care acts as the keystone for Italy's mixed welfare system in its entirety.

A network of relations has developed among these three systems (statutory, independent and informal) in accordance with what typically happens in mature welfare economies. But the distinctive feature of Italy is that these connections can be better viewed as *personal* relations: that is, as initiatives which are not wholly *prescribed* as to the functional roles performed by the multiple agents undertaking them. This can obviously be said about informal agents, but the same applies to welfare professionals. These have generally been able to enjoy relative freedom of action because of the absence of the stringent political and managerial control, although this is now being invoked – for perhaps misconceived reasons of efficiency – from various quarters.

Numerous Italian social practitioners, in fact, have performed a truly 'societal' role, that is, an enabling role with regard to numerous other agents involved in local welfare practices. Often, their action as community 'catalysts' has taken place without full (or even sufficient) cognitive awareness of the intrinsically relational nature of caring situations. Understandably, the greatest margins of freedom are available in the Third Sector. Thousands (literally) of professionals – not only qualified social workers but also other experts (social pedagogues, special educators, youth workers, community psychologists) – have worked together with even larger numbers of volunteers, in collaboration with colleagues in the public services, on the one hand, and with thousands of users and carers on the other. Within the Italian Third Sector has developed an approach to professional practice which falls under the general heading of the 'social model of caring' as opposed to the ponderous 'curing/medical paradigm'. In fact, the system of social (non-medical) expertise in direct practice has been able to play a strongly independent role in the midst of civil society, the management of services, and the policy-making system.

There has arisen over the years something that approaches the ideal type of the 'welfare society'. Following Donati (1991), I call this systemic pattern 'relational' or 'reticular' because it is an 'emergent effect' of the (relatively) free actions of the numerous subjects (including statutory professionals) that weave it together. At least in its more efficacious manifestations in the reflexive sense, this model gives us a glimpse of what the 'civil welfare' or 'welfare society' might be like. Of course, a participatory policy of this scope has not been planned; nor perhaps could it be. It cannot spring from the mind of an enlightened policy maker. The welfare activation of local communities is a process that requires great freedom, and this need not necessarily be free-market liberal or entrepreneurial. It requires a sense of independence rooted in the fabric of society and its cultural patterns. It therefore goes without saying that these are extremely long-term processes specific to national contexts. If we look at the Italian example, we find confirmation of the idea that one of the crucial factors is a certain weakness – or, if one prefers, the limited power – of the public welfare authorities. It is more likely that power will be 'transferred' and diffused in society – to reason with the logic of empowerment – if it is not overly concentrated within one institutional context. But at the same time it is essential that the public institutions should be active and create a solid, albeit 'light', framework of governance, able to support and sustain societal action.

Paradoxically, in Italy the development of a 'welfare society' has been facilitated by the constraints of the expert's technical cultures (managerial and professional) in the conventional welfare state system, despite the indubitable and evident presence of the latter. We may say that the 'actors' concerned, at different levels, have shown 'good will' and a reasonable hope that in the end they will do well, rather than the certainty beforehand that they know exactly 'what' to do and 'how' to do it. In sectors where 'lofty' public policies (based on the hubris and confidence of the planners) have been hazarded, closely targeted on phenomena deemed socially dangerous, and supported by generous public expenditure on highly formal and authoritarian statutory agencies, the results have been generally modest. This has been the case in the field of drug addiction, for example. In contrast, in sectors where the state has done what it could but nothing more, one has seen civil society, when not obstructed by an excessively strong statutory monopoly, being galvanized into action. The public authorities have not suffocated the parallel system of community action. Indeed, they have supported and financed it (with a certain generosity perhaps promoted by political interests, but that is beside the point), and this somewhat confused approach has led to good being done. A case in point is mental health, where the Italian state, with the notorious Basaglia law of 1978, closed down the country's psychiatric hospitals practically overnight. This hasty decision off-loaded onto families, intermediate societal bodies and also reflexively onto itself, a task that was impossible to achieve in isolation, or even initially by all the parties together. The challenge for the state was to meet its promise to introduce on a large scale the community services piloted here and there in local-level projects. There followed difficult years for patients and their families and for mental health professionals as well. However, the need to cope with emergencies and with the problem as a whole, without the illusion that this was going to be easy, spurred the energies of Italian society in an enterprise that was apparently impossible, and even senseless, but which in the end was accomplished by the social body as a whole through a comprehensive learning experience.

A similar dynamic was triggered by the law of 1975 which required the full inclusion of learning disabled children in public schools of all type and level, when the trained personnel required were simply not available. In this case, too, the effort required was enormous (by schools, families, social services and local communities), but equally enormous was the cultural change brought about as regards the 'normalization' processes and the professional growth of the practitioners involved.

The culture of 'care by the community' has developed over the years, giving rise to initiatives that have confirmed its validity. Indeed, the more 'radical' these empowerment and participatory practices among community agents (users, families, volunteers, practitioners, etc.), the clearer the empirical evidence of their efficacy. Of course, this trend has not been a one-way process or without contradictions. There has obviously been no lack of attempts by professional experts and institutional powers to control social processes; indeed, as I have said, in some sectors they have been tenacious. It is precisely this resilience, however, that is useful because it highlights the contrast between the vitality and humanity of shared 'poor' practices and the slow and inexorable entrenchment of numerous authoritarian initiatives of positivist (and also post-positivist) character.

The writing of this book has been made possible by careful observation of the success of relational practices in Italy; one might even say that these successful practices have written the book. At the same time it has been prompted by the need to reinforce such best practices, if possible, by means of a tentative theory that explains and thereby consolidates their functioning. Despite the 'evident' success of these societal movements, their protagonists run the risk to be unable to specify what it is they have achieved, or how they have done so. They are able to see these 'lay' practices work, but they are not always able to give the appropriate importance to them. They conceptualise their actions as those of 'true' specialists and regret the absence of what might traditionally been regarded as technical or specialist skills. They think: 'we're forced to do as best we can on our own, because we still don't have the right specialists. If we did, that would be ideal!'. It is necessary to forcefully argue the opposite: that relational practices work precisely because the specialists, so implacably able to solve problems, are lacking. If they existed, they would impede the lay practitioners in some way, and there would be nothing in their place. Professional interventions in social care seem be effective if (and only if) practitioners humbly acknowledge the limitations of the self-referential skills and seek to overcome them by means of 'external' connection with societal competences.

The book is not descriptive in its intent. Only in its final part do the case studies give a brief anecdotal account of the societal initiative of perhaps greatest importance in Italy: a huge social self-help movement (consisting of more than

1200 groups in every part of the country) promoted by families with alcohol-related problems working with professionals involved on a voluntary basis. The main aim of the book is instead to provide the basis for a mode of reflexive reasoning which, although widely set out in the specialist literature since the pioneering works by Schön (1991), is not always comprehensible to the majority of social workers. It aims to contribute to the growing critique of positivist models of social work practice at the same time as arguing the need for theoretically grounded models of practice.

The Italian version of this book was written primarily to foster basic theoretical insights into relational/reflexive/constructivist practices among students about to embark upon the profession, and who might therefore have the good fortune to absorb this model without the fatigue of first dismantling a 'wrong' one. For them it is vital that the message delivered with their training should be coherent with the complex nature of social care. Secondly, the book was intended for Italian social workers who had already had first-hand experience of reflexive/relational practices. The aim was to persuade them to continue to act relationally – that is, without a solid theoretical-methodological basis of positivist stamp, and without feeling themselves to be any poorer because of it. They have also had the good fortune to live with the postmodern paradox pointed out by Morin (1986), namely that it is precisely the absence of too solid bases (of structuralist sclerosis, one might say) that enables one to do good in the flux of social care. It is this awareness that professional planning must be in flux, too, that should be fostered and made the basis (anti-basis?) of their expertise.

The book was also written bearing in mind those practitioners who are not only hostile to such insights, practitioners 'with their feet on the ground' who do not see how the professional methodology can be written in any other terms than the 'evidence-based' scientific ones considered to be uniquely legitimate in social work. The intention was to open some chink in their basically sensible, but quite ingenuous, conviction.

Why an English language version of my book? In many respects, the reflexive topics new to the Italian public have been widely debated in the Anglo-Saxon literature. However, pioneering debates in journals and books are one thing, the full cultural acceptance of ideas so counter-intuitive is another. Another work which adds itself to this difficult emerging paradigm may not be so superfluous, therefore. The principal purpose of the book is to provide basic insight into the reflexive/relational approach. But it also attempts to carry forward a concrete methodological discourse, to outline a mental framework (a minimum of structure is necessary!) which enables professionals to handle the theory agilely without being mired in confusion. The methodological scheme is centred on the idea of 'relational guidance' and the 'capacity for action' *(agency)* of interest-bearers in care situations. As said, such theory finds informal empirical support in numerous documented exemplary experiences, which in turn are part of a far-reaching international search for a 'third way' in the field of welfare, beyond the 'standard provisions' of the state and of care markets. From this point of view the book may be of interest to social workers in other countries.

As regards the United Kingdom in particular, a number of further aspects require mention. In that country, since the early 1990s attempts have been made to loosen, or even to get rid of, the close statist post-Seebohm constraints by liberalization from laws and ministerial guidelines. Shifting from a conception of the social worker as an across-the-board deliverer of public services, to a case manager who 'purchases' market services on behalf of users, is an approach that undoubtedly breaks with conventional practice. But is it as 'open' and relational as it should be? The liberal option increases the choices available to the service user/consumer, but at the same time vital spaces of autonomy are closed or proceduralized, not only at the expense of professional action. Relational theory interrogates whether it is possible for social workers to be given greater autonomy together with greater accountability (or social responsibility), without the two conflicting.

But is it truly possible to imagine social workers who are fully 'independent' and free in the age of liberalization, and not on the contrary more and more crushed? Is it possible to imagine social workers able to act sensibly without shielding themselves behind the authority that emanates from their public role, and without insulating themselves in the technical efficiency required by the new market ideology? The Italian experience of 'non-liberalist liberty' cautiously suggests that it is possible. The theory of relational agency embraced by this book suggests that social workers should harness their professional action (and there-fore also their certainties drawn from science and conventional wisdom) to facilitate social relations in local communities, with all the unpredictability that arises along the way.

I am grateful to my wife Sandra and to my daughters Lina and Silvia for their support and patience. I am deeply indebted to Professor Ann Davis and Professor Marian Barnes for their invaluable suggestions.

Trento, Italy, April 2003   Fabio Folgheraiter

Relational social work

Introduction

It has always been a commonplace to say that social work 'is at a turning point' or 'is in crisis' (Bamford, 1990; Clarke, 1993). This perennial precariousness of the profession reflects the more generally uncertain fate of the welfare state at large. At the level of both fieldwork and policy-making, the problem of how to devise and implement caring action which society as a whole (citizens, politicians, professional groups) deems sensible and acceptable has never yet been resolved.

An infinite crisis, therefore. Yet we know that no crisis can ever be 'endless'. A 'chronic' crisis is a contradiction. Is the welfare pessimism therefore exaggerated? Is precariousness not the normal state of the social services, something that we must learn to live with, refusing to panic and without wasting time on its discussion? This phlegmatic attitude seems wise. And yet it fails to take account of what has happened in the last decade, when the world of the personal social services (Adams, 1996b), and social work as well, has been turned upside down by a major khunian 'revolution', given that all the traditional and profound bases have broken down (Lesnik, 1998). There have even been authors who have announced that social work 'is dead' (Payne, 1995).

For the first time ever in the European countries, the ethical foundations of the post-war social pact (Thane, 1996) by which we all (the State) assume 'responsibility for our brethren' (Bauman, 2000) have been called into question. The reassuring children's story that we have a *right* to well-being has proved to be precisely that – a children's story. Now we are actually told that our sole entitlement is to efficient services delivered by some or other provider. Our well-being as such we must provide by ourselves. The State does not have the powers of a fairy godmother; the most it can and should do is balance its budget and not over-burden the national economies with taxes.

For the first time, the social professions of the welfare state (Banks, 1999) have been subjected to disenchanted scrutiny and called to account: besides the fine theories they have so ably constructed, where are the results that they promised? For the first time social work has been forced to distinguish their field of action from that of direct helping work. Do not, they are told, confuse counselling (face-to-face helping) with care management, and do not waste scarce resources by failing to understand the difference between situations which require definitive remediation efforts and others which require the efficient management of chronic needs in the long-term care perspective. For the first time, statutory social work has been cut off at its roots. It is under powerful pressure to become increasingly an agent of social control to the benefit of the public authorities (welfare expenditure, risk behaviours, etc.) and to restrict its helping involvement to the benefit of users. And a fortiori to reduce its efforts to induce social and political change to the benefit of the quality of life in local communities (Alinsky, 1971; Selener, 1997; Banks, 1999).

The helping professions have been attacked at their very core, at their most intimately-held assumption. Well-being is no longer an absolute and unconditional end in itself. Rather, the argument goes, it should be placed in close relation to (and often in contrast with) managerial rationality and economic compatibility. The struggle against social hardship is no longer to be waged 'at any cost', and it is no longer to be left to the professionals concerned. Just as warfare is too important to be left to the generals, so welfare has political implications of such magnitude that it must be removed from the discretion of fieldworkers. This is so-called 'managed care' where practitioners are subject to the close control of managers, and service managers in their turn to the close control of policy makers (Lowman and Resnick, 1994; Corcoran and Vandiver, 1996).

As the globalization of economies proceeds (Dominelli, 1999), almost everywhere neo-liberalist thought is poised to take over, albeit in forms that vary considerably among countries. In Europe the doctrine implies the rapid dismantling of the welfare states that have grown and consolidated since the Second World War (Esping Andersen, 1996). If liberalism is not a 'crisis' in the way that social workers are accustomed to seeing themselves, with hopes and despairs related (Jones, 2000), it is difficult to say what it can be.

The reality, however, is even more complicated. Confirming the 'compulsive pessimism' that afflicts social work, one already notes a revolution within a revolution: liberalism is already showing signs of its own crisis.

The case of liberalization in the United Kingdom is instructive. Margaret Thatcher did not hesitate to extend market principles to personal social services with the NHS and Community Care Act of 1990 (Mandelstam and Schweher, 1995). Many of the recipes of neo-liberalist theory have been applied to care through this law, and with a radical thrust reminiscent of the equally famous (in its way) Italian law of 1978 promoted by Franco Basaglia, which closed all the country's mental hospitals (Jones, 1988; Sharkey and Barna, 1990). Just as Italy in the 1980s was a national proving ground for application of the principles of social psychiatry and normalisation (Wolfensberger, 1972; Brown and Smith, 1992), so Britain is now in the eyes of the world a macro-experiment in social care liberalization; or in other words, in the rapid changeover from a welfare system based on public bureaucracies to one based on the 'care market' (Barlett et al., 1994; Wistow et al., 1996).

It is still too early to draw up an exhaustive balance sheet of this experiment, though some verdicts for or against have already been pronounced (Payne, 1999). In general, one may say that social care has proved unexpectedly difficult to liberalize, undoubtedly more so than other more impersonal welfare sectors like transport, telecommunications, although even these have created problems for policy-makers.

A first consideration is the banal fact that the quality of social care depends largely on the availability of public resources (Johnson et al., 1998). The ratio between them is unyielding and no rhetoric can relax it: if you seek to reduce public spending, some needs go untreated; if you truly focus on needs, using the 'needs assessment' procedures, conventional budgets are at risk. Ascertaining whether a budget is balanced is obviously easier than ascertaining whether a need has been objectively satisfied (even assuming that we know what the term means). It is also evident that managers and policy makers are more directly concerned with the health of the public accounts than they are with full satisfaction of consumers (Sherman, 1999), for all the potential opportunities to lodge claims against the local authority diligently made available by the law on community care (Lewis and Glennerster, 1996). Small wonder, therefore, that the short coverage of neo-liberalism is seen as catering more closely to the public economic interest, even though the actual savings made possible by the introduction of 'quasi markets' in the United Kingdom have yet to be demonstrated (Forder, Knapp and Wistow, 1999).

But it is above all among practitioners that the British reform has caused problems – problems that are more conceptual than practical. The market requires that service delivery be standardized (Dominelli, 1998). And the imposition on the social services that their every act must be compatible with the dictates of the economy (Yenney, 1994), so that every individual action is invoiced as it would be in a business, has led to the fragmentation of skills and of helping responsibilities. From a 'commercial' standpoint, the complexity/integrity of the caring process, which is irreducible at the level of the users, breaks up at the level of production. For the providers, every act of care is quantified, and this Taylorization requires practitioners to be increasingly confined within their provisions. Indeed, social work too has become increasingly deskilled, to the point that in many circumstances social workers can be replaced by lower-qualified operators that cost less to the employer (Dominelli, 1996). Under this logic, the classical idea of 'holistic' helping (Butrym, 1976) is lost, and with it one of the mainstays of the work motivation of professional practitioners (Maslach and Leiter, 1997).

The consequence of this fragmentation of supply is that consumers – the entity on which the system as a whole should be focused in a market regime – are in danger of being left alone and disoriented. Users have before them a range of possible standard provisions to purchase. But which they should buy and why, and how they can determine whether it is the most suitable one, they find difficult to understand. Even more so when the majority of welfare users (and sometimes carers as well) would not be such if they did not suffer from distinctive decision-making deficits. Attempts have been made to obviate this structural limit to consumerism in the care markets – even if strong competition were to arise, demand would still be under-sustained – with the idea of case management (Moxley, 1989; Rose, 1992), where an expert social worker acts as a specialized consumer purchasing standard provisions and assembling individualized care packages.

'Entrepreneurial' case management (Payne, 1995), where the case manager is a public employee, acquitted itself very well when it was used in the experimental Kent Community Care Project (Davies and Challis, 1986). However, it has not fulfilled its promise when extended nation-wide. The original idea was that the social worker would simultaneously attend to care and manage a budget, buying provisions in the care market and linking them together efficiently. She or he would do all this while standing 'outside' the helping process and 'centralizing' it on him or herself by means of constant need assessment, monitoring, planning, decision-making, evaluation, and so on. This seemed to be a winning strategy, but in practice it has displayed significant shortcomings. It has had its merits – principally its definitive acknowledgement that the managerial aspects of care matter – but it was unthinkable that this would suffice. And in fact it did not. This difficulty has been mirrored in the progressive bureaucratization of British case management (Payne, 1999): a paradoxical outcome for a liberal procedure, but not a surprising one if we remember that at bottom the welfare 'quasi market' (Wistow et al., 1996) is always a public institution. Very different steps forward in case management will be needed in the near future, if the social work profession is to remain a *comprehensive* activity of human helping and is not reduced to mere manoeuvres of coordination and rationalization, however necessary.

In view of the need for decisive steps forward, which we now await, this book proposes the apparently simple recipe of backtracking and calmly considering the essential terms of the issues at stake.

The tendency to rush headlong into reform of welfare systems when one is dissatisfied with the real well-being of citizens (Marsland, 1996) springs from the outworn prejudice that societal well-being is a strict function of rationality and the efficiency of care providers, whatever form these may take (public, commercial or third-sector). There is no disputing that the quality and efficiency of formal structures are important, but this obviousness conceals the crux of the matter. The problem is how to establish a relation between the artificial (maybe efficient) world of formal social interventions and the world of real life, *so that care arises from this relation* (Donati, 1991; Barnes, 1996). Every self-referential reorganization of the overall welfare system which fails to understand the dynamics of everyday life within which statutory care must 'intrude' (Bulmer, 1987) is doomed to failure, however much 'engineering' expertise may be deployed.

This book essentially says the following: before we start thinking about how to improve and optimize artificial inputs in caring activities, we should ask ourselves how things are 'naturally'. In society's course, 'problems' arise, and 'solutions', or attempted solutions, are devised to deal with them. But what are social problems in themselves, where 'in themselves' means as they appear in the eyes of society before they are perceived as problems by the social services and redefined according to administrative codes and convenience? What are solutions in themselves, where 'in themselves' means produced by society before formal responses are devised, or even before awareness arises that they are necessary? Before we formulate yet another theory or methodology – given that formulating them too impulsively serves little purpose – it would be useful to see how problems form themselves in the 'world of life' (Schütz, 1972), and how problems trigger coping dynamics for their attenuation and perhaps solution. What we do not need is a theory that tells us how to bend problems to our will as their 'official' solvers. Rather, we should let the problems themselves dictate a sensible theory as to their solution; a theory from which all technical reasoning should flow. It sometimes happens that, despite complaints about their inefficiency, formal services nevertheless prove to be efficacious, and when users are canvassed for their views on their quality they declare themselves satisfied. I argue in this book that the efficacy of social work interventions depends on their intrinsic 'value' and in the same degree on the synergy which they have been able to establish with their natural interlocutors, what have been called in different ways: 'natural helping networks' (Collins and Pancoast, 1976; Froland et al., 1981), 'social support networks' (Werger, 1994; Biegel et al., 1984; Whittaker and Gambarino, 1983), 'coping networks', and so on. The efficacy of statutory organizations therefore springs from a virtuous mingling of their value (technical power) with the value (experiential power) of external societal bodies. Usually, the term 'networking' is used to denote efficient linkage between 'sister' organizations and professional workers in the welfare system (Payne, 1993; 2000), but it more generally denotes the mingling of these seemingly irreconcilable spheres of social life. More often, when an appropriate interweaving between 'artifice' (formal services) and 'nature' (social networks) is accomplished (Bulmer, 1987), it is not deliberately sought after. It is an accidental side-product of the unidirectional technical action of services and professional practitioners. The latter concentrate solely on their own work and its direct effects, and they readily ascribe any success to themselves, failing to see the overall action process of which their technique is part. The question is whether it is possible to reverse the terms and to imagine a realistic method able *intentionally* to construct social intervention on relational bases. This method is exactly what is meant by the term 'networking'.

It is not the aim of this book to be prescriptive. Its basic intention is not to tell social workers what to do. It does not invite them to undertake intentional networking if they have never done it before, or if they have no wish to. It only seeks to show that networking – the authentic social relation with reciprocal learning among the parties involved in the helping processes, not the unilateral application of some theory or some technique – is the real key to 'success' in social work. Many social workers may find that they have undertaken networking during their careers without being aware of it or wanting to do it. They have undertaken it whenever their work has been efficacious and they have helped to construct a sensible solution shared by their interlocutors. The concern of this book is to show the methodological (and ultimately practical, of course) importance of relational principles. Unfortunately, they are extremely abstract but it is precisely because of their abstractness, indeed, that these principles can be used to observe 'from outside', with both detachment and profundity, the controversial question of social care (Bowdeer, 1997).

The arguments put forward in this book can be briefly summarized as follows.

(a) At the basis of the 'good' and 'bad' – the problems and solutions – subjectively experienced in social life there lies intersubjective human action. By this is meant on-line action whereby 'agents' are able to work with relative freedom towards achievement of their goals. More than the individual 'essences' of people (character, personality, pathologies, and so on), the social worker must observe their *shared action*, even if it is insufficient at the moment when formal intervention becomes necessary. In the social work domain, the typically sociological (Weberian) concept of 'capacity for action' or *human agency* (Giddens, 1991) links especially with that of coping, or the deliberate tackling of their difficulties, or more in general their meaningful purposes, by all the persons involved in a difficult live contingence. When the people in this coping network are professionals , their action flows over the boundaries of their formal roles and become 'voluntary' (not prescribed) in some degree.

(b) A social worker acts within a networking perspective – consciously or otherwise – when s/he joins a web of pre-existing social action and is able to 'fluctuate' in it without rigidifying its flows and to construct a shared action. Every professional has to introduce his/her own goals and procedures into the helping process, but they should never overlap with nor supplant the goals and plans of others. The social worker's presence gives rise to further relationality by fostering creativity in others which flanks and merges with the technical aspects of his or her role. If the practitioner pays attention to the quality and consistency of coping relations, taken to the extreme of allowing these relations to determine the meaning and concrete planning of the helping process, he plays a role of discreet *supervision*, which in this book is called 'relational guidance'.

The word 'social' expresses shared human actions, rel-actional processes. The rule necessarily applies to *social* work as well (Seed, 1990). It is ultimately a full human activity like all the others, and it is indeed relational in essence. Conventional social work has focused on this broad principle (Bartlett, 1970). The aim of the majority of scholars, however, has always been to provide social workers with a theory (a general prescription) that will enable them to solve social problems, given that it is precisely this thaumaturgic power that it is believed that specialists should possess. But all the theories that have taken this positivist assumption for granted have produced collateral damage, although it is difficult to perceive and attribute. They have induced thousands of practitioners to regard only themselves, not the societal empowerment (power of others outside their professional role). From an extreme perspective, we may say that: if the practitioners applying these theories have achieved any results, they have done so *despite* their strict prescriptions. Technological theories have been transferred wholesale from the health and clinical field, where the power of the practitioner is strong, to the social helping domain, where it cannot be so.

This book is neither the a-theoretical nor anti-theoretical exegesis that might appear from these remarks. But since it proposes a *theory* of 'non-theory-directed practice' or a 'reflexive theory' (Schon, 1991; Clark, 1991) it is theoretical in its essence. It does not encourage the randomness of approaches that postmodernist thought would have us believe is inevitable (Lyotard, 1979; Bertens, 1996). It invites the reader to draw careful distinctions. It contests flawed or improper theories but also argues for the vital necessity of innovative concepts which permit us better observations of the social realities as such. We have necessity of a general reflection which, though at present tentative and provisional, may lead us out of positivism's barren wastes (Parton, 1996). Precisely because postmodern society requires, as Morin (1986) put it, 'foundation-less' procedures, a meta-foundation is necessary (for a paradigmatic rather than prescriptive theory) if we are not to grope our way though errors and the occasional random success, and then find that our trust relationship with the citizen has definitively broken down.

It is not important if this book's thesis, that social work is by nature relational, seems frail and certainly vague in its practical implications. What does matter is whether it can stand as a thoroughgoing alternative paradigm. Crucial scientific innovations have always struggled to gain acceptance (Lenoble, 1957).

All the evidence suggests that relational social work is impossible or impracticable in social services as they are today. The revolutionary idea that helping is a reflexive and reciprocal activity and must be co-constructed as it unfolds, apparently clashes with the stringent constraints of planning and standardization, and also with the powerful interests of care organizations – from the solidarist ones of the Third sector (Brown, Kenny and Turner, 2000) to the more formal ones of the public sector. In the era of the care markets, the relational perspective seems already outdated, if we think that efficiency of care springs from increasing managerial control. However, this realism puts the cart before the horse, so to speak. It is justified, indeed wise, in the framework of deterministic thought, where it is still believed that help is external mechanical manipulation (Gouldner, 1970). But it is exactly this background culture that is under attack, not its applications.

The relational perspective could be the best idea if we think that social care claims for more freedom and more regulation at the same time. We do not know how we can do this at the moment. But we have to hope. The validity of the relational paradigm is not determined by its general applicability for social services in their present form. This idea must first be cultivated, and if it passes the test of collective intelligence – that is, should it be proved that care is truly a 'social relation – then the consequence is ineluctable. The powerful social agencies must capitulate and find new organizational formulas for more flexible fieldwork activities which, though today unthinkable, are nonetheless feasible.

These formulas may be not so comfortable for their managers and professional practitioners, but they will finally be congruous with their external goals. From the point of view of social work the stake is high: it is the possibility itself that the profession may no longer be conceived and practised as an indissoluble whole but fragmented into a myriad of independent technical provisions. If the challenge of reciprocity is not taken up, the idea that people in difficulties can reorient their lives with some help from a professional, risks passing into history as a romantic illusion.

CHAPTER 1

The relational core
of social problems
The joint perception of care needs

1.1. Introduction

This chapter conducts analysis of the point of departure – or better the basis –
of social work intervention: the reality from whose perception every professional
action starts.

Social workers very often assume that they know what the 'problem' that they
are dealing with is. They do not usually take the time to ponder how and why
they sense that a situation is unacceptable and must be changed in a way that they
do not yet know (which is a 'problem' in essence). All social workers (not only
the most practical-minded of them), as well as the methodology handbooks, are
especially attracted to solutions. They seek above all to understand what a possible future different state of the 'bad' situation would be, and perhaps the means
and devices by which this different state can be achieved, or in other words, a
'solution'.

In social care matters, starting off on the right foot – adopting the correct
standpoint – is however advisable. The problems that social workers address
must be conceived as *sui generis* phenomena, midway between the molecular and
the molar: they are not problems that concern individuals, as psychology or
medicine would have it, nor are they problems of collective structures or entities
as macrosociology maintains (Dominelli, 1996).

From the relational perspective, we are faced by a *social* problem when a
broader capacity for action – that is, action undertaken by a 'group' of people –
is insufficient. This is the main idea put forward in this chapter. However,
matters are not as straightforward as they might seem, and before developing this
idea, two specifications are necessary.

Firstly, whether something is 'sufficient' or 'insufficient' always depends on a value-judgement, and therefore on a special relationship between the observer and the reality observed. The observer, a social worker or anyone else, always reflects social categories in his/her perception – s/he looks at phenomena with the eyes (symbols) of the society in which s/he lives. As a consequence, the social work problems are 'social constructions' (McNamee and Gergen, 1992; Parton, 2000) in the sense given to the term by *phenomenology* (Shütz, 1972).

Secondly, when one talks of action, or capacity for action, the Weberian problem of *meaning* immediately arises: actions must by definition be meaningful to those who perform them or to those who undergo them. Otherwise they are not actions. From the professional viewpoint of social work, the focus must primarily be on pragmatic (reality-transforming) meaning, although of course this functional 'focus' is not the only one that exists. One must specify the nature of action in social work, construing it as the relation that holds between an agent's given purpose and the abilities required to achieve it – a relation that in the social work is usually denoted by the technical term 'coping'.

1.2. Construction of the feeling that 'a problem exists': the relational basis

No social problem exists in and of itself: an act of evaluation is required to make it such. This assertion may come as a surprise to those mindful of the harsh and incontrovertible realities of social work. Can one say that an abused child or a neglected old person does not exist? Of course one cannot: they most certainly do exist. But note that I said that they do not exist as a problem 'in and of itself'. Strictly speaking, none of the things and objects of the real world exist in and of themselves (Berger and Lukmann, 1966; Maturana and Varela, 1987), even when reality apparently lies beyond any appraisal of it. *A fortiori,* therefore, *problems* do not exist, since they lie at a different, and more slippery, logical level. The fact is that acts of appraisal almost always take place 'silently' in the mind. Our eyes see external data, never the 'inner mechanism' that render them into phenomenal reality. Thus we trustingly assume that reality is 'objectively' what it appears to be.

1.2.1. *The relationship between reality and the observer*

Let me give an example. I-as-observer see a person staggering along a city street. In truth, it is difficult for the mind to see something as abstract as a 'person staggering'. The mind immediately mixes what is being experienced (the external datum) with inner data ('constructs') creating symbolic associations which for the sake of convenience I shall call 'judgements'. The mind may trigger causal attributions of the type: that man is staggering because he is drunk. And it is this judgement that presents me with what I see: to wit, a drunk. From the outset, I *perceive* the staggering man (that is, I see him rather than think of him) as a drunk. That this perception may be inaccurate – he may be lurching from side to side because he is in the throes of heroin withdrawal or is weak from hunger, or he has been beaten up, or he is acting, and so on – is due to the fallibility of our mental processes and nothing else.

Schütz (1972) calls this mechanism of the mind 'typification' and argues that it is the basis of the way in which objective reality becomes *phenomenon,* or in other words, appears to our mind as perception or subjective knowledge. When the data delivered by the senses to the cerebral cortex reach that highly sophisticated part of the brain, they are fitted into a frame or representative 'type' of that particular phenomenon constituted by a mental construct (Kelly, 1955). These constructs are deeply embedded in consciousness, and they are *taken for granted.* Whatever impinges on the mind is instantaneously compared against this 'background knowledge' (Popper, 1994). The reality that results from this process – the phenomenon that appears to us – is not what it actually is; rather, it is the reality that is recognized as most similar to a pre-existing type.

The perceiving subject can only see external reality; s/he is ignorant of the cognitive processes that generate it. But there is no need for radical introspection required to understand them. Every inner process, or every innate disposition towards knowledge, is by definition instrumental to the grasping of reality, and it would be functionally pointless for it to unfold in the domain of consciousness. This would be useful only in pathological cases like hallucinations, for example, so that the subject could be made aware that everything s/he 'sees' is solely a figment of the imagination. Despite the pragmatic irrelevance of the matter to everyday life, however, it is essential to understand that phenomena arise with the active contribution of the mind. We must consequently take adequate account of it in social work theory, where we consider higher levels of reality like social problems (at the different levels: individual, group, and community).

Let us suppose that the person that we saw in the street really was a drunk. That is to say, let us suppose that, as often happens, the typification worked, in the sense that there was an 'exact' correspondence between the mental category activated and the objective phenomenon perceived. The staggering man really had been drinking. But can one say that this is a *problem?* To answer the question, we must settle a preliminary issue: what type of problem are we talking about?

Like any other sense datum, the sight of a drunk can be transmuted into a problem by two different kinds of observer judgement, one moral and the other technical. Of the two, only the latter seems to be of specific interest to the social professions, and yet the former has more relevance than might seem at first sight.

1.2.2. Constructing a problem according to the moral code

A moral evaluation is made when the judgement informing the perception concerns the goodness or badness attributed to the phenomenon of which the observer becomes aware (Sacks, 1992). A *problem* obviously implies a *negative* judgement – that is, it is a reality connoted by badness, experienced not so much as unsatisfactory or unacceptable as contemptible or despicable. If I see a man staggering along the street in front of me, and if he arouses a negative moral reaction in me, then I no longer see him as a man who is drunk – as happens when only a simple cause-effect judgement is performed – but as a *drunkard*. 'Drunk-ard' is a word laden with disapproval or distaste – that is, with negative feelings correlated with an already-possessed notion of badness. Calling the staggering man a drunkard implies, amongst other things, that he is such intrinsically, independently of the particular circumstances in which I see him (and in which his behaviour might even be...excusable). The tendency to drink to excess, I feel, is typical of the man, and this tendency is 'not good'. Further evidence will convince me even more firmly that the man is morally flawed and that his behaviour is reprehensible: he is a person who cares nothing about his integrity (and is wrong not to do so), about his dignity (and he is wrong), or about the integrity of others (and he is wrong), and so on. I see a problem, morally speak-ing, when I think/feel that the drunkard before me should be other than what he is, and that it is his responsibility/fault – or perhaps someone else's (his family, society, etc., but at any rate some identifiable entity) – that he is what he is; when I think that he, or I, or society, or anyone at all, would benefit if he were not what he is (or better, what he appears to be).

The blame placed on somebody, like the sense of blame that the latter inter-nalizes, is a social event. When the observer attributes blame, s/he classifies the phenomenon at hand within a mental framework which, although it may be private to him/her, is more usually shared. If this framework is rooted in the culture, it simultaneously resides in the heads of others, and it is activated in largely the same way. One could discuss at length about the objective valence – functional or utilitarian – of these moral judgements which arise in several minds. Often the utility of generalized disapproval, for example of drunkards, can be easily discerned. One can posit that certain collective attitudes are selected in Darwinian manner in order to ensure the better survival or greater well-being of society as a whole, and that this is a necessary process. In the case of alcohol abuse, for example, there is general consensus on the fact that it should be curbed (although it is debatable whether encouraging social disapproval serves this purpose). But the fact remains that these value-judgements may be reversible, or may change from one moment to the next. They may have been different in the past, or they may be different today, or they may be different in certain subcultures comprised within the dominant culture. In the subculture of alcoholics, for example, alcohol is presumably regarded as a good thing. Indeed, different value-judgements may coexist in the head of the same observer, who in this case would be a deviant or creative observer.

It is often the case that when two different observers are confronted by the same phenomenon, although they do not see different things (because they have the same objective perceptions of reality), they nevertheless see different *problems*. Or, as sometimes happens, one of them sees a problem while the other does not, or instead sees the opposite of a problem, namely something desirable. When I encounter a man in the street who has obviously been drinking, I may pass the moral judgement that he should stop. The next person to see him may simply not think anything, or consider it to be purely the man's business. Those who follow may think that the occasional bender does one good; that the man sometimes has a few too many and feels better afterwards. The same thing, therefore, may be seen as bad, as neither good nor bad, or as good: the same thing, note, not just in different persons but in the same person at different times. Without lapsing into moral relativism – that is, without justifying the absence of acceptable judgmental criteria – we must accept that this phenomenon is an integral part of reality.

When a problem is addressed by a social worker, and not by a generic 'observer', there is still a moral judgement involved. The stereotype of the professional practitioner is that of the ascetic technician, but deep down he or she is also a man or a woman and unconsciously compelled to define problems according to moral sentiments. For him or her, too, a problem is something felt to be wrong. Of course, an expert practitioner is ethically obliged to abstain from moralism. S/he must not apportion blame or feel resentment, which are inferior forms of moral judgement. However, firstly, refraining from such behaviour is not always easy (which is why all codes of behaviour enjoin it), and secondly not being angered or made anxious by the situation is perhaps the necessary basis for action which is humane and not just technically correct.

For many practitioners with long years of experience, contact with problems has become a matter of course; consequently, taking action against them is more routine than stressful. In this case too, however, we should bear in mind that moral sentiments are nevertheless present as the deep-lying 'archetypical' motivators of the practitioners' action. The social policies of the welfare state that frame these routine actions have arisen from a moral impulse in society. They spring from a sense that certain situations are unsatisfactory or intolerable. This moral rejection by the collective consciousness is symbolically embodied in every individual dealt with by every institutional practitioner, or more in general in every administrative act performed by the welfare state, as Ignatieff explains.

> My encounters with them *[with elderly people in his local community, NdR]* are a parable of moral relationships between strangers in the welfare state. They have a needs, and because they live within a welfare state, those needs confer entitlements-rights-to the resources of people like me. Their needs and their entitlements establish a silent relation between us. When we stand together in line at the postal office, while they cash the pension cheques, some tiny portion of my income is transferred into their pockets through the numberless capillaries of the state. (Ignatieff, 1984, pp. 9-10)

1.2.3. *Constructing a problem according to the technical code*

There is another code besides the strictly moral one that raises problems in the mind of the expert practitioner: the technical code. The sight of the man staggering along the street may induce a professional practitioner to see a problem (should s/he want to) from a different point of view: not with displeasure, anger, distaste or frustration, but rather with the 'detached' perception of a dysfunction, for which s/he formulates what in technical jargon is called a *diagnosis*. Goffman carefully distinguishes between the two levels.

> What psychiatrists see as mental illness, the lay public usually first sees as offensive behavior-behavior worthy of scorn, hostility and other negative social sanctions. The objective of psychiatry all along has been to interpose a technical perspective: understanding and treatment is to replace retribution; a concern for the interests of the offender is to replace a concern for the social circle he has offended. (Goffman, 1967, p. 137)

Diagnosis always requires some sort of hermeneutical processing. The external datum is not 'automatically' fitted into a mental slot, as in the case of empirical perception or moral judgement. Its collocation instead requires a specific act of reasoning, an intentional cognitive process. To diagnose is to identify a pathology or, by extension, a dysfunction. It involves not the feeling that an offence has been committed against universal justice or against the social order, which is generally self-evident, but that a person harbours a dysfunction which requires reasoning and method for its identification. Popper defines the diagnostic procedure as follows:

> [The diagnosis is] a trial-and-error affair which proceeds systematically – as many trial and error do; by no means all are random-according to a plan which in itself has developed out of trial and error. The doctor has learned a kind of programme of the questions to be asked. There are some very general questions about age and so on to be asked, and then some specific questions about where the pain is felt and what is wrong with the patient, and so on. By a systematic trial-and-error method, and a special systematic error-elimination method which is learned from books or learned in the clinic. By a systematic trial-and-error method, and a special systematic error-elimination method, he then comes to a small number of possibilities. And from here on, the process is then, as a rule, again elimination of one possibility after another of the small number. Let us say, by blood tests, or whatever it may be. And then remains the diagnosis. (Popper, 1994, p. 127)

Beneath the outward appearance of the man staggering along the street an expert clinician may discern an *alcoholic,* that is, a person addicted to alcohol. If superficial appraisal is not enough to attach this label, more careful investigation will be needed to bring out hidden information by means of direct observation, interviews, physical examinations, tests, and so on. This hidden information does not emerge by itself. By its nature it evades observation. Whether or not it is perceived depends on the method of inquiry, on *how* the observation is made, on *what* is observed, and also on *why:* all of which are variables which do not reside in things but in the subjectivity of the diagnostician.

Technically, we may say, the problem exists when diagnosis detects it. Or better, the problem exists in *how* it is detected. We should not be overawed by science and believe that diagnostic technique always reveals the reality and does not partly create it. For it does create it, not only for the obvious reason that the same objective datum may be allocated to different mental slots, according to how it is interpreted, but also for the more radical reason that the search for pathologies or dysfunctions – which is the essence of diagnosis – presupposes the creation of pathology itself as a notion, as a judgement of abnormality/normality that must preexist and therefore *a fortiori* cannot reside in things.

Cholesterol found in the blood at a certain level of concentration is only cholesterol in the blood, nothing more. Why then does its concentration above a certain level constitute a 'pathology'? Because doctors have formed a pact to determine that it is so; because they have fixed a threshold above which the concentration of cholesterol in the blood becomes a pathology. Just above that specific parameter the datum is tinged with badness, perhaps with nobody knowing exactly why, and maybe with the judgements changing in the course of time.

There is no denying the huge variety of pathologies officially codified by medical science, despite what has been said so far. The amenability of these pathologies to positivist prediction – that is, our ability to say 'under these conditions, these pathologies' or 'with this pathology, these outcomes' – within certain limits undoubtedly gives them the 'privilege' of objective existence.

The fact remains, however, that every medical pathology is the consequence of definitions: if nobody defines a pathology, it does not exist. Or it is as if it does not exist. Conversely, if someone defines a pathology, it exists even when it does not. A classic example is the hypochondriac, who imagines his pathology after having defined it by himself, whereafter he effectively lives out the illness while constantly seeking an expert to confirm his belief. Indeed, a pathology is created when someone *believes* that it has been defined, as in the following comical episode reported by Mucchielli (1983). A doctor was exhausted after working through the night. While examining his tenth patient and listening as he re-counted his problems, the doctor felt an uncontrollable urge to yawn. He managed to restrain himself, but so great was the effort that his eyes began to water. The patient stopped talking and burst into tears. When he had pulled himself together, he explained that, on seeing the doctor so moved by his story, he realized that he was so dreadfully ill that there was nothing to be done for him.

As one moves away from medicine and enters the notoriously uncertain field of *psychological or social diagnostics*, it becomes increasingly difficult to define what a dysfunction actually is, and equally difficult to determine whether or not one exists. Discussion of the objective nature and real consistency of a psychological or social dysfunction could truly continue *ad infinitum*. Often, one cannot find a more reliable benchmark than the norm – how everybody, or at least the majority, normally behaves – to define by default an attitude or form of behaviour as pathological or, in this case, deviant. To refer once again to alcoholism, which is a pathology midway between medical and psychosocial, it is plain that its essence *(dependence or addiction,* the difficulty or impossibility of doing without alcohol) is a pathology only if we agree that it is one. Everyone (or almost everyone) agrees that it is a pathology because alcoholics are a minority, and hence we have the statistical solace that the norm is breached. However, there are other obsessive forms of behaviour apart from addiction which brighten up our lives without their being labelled as pathological: going fishing or climbing mountains, collecting stamps, and so on. The fact that an obsession with drinking causes more damage than an obsession with fishing is no reason for condemning the one form of behaviour or extolling the other. In and of themselves, they are of equal merit.

Another important field where the *relative* nature of social problems – even those dramatic ones that seem self-evident – is apparent is child abuse. Cases of this kind are constantly on the increase, but one may ask whether child abuse is objectively more common, or whether it is statistically increasing because those who carry out assessments are more skilled at detecting the problem.

> A number of authors... have argued that the phenomenon of 'child abuse' is not an objective condition but a social construction, the meaning of which arises from ever-changing social values. Standards of acceptable and unacceptable child care have evolved over time in response to new knowledge about children's needs and development and changing attitudes in society toward children and families. However, the distinctions remain blurred. Extremes of child maltreatment can be recognised unequivocally, but when does neglect become critical, or psychological tormenting too severe? (Peter Reder and Clare Lucey, eds., 1995, p. 14)

I am not saying that it is unreasonable or wrong to maintain that alcoholism, child abuse or other social ills are pathologies or dysfunctions, in short 'negative' phenomena. I am only saying that this status is attributed to them by an act of *judgement:* it is not intrinsic to them.

What are the implications of the foregoing, rather banal, discussion for social work? It implies that the social worker, too, like the common observer, sees and does not see, sees too much or too little. The observation of problems and their definition in turn constitute a problem. It seems that problems are objectively *there*, and that those who see problems have no bearing on their existence and need merely take cognizance of them. But this is not how matters stand, although of course they often seem to do so in practice. From a logical point of view, one should always bear two things in mind. First, who knows how many problems there are that social workers fail to see? Second, who knows how many problems social workers see which are not problems when considered from other standpoints, or within different sociocultural coordinates? The expert always creates his or her problems, whether or not they actually exist.

Problems are often delivered to practitioners for solution after they have already been prepackaged by the culture, or by administrative custom. Generally speaking, social workers deal with problems that have been codified and defined by the tradition of their service, or by the law, or by the users themselves. This too is a routine aspect of their work, in practice but not logically: to do true credit to his or her qualification, the professional practitioner should dispute certain definitions of problems. It is difficult to provide examples because we are too closely bound up with our problems, which seem to us entirely incontrovertible, but why or in what sense are children who do badly at school – those whom Cordié (1993) calls the 'dunces' – a problem? Or why is Down's syndrome a problem, or at any rate something so exceptional that it requires special care, intensive training, confinement in institutions, and so on: treatment which is not meted out to other people with other shortcomings. Why is there so much alarm over Down's children?

1.2.4. *Relations between expert and subjects: the formal problem*

Alfred Schütz has drawn a number of distinctions of great analytical (and operational) importance. He has shown that the meaning of action may not be the same for the acting subject in the course of an action and when it has been completed. Likewise it may not be the same for an interlocutor (if communication is involved and the action is directed towards another person), nor, even more so, for those who observe the action from outside without being affected by it.

Thus far I have referred to the detached observer, and to how she or he gets the idea that there is a problem – and I have also shown how, before and after its formation, this idea is shared or sharable by other observers, or in other words, is a social 'fact'. I have taken a step forward from the idea so dear to us all, and so reasonable, but also insidious, that we see problems because 'they are there'. I have emphasised the active role that the observer plays in creating the problem by interacting with sensible reality and attributing meaning to it. Yet, in the end, all these considerations are counter-empirical. They serve to make professional action methodologically better, but they cannot detach it from common sense.

All the arguments put forward thus far are operationally useful because they focus attention on 'the problem that is not'. In other words, they are useful because they extend the practitioner's field of experience to include *possible* problems, those that are not in their perception (Popper, 1994), or those that do not yet inhere in things or do so only symptomatically. These arguments also usefully point up the idea that a problem perceived may also be considered critically and, if need be, gainsaid. However, we must be clear on the matter: all the problems that impinge on and affect the consciousness are there before the observer and carry the same weight as reality. Whether 'they are' or whether they are 'constructed' by the mind/reality relation is only a theoretical issue. In fact, it makes little practical difference to the practitioner who has to deal with them: it is 'as if' problems are objective. The true empirical leap comes when one answers the question: 'For whom are they problems?'.

A professional practitioner must be especially wary of the idea that a problem – once it has formed within his or her head despite all the warnings issued hitherto – needs nothing more than this to stand by itself. This is the cause of all practitioner errors, the assumption that fills the graveyard of good intentions. Let us see why.

An expert practitioner looks at the poor drunken man (this is a moral judgement!) in our example. Let us suppose that he or she realizes immediately, on obvious semiotic evidence, with no need for laborious diagnosis, that the man is an alcoholic. The practitioner therefore sees a *problem*, technically speaking. But what does this fact – that s/he sees a problem – mean? Let us endeavour to set aside all the arguments put forward so far, for they will only cause uncertainty as we proceed further. So we discard the idea that *in reality* an alcoholic is simply a person in a particular state just as we all are at every moment, and that 'alcoholic' is a label. Let us also forget that this label is unreliable because other practitioners, our colleagues, may fail to see it, because they are distracted, or because they disagree in their interpretation, and so on. Even though a problem takes shape in the mind of a practitioner, and even though this practitioner finds that other experts are of the same opinion, so that one can say that in practice the problem really exists, the practitioner does not have a great deal to go on. But let us have no doubt that the man is an alcoholic. There he is and that is enough. However, even now the problem has only been defined (or construed) by half.

A practitioner may be prompted to act on a moral impulse, compassion for instance, or s/he may act out of official duty (if, for example, s/he is the social worker for the neighbourhood in which the alcoholic is seen staggering down the street) or because s/he has been paid a fee (if s/he is a therapist hired by one of the man's relatives, for example). Whatever the case may be, if the practitioner decides to tackle the problem that s/he believes objectively exists, s/he may commit the crucial professional error of believing that the problem 'exists' just as s/he perceives it. Given that the practitioner can see it, s/he may conclude that this is all that is needed for intervention to begin. The notion that what the individual expert sees is the underlying reality (the problem) addressed by the social intervention is too simplistic an idea to be true (more mistaken than it is possible to explain in words).

We must obviously not underestimate the power of 'therapeutic labelling' or the potentially perverse effects of so-called professional 'take-up'. When experts get it into their heads that there is a problem as they see it, there is usually little to be done: there is no escape for the problem, for now it 'exists'. And if they set their minds to solving it, the problem exists even more. Simmel understood this apparent paradox long before the welfare state – which is legally compulsory 'take-up' – was even dreamt of. He writes:

> [...] the fact that someone is poor does not mean that he belongs to the specific category of the 'poor'. It is only when he (the poor man) is assisted [...] that he begins to belong to a group characterized by poverty [...] Poverty cannot be defined by itself as an objective situation of objective type, for it is only a social response to a particular situation. Poverty is a singular sociological phenomenon: a set of individuals, independently of purely personal destiny, occupy an entirely specific organic position, which is determined not by this destiny or by this condition but by the fact that others will endeavour to put this condition right. (Simmel, G.,1908: chapter seven)

Simmel warns us that the solution may create the problem: in other words, that a problem may be created or exacerbated by the mere fact that attempts are made to solve it. This paradox is amply confirmed by experience in social work, only that in this case it occurs when solutions are applied to ill-defined problems, ones conceived with the simplistic idea that they are objects to manipulate.

Something so inchoate – an object which a solitary expert brings into focus so that it can be solved – supposing that it exists, can never be a social problem in the sense with which the expression is used here, namely as the basis for formal social intervention. A social problem must have a whole set of characteristics, the first of which (first in the sense that it is the basis for all the others) is that it must be an *intersubjective* reality, and in particular shared with the person who 'has it'.

An event or a configuration of events may be dignified with the title of a 'true' social problem when its definition (or construction) is a joint undertaking – albeit one that starts from different codes – by all the subjects that Schütz envisages as involved in every action: not only (a) the observer but also (b) the perpetrator of the action or (c) the person affected by it, even potentially. In the case of social intervention, which is of interest to us here, we may say that there must be a conjunction between the expert practitioner, the designated user and his/her significant others (when there is a proclaimed user). Or, when – as it may happen in social work – there is no user or it is preferable for the practitioner to act *as if* there is no user, we may say there must be a conjunction between the practitioner and all his/her interlocutors in action, even potential ones. Although the problem will be viewed or conceived in a different way by each actor – in particular even if the practitioner grasps its 'technical' sense on his/her own – the *sense that a problem exists* must be shared. If this sense is fragmented and exists only for some and not for others, and is therefore not shared, then it is not a mature problem – it is not mature in the sense that it is not yet ready for formal intervention. If the practitioner's action starts in the absence of this minimal condition, it is likely to be mere wishful thinking. (In any event, it will not be a social intervention).

1.2.5. *Practitioner/user dual sharing*

The idea that before any intervention the actor and recipient must form some sort of unit of consciousness, as far as this is possible, and that this unit creates problems, has been marvellously expressed in a short novel by Thomas Mann. The young hypochondriac Shiraman is convinced that he is terminally ill. He tells his inseparable and plain-spoken friend Nanda that he wants to die, and tells him to build a funeral pyre. Instead of complying, however, Nanda answers as any social worker should:

> You may rest assured that if your disease is truly incurable, and I have no doubt that it is, given your assurances to me, I shall not hesitate to carry out your orders and build the pyre. Indeed, I shall make it so large that there will be room for me as well [...] Except that, for this reason, and because I'm involved as well, you must first of all tell me what you feel [...] If I put myself in your place and for a moment try to think with your head, as if it were on my shoulders, I'm forced to admit that my [...] I mean to say, your conviction that you're incurably sick should be examined and confirmed by others, before such an important decision as you have in mind can be taken. Speak therefore! (Mann, 1966, p. 281)

In answering the question 'problems for whom?' we may say when reasoning in relational terms that the user's problem must also become the practitioner's problem, and vice versa, so that it is a problem for both of them. This intuition goes well beyond the classical notion of *empathy* as Kierkegaard long time ago recommended (Hobbs, 1992) and which is now treated by every handbook on social work.

> If you want to help somebody, first of all you must find him where he is and start there. This is the secret of caring. If you cannot do that, it is only an

illusion, if you think you can help another human being. Helping somebody implies your understanding more than he does, but first of all you must understand what he understands. If you cannot do that your understanding will be of no avail. (Kierkegaard, 1849; quoted in Hobbs, 1987: XV)

The basis for a helping relationship, if it is to deserve such label, is precisely this kind of human understanding: the helping should be 'given' only when the practitioner 'feels' accurately the person and his or her problem. This is an important rule, for it states that the expert is obliged to connect with the 'true' problem as it is presumably felt in its true nature by the person concerned.

The relational perspective shows us another side of the empathy rule (or another directional flow) which is not always well understood. There is also the reverse requirement that the practitioner's problem, if s/he alone is aware of it, must also become the recipient's problem, if s/he is not aware of it or does not see it, or sees it inadequately or distortedly. It is not important only that the expert should have a clear and comprehensive idea of the user's difficulty from the latter's point of view; it is also and equally important that the user should have an idea of his/her difficulty as it has taken shape in the expert's mind. If the answer to 'problem for whom' is 'problem for both' (in the particular case of a dual relationship), this should logically follow.

Creating this shared basis is often a difficult task for the social worker. It is a task whose purpose is paradoxically to *create* the problem (relationally under-stood), rather than – as it might seem to the practitioner – to resolve it. Obvi-ously, creating a shared problem means creating better conditions for its solu-tion. Consequently, the idea that one sets about resolving a problem while still laying the intersubjective basis from which to start is not entirely mistaken (only somewhat ingenuous).

Once again the example of addiction helps illustrate the point. In this case, the subjective distance between the person suffering from the problem and the expert who wishes to help him or her is huge. The drug addict and the alcoholic live in a 'pre-contemplative state', to use Prochaska and Di Clemente's expression (Miller and Rollnick, 1991): they are unable to 'see' (to contemplate) the prob-lem that afflicts them. Or, put otherwise, they are individuals caught up in a mechanism of *denial,* that is 'an unconscious or semiconscious defense [...] an inability by the individual to see the reality of his/her situation, although this reality is often apparent to others' (Amodeo, 1995, p. 98).

Even if the expert sees the problem very clearly, s/he must keep calm, so to speak. And the expert must not only restrain him/herself when s/he sees these individuals in the street as an observer, but also when they come to him and her as users with an incipient awareness that they need help. The practitioner must also proceed with caution when the motivational counselling begins (Miller and Rollnick, 1991). A more or less long initial phase of help must be devoted to fostering the motivation to change. The aim of this initial phase, that is to say, in the light of the concepts presented here, is to enable the problem to emerge in the mind of the person afflicted by it.

The mental interconnection between expert and user – more than the one that operates in reverse between user and expert – is a process that should be managed with great delicacy. When, as in the case of addiction, the problem lies within the user, s/he often sees nothing – in the same way, for example, that we see nothing of our face when there is a blob of ice cream on our nose. Just as it would not make a great deal of sense to insist on describing a blob of ice cream on someone's nose in words – rather than by simply holding up a mirror – it would be equally senseless for an expert to try to give a verbal description (no matter how detailed and precise) of the other's problem that he or she can see. To shed light on (or give insight into) a problem, a mirror is required, just as a mirror is required to see one's own face.

Technically speaking, what does using a mirror in help actually mean? The answer is somewhat long and complex, and it is only outlined here (it is dwelt upon at length in Chapter 3). The expert must reflect or reformulate the statements made by the user which signal some sort of awareness, even minimal, of his or her problem. The latter's incipient self-awareness, together with a great deal of other irrelevant material, impinge upon the consciousness of the expert, who recognizes them and purges them of everything else. S/he then restates them in other words and relays them back into the communication as small 'bundles' of meaning. These products of the practitioner's consciousness, which are in fact processings of the interlocutor's consciousness, are returned to the latter in the well-known counselling formulas of 'You're telling me that…' or 'I understand that you…', and the like (Carkhuff, 1987).

In this way, awareness of the problem is reinforced in the consciousness of the person after it has been expressed and then reflected back in the words of the practitioner. The words of the practitioner encase those of the user's to constitute an intersubjective unit, something that is thereby objectivized. We may say that the person is able to see the problem as if it was external to him/her, as if the person were an external observer of him/herself.

Here I am talking about mirroring as a technical process used by a practitioner who acts intentionally. But mirroring may also be an immediate fact, an image suddenly reflected on the face of a significant other. This is how an ex-alcoholic described to a self-help group how he became aware of his problem:

I had carried on for years with no sign of any chips in my denial. I insisted, or screamed if necessary, that I could control my drinking and that everyone should mind their own business. Then one day I saw hurt on my daugther's face as I staunchly upheld my right to drink. Her look bore the truth as I could not see it in myself. I knew I was an alcoholic and I could not control my drinking. I have not had a drink since that afternoon. (Brown, 1995, pp. 35-36)

For a professional helping relationship, a problem exists when the practitioner sees it, when the user sees it, and when each of them knows what the other knows or sees what the other sees. I shall use the expression 'relational basis' to indicate not only that both of them are aware of the problem but also that they are to some extent aware of their (reciprocal) awareness. While a clinical definition of the problem may not comprise this relational embedding – in the sense that the therapist may also start from his or her own viewpoint or diagnosis – a unilateral definition by the expert would be meaningless in social work. If this shared sense of the problem is lacking, then work is required to create it. And it is of no importance whether we already want to call this preparatory work 'intervention' or whether we do not.

1.2.6. *Practitioner/persons involved multiple sharing*

In social work practice, full expert/recipient interconnection is a necessary but not sufficient condition. As Rogers has shown, this interconnection may be present in traditional clinical counselling as well. It is therefore clear that the dual sharing of the problem – the fact that both the expert and the user are mutually interconnected – is still not what we are looking for. As already said, the 'social' manifests itself when the basis of sharing is broader than two (from two to n).

An extended basis for sharing means that shared awareness of the problem, which we assume already exists between expert and recipient, should come about with the largest possible number of persons involved in events – or in other words, standing in relation. A social worker must always remind him/herself that the true answer to the question 'problem for whom' is 'for the greatest number of people that can be realistically conceived as *capable of* feeling it'.

Social workers often find themselves in situations similar to sitting on a stool with only two legs. It may happen that they see the problem, but the persons concerned and their families and friends do not: for example when a neighbourhood social worker sees children constantly wandering the streets unsupervised by an adult. Or the problem may be seen by the social worker and the friends and family of the person concerned but not by the latter: as when a mother tells the social worker of her suspicions that her husband is abusing their daughters. On other occasions the problem is seen by the person concerned but not by the social worker, who indeed may see nothing at all, or something different: as for example when a still self-sufficient elderly person asks for home help.

Whenever awareness of the problem is partial, it is necessary to work with the apparent paradox of creating the problem as a social fact, starting from fragmented perceptions or no perceptions at all. This is work on perceptive sharing.

1.2.7. *'Social control' situations: is sharing possible?*

The sharing rule applies when we are dealing with helping in the proper sense. The problem must be a shared construct when it is the raw material of professional care conceived in the best interests of the persons concerned. But we know that social work may not be of this type. This is when we talk of 'control' rather than 'helping'.

Social workers are sometimes unable to act on the basis of their beliefs or their 'therapeutic' mandate. Instead, they are obliged to act in favour of one party against another, or in the interests of society as a whole in pursuit of the higher exigency of collective welfare. There are frequent and well-known assessment situations (tasks) in which a social worker is compelled to perceive social problems and to take measures *contrary* to the perceptions or feelings of the person concerned. In the case of child neglect, for example, the social worker must intervene even if the children, parents, neighbours and others are against it (Stratton and Hanks, 1995). In these cases, if we ask 'problem for whom?', we must answer: problem for society, for that impersonal social order which protects its own welfare as embodied in the objective welfare of unaware subjects, namely the neglected children in the above example. The construction (definition) of the problem, and the action to be taken, are fixed by law: the discretion of the social worker – although s/he takes the decision whether or not to intervene – is limited, but even more limited is the discretion of the persons in whose regard adverse measures are taken.

Breach of the sharing rule always causes suffering, even when it is reasonable and justified. If the breach is total – as in the case of forcible removal incomprehensible to those involved – then the situation is more accurately described as a technical-administrative problem rather than a social one. The presence of social workers in these assessment procedures is intended to ensure that the logic of social care – which should be based on sharing – is nevertheless present. No matter if little or nothing can be done: the role of the social worker, compared with those of the judicial authorities and of the law enforcement agencies for example, necessarily requires that an attempt must be made.

1.3. The social problem as inadequacy of action

To sum up: a social problem is not an objective phenomenon amenable to solution by anyone who, say, sees it in the street. Nor is it like a mathematical problem set for a child at school with its canonical solution at the end of the book. A social problem is a complex of perceptions and judgements of inadequacy/difficulty – that is, a complex of subjective experiences connected with more or less definite conditions or circumstances. It is a problem laden with subjectivity, but when it is sufficiently shared – when it is not a problem only for the person affected by it or for the person appointed to solve it – it may become a less uncertain reality, something that can be intentionally addressed, and perhaps even solved, as every problem should be when we imagine it intuitively.

One important criterion for distinguishing a social problem has just been discussed: the extent to which it is shared. The more people recognize a problem, the more it becomes a social problem. Is this enough? Is any problem at all, as long as it is shared by a sufficiently large number of people, a problem that falls within the domain of social work? The question can be addressed by reversal. One can certainly say that if there is no sharing of sentiment, a difficulty experienced by a person in isolation is *not* a social problem. A social problem is such for two reasons: because there is an interweaving of minds that grasp it (on the structural level), and because there is something else lying at a more substantial level. This something else is action and its shortfalls.

Elsewhere (Folgheraiter,1998), I have defined (in)capacity for action to be the subject matter of social work. By this I mean that a problem of interest to social workers is not a *pathology*, or a static state of affairs, but a dynamic difficulty: an impediment against the achievement of goals.

A common sense view might consider a pathology in the strictly medical sense of the term (a tonsillitis, a hemiparalysis, a manic-depressive psychosis, etc.) to be a 'thing', a concrete entity located in some bodily apparatus or organ in the form of bacterial or viral attack, of a biochemical imbalance, and so on. In reality, all the arguments put forward so far can be applied to medical pathologies, since these too only become problems when the processes of appraisal and classification that we have defined as diagnosis have been performed. However, it might be objected that expatiating on the existence of a concrete and full-blown pathology is a waste of time. Although this pragmatic impatience may be acceptable in health care, where pathologies are at issue, it must be held in check in the social work arena, where actions are at issue.

An action may be impeded by a pathology but it is never itself a pathology. Nor is it any other concrete thing that may resemble it. An action is not a

phenomenon that *concretely* exists, unless it is confused with the muscular movement by which it is performed (and an action, as we shall see, may also be non-
material). An action is a (more or less) intentional project: it is the striving of an
organism towards a goal that it wants to or must achieve. The meaning of an
action – that something which, as Schütz reminds us, varies according to the
points of view of the actor, of the subjects involved, and of the detached observer
– resides in its directedness towards a goal, which may be a physical object or a
mental fact like an aspiration or an emotion. It is as if the goal, once achieved,
is stamped on the action that accomplishes it, causing it to change nature from
its previous formlessness through the acquisition of meaning.

The action is not the visible act (the muscular movement or the behaviour)
that achieves the goal; rather, it is the profound relation between actor and goal:
it is both of these entities merged together. Consequently, to describe a problem
as an deficiency of action, rather than as the presence of some morbid state, is
truly a judgement in the pure state: a problem arises when someone (who?)
decides that an expected end (expected by whom? why?) has not been accomplished, with all the related implications.

1.3.1. *The agency assessment in social work: the critical points*

Conventional social work assessment may be conceptualized as a complex process of judging which frames and specifies social deficiencies, or in other words,
failed actions. This procedure differs from diagnosis. Diagnosis involves a direct
judgement in that its purpose is to establish whether or not a 'thing' (a pathology)
exists; whether there is a coherent set of signals (symptoms) such that the observer may state 'I'm certain: it's that particular pathology [causing the distress
or dysfunction]. It wasn't visible to the naked eye, but after collating all the
symptoms, I can declare that it exists, and that its name is certainly such and such'
(Of course the argument can be attacked on logical grounds, but it works in
practice, and that is what matters). Once the diagnosis has been made, the
problem exists and is manipulable; and often the solution as well, given that in
medicine diagnosis and solution are frequently one and the same thing: 'head-
ache' means aspirin; 'appendix' means its removal, and so on.

The judgement involved in action assessment is different. The process does not
merely establish whether or not a certain thing exists as in the case of pathology. Nor
does it ascertain whether something is actually lacking (i.e. a need) as happens in the
more traditional 'needs assessment' (Davis et al., 1997). It instead determines whether
or not a certain *relation* exists among two abstractly correlatable entities, namely a
motivational state (a need, desire, aspiration, etc., i.e. a subjective ends) and an

Motivational states		Factual states	
A_1	Imposed obligations	B_1	Personal capacities/constraints
$A_{1.1}$	Bio-psychic needs endo-genous to the actor	$B_{1.1}$	Physical health
		$B_{1.2}$	Mental health (personality)
$A_{1.2}$	External (but internalized) demands, pressures and challenges directed at the actor	$B_{1.3}$	Information, knowledge, abilities
A_2	Freely-assumed obligations constraints	B_2	Resources/environmental
		$B_{2.1}$	Social (other persons)
$A_{2.1}$	Expectation, mental stan-dards, desires	$B_{2.2}$	Institutional/cultural
$A_{2.2}$	Goals, plans, projects, etc.	$B_{2.3}$	Physical/mental

Fig. 1.1 The four fundamental variables of action

actual state (the objective prerequisites/premises for the action intended to accomplish the end). The dynamic connecting these two entities is what is conventionally called 'action', and it is this dynamic that the expert assessment must evaluate in order to give a technical definition – which may or not be shared with those concerned, according to their codes – to a social problem.

In more concrete terms, and to simplify the discussion, I shall try to specify the critical points of assessment with the help of a diagram (Figure 1.1). By 'motivational state' is meant everything that has to do with the meaning in the 'mind' of a person of a task to perform: what I have called 'aim' or 'purpose'. We may distinguish tasks between a 'must-do' imposed by (intrinsic/extrinsic) necessity and a duty assumed by free choice or by free will. This distinction is analytic, given that in reality the two states tend to merge together.

The task imposed by necessity (A_1) we may call an *imposed obligation*, and it is everything that a person feels obliged to do at a certain time. We may crudely divide it into two levels: (a) the need to respond to impelling bio-psychic needs which arise within the person, in his or her physiology, so to speak; (b) the duty to respond to more or less binding requirements/pressures that originate from outside the person, environmental entities which imprint themselves on the mind and motivate action in the same way as needs.

I shall call a self-imposed task (A_2) a *freely-assumed obligation*. The term refers to both unconscious variables like expectations/desires/ideal standards, and so on, and to more rational and intentional variables like the goals, plans or programmes that a person somehow freely assumes; or better, goals which s/he was originally not obliged to pursue, but which once they have been psychologically 'fixed' may become binding for the person and therefore real motivators of action.

By 'factual state' I mean the ascertainable existence of resources or constraints which may stimulate/aid action or alternatively obstruct/restrain it. These states can be distinguished into *personal* (B_1) and *situational* (B_2). Personal resources or personal constraints are strengths or weaknesses in those areas of the person (discussed in detail in Chapter 4) that pertain to the biological, emotional/affective and cognitive-behavioural. Situational resources and situational (or environmental) constraints are structural or conjunctural features that are external to the actor although they affect him/her in various ways.

Action is effective when the sense of must-do (subjective state) – which may be present or absent, with all possible intermediate gradations – is combined with the actual possibility of doing something (objective state), this too with multiple variations. A social problem arises when an action is limited or impeded with perceivable and communicable consequences. According to the above diagram, a deficiency or absence of action can be brought about by two main causes:

1. *The state of fact is lacking*: a duty or obligation, and the subsequent motivation to action, is not matched by a set of resources so that there are objective obstacles against its fulfilment.

2. *The motivational inner state is lacking*: according to an external observer, the duty or obligation has not been internalized, either wholly or in part, regardless of the state of fact of resources/constraints that may help or hinder its fulfilment. Strictly speaking, involved here is not deficiency of action but an action not performed because of a teleological void, or in other words, because of a lack of purposiveness.

Let me give an example of the latter point. A boy in the second year of lower secondary school who has no desire to study, plays truant from school and spends the whole day riding around on his motorcycle. He thus evidences a social problem caused by a lack of a commitment to study – that is, to the obligation imposed on him by others – more than by the absence of the means to do so. The existence or otherwise of the boy's ability to study is secondary to his motivation, although the two variables are obviously correlated: an inability to study may reduce motivation, and vice versa.

Point 2 comprises a type of social problem which is apparently not included in the above diagram. I refer to dysfunctions which originate in effective actions, i.e. when a person is able to do something but the consequences of this 'successful action' can be evaluated – immediately or in the long term, by the actor or by observers – as negative, in the sense that they are destructive or reduce wellbeing (that of the actor or others). With respect to the definition of a problem as a deficiency of action, these actions are important. Not because they are absent, obviously, but because of the lack of their opposite, namely desirable actions.

Let us return to the example of the boy who rides around on his motorcycle rather than go to school. His problem, in fact, could be conceptualized as an *excess* of ability: his desire to ride his motorcycle is manifestly connected with ability, given that he is a skilled motorcyclist. The fact that the boy is able to perform this action well is harmful to him (in the view of others, given that for him his ability is only a source of self-esteem). If the motivational state of desiring the motorcycle were not conjugated with the ability to use it (lack of personal capacity B_1) or the physical availability of the motorcycle (lack of environmental resource B_2), phenomenologically the problem would be otherwise. However, the boy's situation can be equally well conceptualized as a lack of the opposite tendency, or of purposiveness, namely the absence of a desire to study. This, in truth, is the *essential* manner of defining it. If a demotivated schoolboy does not possess a motorcycle, or does not know how to ride one, the problem does not disappear: he will soon find another amusement to keep him away from school (McCombs and Pope, 1994; Carr, 1994).

Similarly, a drug addict may be such – that is, may have or be a problem, for himself or for others – in that he effectively perceives the need induced by drugs (motivational state) and effectively satisfies it by regularly managing to procure his daily dose (factual state). Alternatively, one can focus on the other side of the problem, and call him such because of his inability to perceive the opposing need for moderation or abstinence. Any ascertainment of his gifts of personality that might help him overcome his addiction, as well as of environmental resources (the availability of care services, for example), is secondary: these objective prerequisites may be present, but only motivation or awareness of the problem will bring them to bear.

The two broad categories of problems identified here – a problem as a lack of state of fact or as a lack of motivational state – prompt considerations concerning the role played by the actor's awareness. When the problem is caused by the actor's inability to fulfil an obligation of which s/he is aware (that is, when the problem is caused by the absence of states of fact), it is likely that the actor will also be aware of the problem – that is, aware of his/her inability to meet the requirements made of him/her. The actor sees the difficulty in which s/he finds him or herself, and so does the social worker. When conducting an assessment, the social worker must fathom the bilateral components of the problem: those relative to the sense of task, or the characteristics of the *requirement* for action, and those relative to personal capabilities and the situational resources available. S/he is aided in this task by the fact that the components of the problem are to some extent tangible, and that the subject can help define them.

When the problem arises because there is no expected action, and this action is not performed because it is not perceived as necessary – the person does not see why s/he should perform it – the problem becomes more complex, and so too does the assessment. A person who lacks awareness of a goal, necessarily also lacks awareness of possible failure to achieve that goal, namely the problem. What others may see as his or her problem, for him or her does not exist (it cannot be). The purpose of assessment is not only to unravel the objective terms of the problem, but also to single out a mental dimension: an inability to see things by oneself.

These two types of problem may be comprised in a single event. For example, during a home visit, a social worker enters the flat of an elderly man and finds it dirty and neglected. The man is evidently unable to cope with the task of keeping his home tidy $(A_{1.2})$ to the standard required by social custom. This dysfunction may be due to objective personal or situational hindrances (e.g. bad health or a depressed state; lack of money or equipment, etc.) that prevent him from acting even though he is well aware of the need to perform the task. Alternatively, the dysfunction may depend on the fact that he is not aware of the task required of him: he simply cannot see it. Whether the flat is tidy or not is a matter of indifference to him. As we can see, these are two different kinds of problem, though they may have the same outward appearance.

The analytical distinction between motivational states and states of fact may remind the reader of the fundamental dichotomy between subjective and objective. But caution is required. The category 'motivational states', which seemingly comprises only subjective elements internal to a person, also includes the notion of an external requirement or pressure or challenge $(A_{1.2})$. As said, these are elements that (a) reside in the environment and (b) may be strongly objective. Here they are classified as 'mental' events, because environmental requirements (the obligation to repay a debt, for example) may become action only when they are internalized. On the other hand, the category 'factual states' comprises intrapersonal abilities (B_1) which are usually regarded as subjective, not as elements of the environment. Here they have been classified as 'states of fact', and therefore as objective states to some degree, because they are perceived by the observer as 'given', like the concrete features of the environment. The B_1 abilities can be subjected to objective assessment by means of specific instruments, even for quantitative measurement, like checklists of skills or attitudes, indices of functional self-sufficiency, and so on (ICF, 2001).

1.3.2. *The relationship between a task and an agent: dual coping*

The scheme of action presented above in quadrangular form $(A_1 A_2; B_1 B_2)$ serves mainly analytical purposes. In order to provide a more immediate understanding, one that is more operationally applicable, the diagram can be simplified into a relationship between only two key variables, task and person, as in Figure 1.2.

This simplified model of action goes by the name of 'coping', a central concept in social work (Bartlett, 1970). This classic representation of action, and of its functional deficits, may be useful despite its conciseness provided that those who use it bear in mind what was stipulated above, namely that (a) by 'duty' is meant not only the objective (though internalized) environmental situation but also projects generated by the mind, and (b) by 'person' is meant not only the actor's subjective capacities/incapacities but also the concrete constraints and resources of the surrounding environment – elements which integrate with the person and become almost an extension of it.

Fig. 1.2 Personal coping as the minimum perceptible unit for a social worker.

Inspection of the coping model shows that a social problem cannot be defined unless the unit comprising both the task and person is considered. It is not possible to define a problem solely on the basis of 'task', saying for example that Mary asked for help from the social worker 'because she must look after her sick husband'. Looking after the sick husband (task) is *one* component of the problem. It may be the most evident and tangible one, but it does not suffice unless it is combined with Mary's specific situation and her capacity for action as such. The problem is 'Mary *vis-à-vis* the duty of looking after her sick husband'. It is not Mary in herself, because she may be able to cope with thousands of other tasks in her life. It is not looking after her ill husband, because thousands of other wives look after their husbands without seeing it as a problem (perhaps they find it difficult, but it is not a problem).

We have a social problem when someone – an observer – decides that a task is greater than a person's ability to handle it. The observer may be the agent (the person) him/herself, who acts as judge of his/herself by assessing his/her ability to achieve a goal, or it may be an external perceptual system, which determines whether the person has set goals for him/herself or not, and whether s/he is actually striving toward their achievement. In its turn, this observing system may be observed by another more external one, which examines whether the observer performs his/her duty correctly or whether he/she too has 'problems' in his/her ability to act (in this case merely 'speculative'), and so on.

To summarize, every problem is defined by the conjunction of three variables. As regards its objective difficulty/gravity/complexity, the *task* can be imagined as located along a *continuum*: the observer may see it as extremely simple or as extremely complicated, or somewhere in between, according to a set of evaluative parameters. Also the *person*, as regards his/her potential endowment with internal and external resources, lies somewhere along a continuum. Every concrete action can be located at a particular point along the task cline, and also at a particular point along the personal capacity cline. If we used a double-entry matrix, we could differentiate among problems by locating them at different spatial points. However, bearing in mind that very different definitions are given to a problem according to *who* observes it – the person concerned or external observers, or both – a three-dimensional descriptive model is more suitable (see Figure 1.3).

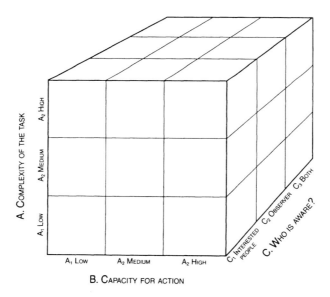

Fig. 1.3 Classification of social problems on the basis of a three-dimensional system (task/person/ observation system).

Let me give an example. The problem of a young drug-addicted mother who does not feed her child properly and sometimes forgets to take him to school, can be represented by coordinates A_1, B_1 and C_2 in Figure 1.3. The task of 'feeding her son properly and taking him to school' is objectively of low complexity (A_1). 'Objectively' means in the eyes of an external observer, who judges according to a statistical yardstick or mean: the majority of mothers, in fact, handle this task without difficulty (That the young mother in question finds the task difficult is a different matter; and it is taken for granted, given that she is unable to perform it). The young mother's objective capacity for action – which in this case is a capacity to provide parental care – is limited (B_1), if nothing else because of her drug addiction.

The observation system is restricted to the external observer alone (C_2), for neither the mother nor her friends, if she has any, are aware of the task or of the problems that derive from its non-fulfilment.

An entirely different type of problem arises in the case, for example, of an unmarried fifty-year-old man who must look after an elderly mother suffering from advanced senile dementia. This problem can be described with coordinates A_3, B_3 and C_3 in that: (a) the task of looking after a completely non-self-sufficient elderly person on one's own is objectively complex (A_3), (b) the son is – let us assume – well able to look after his mother (B_3), but (c) both he and the social worker to whom he has applied for help are aware that he cannot do so for very long (C_3).

The term 'coping', as said, denotes a reciprocal observed challenge between task and person. The idea of 'challenge' entails that coping can be conceptually evidenced only when the action breaks down, at least for a while, and becomes difficult. For there to be coping, the task must be intractable and the person must not immediately know how to deal with it. There must be some difficulty in the action. When instead the task confronting a person, or the task which s/he freely assumes, is dealt with immediately, we have an efficacious action which proceeds smoothly and straightforwardly. In this fortunate case there is neither a challenge nor, even less, a problem. People's lives comprise numerous actions directed towards achievement of conscious or unconscious goals where these actions come about by themselves without hindrances.

This specification enables us to give more precise definition to concepts that are easily confused. We may distinguish, in fact, between *immediate action* and *coping*, where the latter is understood as the handling of a task which is slightly more demanding than the capacities available to deal with it, and then between *coping* and *problem*, where by problem is meant a coping which is thwarted, i.e. when the agent's ability, even if solicited by the task, does not increase accord-

ingly and the agent or the observer come to believe that it will not arise spontaneously.

We can also distinguish among *individual problem* (i.e. an deficiency of
coping where awareness of inability to perform the task is restricted to the person
confronted by that task), *social problem* (where the problem or crisis is perceived
by the various people involved, or by external observers), and *formal social problem* (when one of the observers is a professional practitioner for whom the
difficulty of the persons involved, and which s/he helps them to overcome, is a
not immediately resolvable *challenge*). I shall return to this last distinction below.

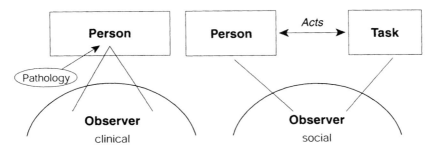

Fig. 1.4 Comparison between the minimum units of observation of a health worker (left) and a social worker (right).

The simplified coping model sheds clearer light on the question of the
specificity of *social* observation. We may say that the task/person relation is the
minimal unit of observation for social workers. They cannot focus on elements
smaller than this unit. Were they to do so, they would be breaching the bounds
of their professional domain. Note, however, that the elementary coping relation
– the task/person relationship – should then provide the *basis* for broader-gauge
observations which focus on wider relations. But, as said, social workers cannot
penetrate below this basis. If they do, they encroach on areas of clinical
competences, where medical rather than social criteria apply. Figure 1.4 com-
pares the different standpoints of the clinician and the social worker. It will be
seen that they employ what are almost reverse methods of observation.

The clinical observer sees keenly; the social observer extensively. The former
sees (or thinks that s/he sees) a state within a person's skin, a pathology, and
eliminates action. The latter sees the action, that ideal dynamic appendage of the
person that ties him or her to a task, and determines whether or not there is a
problem by establishing whether or not this action is efficacious.

Obviously, the expert social observer, besides seeing differently from the
health worker, also has a view different from that of the person immersed in the

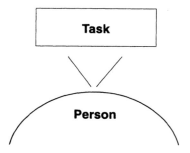

Fig. 1.5 The task observed from the point of view of the person concerned.

problem – that is, the 'user' if the observer is a professional practitioner. The person involved *feels* that s/he is in difficulty (when the difficulty is perceived), rather than observing or clearly understanding the insufficient action dynamic in which s/he is caught up.

Should we want to be more specific, we may depict his or her standpoint as that of the external observer in the above diagrams. What does s/he see? More probably only the *task*, not him/herself. Unless an observer makes a conscious and difficult effort of self-observation, s/he is generally unable to see himself or herself while observing. S/he sees only the object in his or her range of vision. (These points are illustrated by Figure 1.5). A person immersed in his or her problem 'sees' it in more focused and restricted manner than does (or should) the methodologically sophisticated professional social worker, although the latter has a better viewpoint because s/he is external to the coping behaviour being observed.

Evidence that the person concerned possesses a more concrete and more focused view of his or her own problem – given that s/he is immersed in it – is provided by the typical format of the initial phase of social work interviews. These usually begin with the client reporting (complaining about) concrete facts to do with external circumstances: a violent husband, children doing badly at school, the loss of a job, and so on. For her, only these concrete phenomena constitute the problem; it is only these that are wrong. She is more often unable to see her own possible contribution to the problem (that is, her lack of action). In these cases, the social worker must initially support this view of the client, but thereafter, as counselling progresses, he or she must shift the helping focus to the client as an agent itself, through appropriate reformulations. For example, according to the procedure described by Carkhuff (1987), s/he may begin by mirroring the contents (the facts) told by the client *(content reformulation);* then

Fig. 1.6 The inner task observed from the point of view of the person concerned.

s/he may elicit the client's emotions and feelings about the task *(meaning refor-mulation)*. Or s/he may use a technique known as *personalization reformulation* to make the connection between the problem and the client's structural charac-teristics as an agent explicit. In each of these cases, the expert encourages the client to see the connection between himself or herself and the task, a connection which was initially perceived by the expert alone.

Another specification is necessary. As said, a social worker sees a social prob-lem at the moment when s/he perceives an uncoupling between the task and the person. No longer the problem of an individual person, a difficulty becomes a *formal social* problem, and therefore a *problem* for the practitioner as well, when the latter not only perceives it but also fully understands it out of empathy and therefore shares it with the person concerned – when, that is, the social worker agrees that what s/he sees, or what s/he is being told, is truly a problem. Yet a problem is by definition 'something that one does not immediately know how to solve'. Strictly speaking, therefore, a client's problem also becomes a problem for the social worker when a further necessary condition holds: that the *solution* of the dysfunctional coping discerned by the social worker does not *immediately* spring from his or her perception of the problem. In other words, the social worker must perceive the coping difficulty but without having the solution to it directly to hand. If s/he can say 'To solve your problem do this or that', then strictly speaking this is not a problem for him or her. It is a problem for the person who does not know what to do – who has been defeated by the problem – but not for the professional, who immediately knows what is required. Hence, ac-cording to the theory set out above, what we have here is not a true formal social problem. A social problem must be an *enigma* for all those affected by it, the social worker included. It must presuppose that it is necessary *to search* for a joint solution, rather merely apply one already available.

A different case arises when despite the social worker's best efforts the search for a solution proves fruitless, and the problem is not resolved or ameliorated. Therefore, besides being a social problem in the sense with which the term is used here – namely, as the basis or raw material for formal intervention – we have a technical problem for the social worker, a persistent professional difficulty. An even more external observer, a supervisor for example, may view the social worker with coping difficulties as a task for himself or herself. The supervisor sees a coping difficulty (a problem) raised by the power of two: inadequate coping by a social worker, the content of which (task) is in its turn inadequate coping by a client.

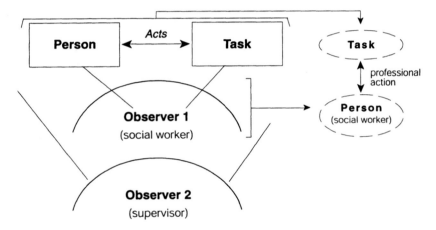

Fig. 1.7 Multiple model of social problem observation. Observer 2 (the supervisor) sees the problem of an operator (observer 1) who sees the problem (difficulties in coping with a task) of a person.

This backward shift in the point of observation – so that observation of an observer (the social worker) takes place – is depicted by Figure 1.7, which illustrates in abstract the process of professional supervision. (If we take a further step backwards – so that the supervisor, too, has difficulties in observing and understanding the social worker's difficulty – we have third-degree coping; and so on). The supervisor observes inadequate coping behaviour, the object of which is again inadequate coping, and s/he discerns a professional difficulty, which in the long run may also become a personal difficulty. Thus, a personal difficulty triggers the process of dwindling motivation and mental exhaustion known as 'burnout' (Cherniss, 1980; Maslach and Leiter, 1997; Berstein and Halaszyn, 1999).

1.4. A higher level of observation: relational coping

To sum up the argument so far: a social problem is a relation, in the broad sense, for three reasons. Firstly, because it to some extent depends on (emerges from) the way in which reality interacts with the observer, so that a problem is the reality that the observer or observers agree that it is. Secondly, because the evaluation which determines that a person has a problem must necessarily – for the problem to become a formal object of social work intervention – be shared by several persons standing in relation and immersed to varying extents in the problem (as the 'bearer' of the problem, the others involved, and the expert observer). Thirdly, because if we delve deeply and examine what actually constitutes the problem-creating evaluation, we find that it hinges on the relationship (inadequate or non-existent) between two variables, task and person, in the ideal interaction that is coping.

We may now develop the argument in more concrete terms. The foregoing, rather metaphysical discussion, has shown the relational matrix in which a problem can be framed theoretically. But a social problem is relational in a concrete sense as well, for it consists of real relations between people of flesh and blood. This brings us to the crux of the matter: coping, as abstractly defined in the previous section, is in reality substantiated by relations in both its components, task and person (or better, persons). The majority of the *tasks* that a person must cope with are constituted by, or derive from, interpersonal relations. That is to say, they are pressures or challenges which involve persons in the life-environment of our hypothetical coper. But above all, every task, as we know, prompts to action not just one person, but a number of persons in a *networking process.*

Once again, an important specification is required before we proceed. I must clarify a point which causes much mischief in the analysis of relations in social work. The point to bear in mind is that relations have a bearing on a problem not so much because they *cause* it (or more precisely, not because they cause dysfunctions in people) as because they constitute it.

1.4.1. *A social problem is not an individual disorder caused by relations*

The systemic (family therapy) approach has been used in psychotherapy since Bateson's seminal works that gave rise to the clinical technique of the Palo Alto School (Piercy et al., 1996). This clinical method has also been applied, sometimes ingenuously, in social work (Coady, 1993). It is therefore necessary to clarify the difference between this widely-known psychotherapy 'philosophy', sometimes considered to be the relational approach *par excellence,* and the networking approach, which is the relational view purged of clinical content presented here. There are obvious similarities between them, first and above all the idea that the social relationship is the cornerstone of theorization, yet it is important to emphasise their differences in order to forestall conceptual confusion, and perhaps to prevent errors from being committed in practice.

The most evident differences are apparent in the way that the two approaches use the concept of relation with regard to the dynamics that generate solutions. This topic will be dealt with in detail in the next chapter. For the time being, I shall show how the approaches differ in their conceptualization of problems.

1.4.2. *The family therapy and networking approach: differences*

For the psychotherapeutic (systemic) relational approach, the 'problem of problems' (we shall see below what this means) is once again a mental *pathology* – a schizophrenia, a depression, a neurosis, and the like – or a major behavioural disorder. Its point of departure is essentially that of any other psychotherapy school: all of them, psychoanalytical, behavioural, Rogersian, or whatever, view the problem – the reason why help is given – as an individual clinical fact, or in other words, as an alteration in a person's mental processes manifest in one or several external symptoms. What distinguishes the systemic approach from the others – to the point that it claims radical epistemological diversity – is its conception of the causes of pathology. But it is identical with the others in its assumption that a problem is a pathology. The networking approach instead rejects this axiom, and in doing so sets itself radically at odds with *all* psychotherapies, including those, like the systemic approach, which in other, more superficial respects resemble it.

The systemic (family therapy) approach maintains that a pathology is *created* by interpersonal relations. A person becomes mentally ill or suffers from chronic anxiety or behaves dysfunctionally *because of* the structure of human relations surrounding him or her. Put otherwise: people are influenced, or 'conditioned' in behaviouristic terms, in their mental structures or personalities by the form and content of their everyday communication with significant others.

Consider for example the case of Anna, a young girl with a serious eating disorder. She rejected food and dawdled over her meals for so long that constant help was required from her parents, especially the father. Mealtimes lasted hours as the parents urged Anna to eat and made sure that she did so. Even intuitive analysis of the systemic form of the girl's relations showed that the parents' concern over her disorder – and therefore the fact that the father related to her only *because* she was disturbed – induced Anna to see her symptom as an advantage, and that she refused to relinquish it despite (indeed because of) the father's pressure on her to do so. The type of parent/child relation entirely explains why this specific dysfunction arose and persisted until it became chronic.

The systemic (family therapy) approach has two noteworthy features.

1. The observer does not merely see the dysfunction or, in other words, 'diagnose' it by saying whether or not it exists and whether it is one thing rather than another. Such is, it will be remembered, diagnosis in the strict sense. The observer also interprets the problem and explains it in terms of causes, which in this case are relations which do not work. Causal attribution whereby 'that pathology derives from those relations' is the overriding concern of the systemic clinician. As the approach rightly claims, the true diagnostic focus is the structure and dynamics of relations, the aim being to discover the nature of the entities which – by creating the reality *sui generis* constituted by the relational system – cause the problem, namely the pathology. The 'enlightenment' curiosity to find out how and to what extent relations are 'sick' becomes crucial (and in some cases, we may say, self-referential). However, even granted that pathological relations are the problem, this certainty is always significant because it informs us about the cause of the individual pathology which sets everything else in train (which is why I previously called this individual pathology the 'problem of problems').

2. The only causes considered are relations – to the point, one might think, that they are taken to be the cause of all conceivable pathologies. This statement obviously requires immediate clarification.

1.4.3. The aetiology of individual problems: the individual and the social-individual problem

A given individual structure – also a dysfunctional one if we think of pathologies – may arise for endogenous reasons (i.e. internal causes) or for exogenous ones (i.e. external causes). A pathology is by definition an inner state clearly attributable to the person. It is therefore commonplace to associate a pathology intuitively with endogenous causes. Consider, for example, a mentally disturbed woman who raves to herself as she wanders the streets. We automatically assume that there is something within her that makes her behave in such a way, and that this something derives from something else inside her, and so on. This was for long the only plausible key to interpretation of mental pathology, and it drove research into possible endogenous causes and their clarification. Investigated or hypothesised were genetic, biochemical, and traumatic causes (pathologies), and others besides (metabolic disorder, etc.).

The systemic-relational revolution turned this mode of thought on its head, also encouraged by evidence that these endogenous causes are not easy to identify, and it is just not possible at all. It showed that a chronic inner state, like a pathology or an entrenched attitude, can be produced by relations. Put more precisely, it showed that such a state could be understood in the light of its communicative function – in particular the function of preserving a sense of identity and personal integrity threatened or pressurized by the attitudes of others.

With this interpretative key, certain forms of behaviour which common-sense found incomprehensible without the use of facile and often tautological explanatory devices – like the concepts of mental pathology or personality disorder – became intelligible and coherent. The systemic approach showed that it was not the disturbed person alone that should be observed and perhaps scrutinised internally. Instead, the unit of observation should be that person and someone else: that is to say, a pair (or more) of actors in stable interaction. The ways in which relations structured themselves or acquire specific *form* explained the person's overt behaviour.

Space precludes further discussion of these concepts (The reader may gain an idea of their range and impact from the case study in the last chapter of this book). What I wish to emphasise here is that no matter what the causes of an individual dysfunction may be (mental, behavioural, or whatever), *even if they can be clearly linked with relations*, the dysfunction is not a problem that should specifically concern social work. A problem that can be described as a *disorder* (in a person's mental structure) is not so much a social problem as what we may call an *'individual* problem' to indicate that it concerns 'that person there' with a name and surname. To be exact, we may at most say that a structural alteration in a person *due to the effect of relations* should be called a 'social-individual problem', thereby emphasising that the social (the relation) is one of the causes of individual disorders. The label 'individual problem' should be reserved for those disorders due to evident endogenous causes – that is, when the role of relations is not discernible (see Figure 1.8).

1.4.4. *Relations which cause and relations that prolong an individual problem*

Innumerable individual problems are generated by endogenous factors where external influences (by social relations) are not directly involved. Not always, therefore, does it make sense to search for relational causes. This is quite evident in all psychophysical handicaps with an evident organic basis. On other occasions, the search for pathogenic relations may be extremely laborious and complicated, and often it only yields a handful of feeble hypotheses. Giovanni is a five-year-old boy suffering from severe autism (Schopler, 1995). Although there are theories that contend that autism is caused by an unsatisfactory relationship with the mother in the early stages of development, it is obvious that such severe forms of handicap cannot depend entirely on this relationship, however fundamental it may be (amongst other things, Giovanni's mother, who presumably brought all her children up in the same way, has two other healthy sons). By contrast, as in the case of Anna who refused to eat, and in many other cases besides, it frequently happens that the dynamics of the interaction are evident and immediately perceivable. *Primary educational* relations are obviously important in determining specific personality traits or persistent problematic behaviour, or the persistent attitudes of adults towards children. Relations of particular significance for social work are those that arise in concomitance with, or *as a consequence of*, endogenous pathologies so that constant or at any rate 'special' treatment is required for a person whose problem 'arises from within'. It is frequently the case that these relations aggravate or give greater salience to the manifestations of a pathology which in itself does not derive from them. When an individual problem is observed after a certain lapse of time, it is frequently seen as 'encrusted' with relations which in fact only spring from the attempt to deal with it. For example, a hyperactive child with attention deficit syndrome (Woods and Ploof, 1997) who never sits still for a moment at school may activate relations with his teachers or classmates which *reinforce* his motor hyperactivity (he may attract attention, for example) although it is caused by a neurological deficit. In such cases, it seems that the problem is due to relations, but one must know how to distinguish precisely between what causes a problem and what exacerbates it.

Let me repeat: searching for these causes – trying to explain why a certain person is the way he or she is – is not the job of a social worker, although it is a temptation difficult to resist. There are two temptations, in fact: one is to concentrate on a person's *anomalies;* the other is to seek an explanation for the origin of these anomalies. Nonetheless, the social worker should not spend too much time on searching for the causes (endogenous/exogenous) of a personal anomaly. Although these anomalies are the social worker's bread and butter, so to speak, and should certainly be taken into account, he or she is concerned with other types of problems.

Social problems are difficulties which are produced, and which therefore should be investigated, downstream from an individual difficulty, not upstream of it. The *product* of past dysfunctional relations (a child suffering from a personality disorder, for example) is not the social worker's problem. The problem is the *lack of adequate* relations in the proximate future. If we conceive of relations not as 'causes

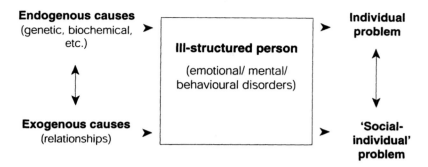

Fig. 1.8 Distinction between an 'individual problem' and a 'social-individual problem' according to its type of cause (endogenous/exogenous). The two-way arrows between the two types of cause and the two types of effect indicate that they may interact.

of' but as 'actions necessary for', to say that a problem is *social* or to say that it is *relational* is exactly the same thing. Whilst, as we have seen, a human problem may or may not be a relational outcome – that is, it may or may not be the consequence of relations – a social problem is relational in the fullest sense of the word. It is the inadequacy of the social (of persons standing in relation) to manage (cope with) a joint action dynamic projected into the future. In the social sphere, a problem should be seen above all as a joint action which at present is lacking.

1.4.5. *The methodological features of relational coping*

To understand the point fully, we must return to the conceptual model of coping. It will be remembered that we considered a problem to be an infelicitous combination of a particular person with a particular task (or coherent set of tasks), or in general an inadequate capacity to act purposefully. However, we have also seen that the dual coping model *(one* task and *one* person) does not describe reality exactly. Indeed, it does not describe it even approximately.

With regard to the two main variables that constitute the coping process, we may ask 'what are tasks in actual practice?' And what is this curious creature, the individual person, who copes with them? The key questions are these: whose capacity for action? Who is the 'agent' that the expert observer must frame in his mind in order to visualise a social problem, if there is one?

A concise answer to these questions might run as follows:

> A social problem is a generalized difficulty ('generalized' in the sense that it is felt by several people) due to a task *potentially* ascribable to several persons but which they are unable or unwilling to cope with adequately.

Whilst it is easier for an observer to conceive or perceive the coping process in the singular, i.e. as one task and one person, this is not the way things operate in practice. The reality of coping is plural, and even if it were not, in some circumstances it would be more fruitful for the social worker to view things in this way.

The broad-gauge model of coping is depicted in Figure 1.9, where the coping subject (the effective agent) is a *set* of persons. I have called this set of persons linked (or ideally linked) around a task a 'coping network'.

When an observer looks at a coping network, s/he must be trained to see it, for it requires a perception that is largely abstract. Observing the task/person interaction is already difficult, because it involves seeing something that does not exist. A task is a mental (intangible) construct. Consequently, one never sees a person handling a task as one sees a carver handling wood. A person, at any rate, is at least a concrete and observable entity.

But what can one say about a network, about a set of interconnected persons? A network is anything but a sensible phenomenon that can be seen and touched. It is a conceptual entity, a pure abstraction. If the illustration provided by Figure 1.9 is accurate, when we say that a problem is 'seen', we are saying that the observer perceives it not with real eyes but with the mind's eye.

What can be 'read' from these two diagrams and their depiction of the coping *subject* as a network? A number of things:

1. The action observed in network coping is a 'cumulated' or joint action. The simplest way to understand this concept is to imagine a *sum* of distinct actions (strain toward goals) tied together by an ideal bond, namely the task. A more

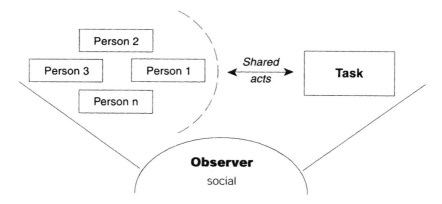

Fig. 1.9 Networking or relational coping.

sophisticated way is to imagine the *product* of numerous interconnected in-dividual actions ('inter-actions') whose criss-crossing and interweaving create a new entity, greater than the sum of its individual components.

Whatever the case may be, all the interactions associable with the task must be combined into a single view.

2. As regards the onset of a problem (deficiency of action), it is improper to say that a problem arises when Ego (person 1) fails to cope with a task. In reality, when a person is unable to do something, there are always other actions by other people (person 2 or person 3, or others besides) who intervene between him or her and the perception of the difficulty by a social worker. These other people set about, largely spontaneously and more or less efficaciously, to compensate for person 1's inability. *The problem arises when this cumulated action is not enough, or when it does not exist.* Instead, if the necessary action is taken the individual problem may never turn into a social problem (because, in effect, the 'social' does not have problems). Even less will it turn into a *formal* social problem, because there is little chance that it will attract the attention of a social worker in a statutory care setting.

3. It should be pointed out that the network may operate so that the compen-satory inter-actions are activated not only *a posteriori* of Ego's (person 1's) evident coping difficulty. The scenario of 'person 1' struggling entirely alone with a task, after which, should s/he fail, the members of the network take over to do it themselves is not appropriate. This may happen in some circum-stances; but more frequently coping, when it works, is more subtle: from the outset the task is addressed with immediate synergy, in the sense that the compensatory actions are triggered at the precise moment when they are needed. One is matched by another, one is set off by another, so that there is truly *comprehensive* action (by the social as a whole) comprising each small action of all those involved (from person 1 to person n). Every action or

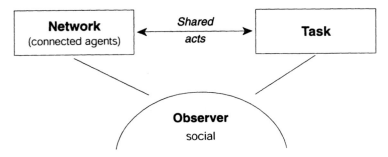

Fig. 1.10 The coping network in outline.

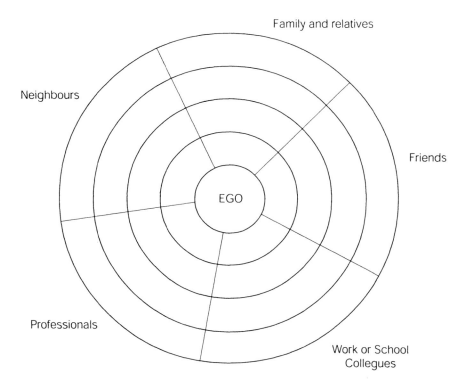

Fig. 1.11 The social network map proposed by Todd (in Maguire, 1983).

interaction is triggered not by the perception of blatant failure by 'person 1', but by the simple perception that there is something that needs to be done. It may happen that the crisis (of person 1) does not occur because it has been preceded or attended by immediate and synchronic actions which have fore-stalled it (rather than remedy it *a posteriori*). These *ad hoc* actions which wrap themselves around the person and protect him or her in a buffering way provide what is technically called 'social support' (Pierce et al., 1996).

If instead the crisis did occur, one must ask why it was a crisis for person 1, assuming that third parties were involved, or should have been. Why was it a crisis for person 1? In more precise terms, one should say that it was a crisis for the network – according to the observer – for the relational entity which did not function properly.

4. According to the relational coping model, a network must always and exclusively be defined with reference to the logical category of 'task'. This entails that the network cannot be viewed as a static and permanent structure. A

network-as-structure is defined with reference to one person and to the social ties that this person *possesses (egoical* network, i.e. centred on an Ego). A network of this kind usually has a graphic representation similar to fig. 1.11 (Maguire, 1983). A network-as-dynamic (a coping network) instead relates to a task and to the inter-actions that this task weaves together and directs towards a goal. Let me give an example. If we say that Luca has a wife, two children, a father and mother, two parents-in-law, five brothers and sisters, a large number of relatives, numerous work colleagues and friends, we convey an idea of his relations. Other relations may be added to these, while others may be lost, but in substance Luca's network of possible stable interactions consists of these people. On observing Luca from time to time, it is more likely that we shall find him involved in interactions within this circle of relations than without it. And we may assume that this circle is (relatively) stable, in so far as it is the same today as it will be tomorrow. To refer to 'Luca's network' is to evoke all the persons of significance in his life, the persons with whom he is most likely to interact.

As such, Luca's social network has no dynamism, because it a set of ties that tend to be self-maintaining: it is a structure. We instead have a network-as-dynamic when we imagine an action or a coordinated enterprise undertaken by persons with a view to achieving something. In this case, we consider the real *content* of relations, the particular communications or concrete actions that are activated in the course of time. We consider the movement of numerous individual actions which interweave with each other as they are driven by their underlying logic. The catalyst of these actions, the element that ties them together in the logic of social work, is the task, that which the network is 'required' to do. Convergence or otherwise on the outcomes prescribed by the task provides the feedback which ensures that we are moving in the right direction and not losing the sense of what we are doing. When the task fades away, i.e. when it is no longer the concern of the persons involved (either because it has been accomplished or because it gradually loses its relevance) also the inter-actions required to perform it, and consequently the network, disappear.

If, for example, Luca falls ill for a certain period of time, and his wife has to nurse him in hospital while someone else looks after their small children, Luca's extensive network, as a structure, does not have much significance. We must determine whether there is a sufficient dynamism to induce some of the people in the network – not all of them and never all of them together – to take appropriate action with respect to the task perceived.

5. Figure 1.9 shows a plurality of persons addressing *one* task. However, a task is often a series of interconnected tasks, so that a real coping network has a

plurality of tasks addressed by a plurality of persons. For example, the task of 'running the home' is defined in the singular only when it is understood as comprising a broad set of correlated sub-tasks: cleaning, ironing, shopping, paying the bills, and so on. The macro-task of care – the task, that is, of helping the person in difficulties – also consists of a wide variety of duties, some of them predictable, others less so.

> There is a great variety in the times of day or night at which help is most effectively received: in the care tasks required (from light household chores with frequent supervision, to intimate, heavy, messy and repugnant personal form of care); in the minimal frequency with which tasks are performed and the predictability of the most effective time for undertaking them; in the duration of each episode of caring (from a few minutes to almost continuous attention); in the affective and relational needs of the recipient influencing their morale and will to function independently; in the personality and behavioural traits of an elderly person affecting the ease with which he might be helped, the gratification of those who do the helping, and the type of helper who would contribute most to the client's functioning; in the amount, complexity, nature, quality, reliability, and potential of the support and care received from family and other informal sources; in the presence of ambivalences, misunderstanding and exploitation which affect relationships in the informal system; and in the needs of the client for brokerage and advocacy, to achieve effective access to specialized resources and services. (Davies and Challis, 1986, p. 5)

We talk about a 'single' task only for the sake of convenience. A network usually has to cope with several types of sub-tasks simultaneously, so that a more accurate model of coping is that provided by Figure 1.11. We may consequently specify further that a social problem arises not only when the network is unable to cope with *one* task, but also when it is unable to cope with a *quantity* of tasks. It may be easy to deal with each task taken individually, but not all of them together.

6. The explanatory fiction of the 'coping network' enables us to imagine a task 'as if' it always confronts the network as a source of 'external' pressure. In social work, and more generally in caring work, this assumption states that the pressure external to the network that we have called a 'task' is a 'user', a person unable to cope on his/her own and who must associate with other persons in order to receive help. In other words, we tend to think that the agent component in the coping network is constituted by the persons who provide assistance, whereas the task (or the problem to be solved, or the burden to be born)

is the assisted person. However, this conclusion cannot be drawn logically from the relational coping schemata in Fig 1.9. It is instead a figment of our imaginations, unconsciously biased as we are by the one-way model of helping so deeply rooted in all of us. In a coping network, the user does not exist, even when she actually – and unfortunately – does so.

I have already referred to a network's task as a shared psychological state, as an inter-mental dynamic within the network, as a joint perception/motivation to do something. Take, for example, the case of Rodolfo, a mentally disturbed adolescent. Rodolfo can be considered a task for his network – as someone who produces needs and responsibilities for those close to him – only in the extreme case where he has absolutely no awareness of the need/duty to do something for himself, i.e. the same concern that his carers have. Should he share the perception of the task, or even just some of it, and thus express some sort of purposeful coping action, he too must be regarded to all intents and purposes a member of his network, an agent himself for the common good. Note also that the schemata of relational coping, in order to be a generalizable 'theory', must be relevant to every operational setting of social work, and especially to those where the client does not really exist, like community development proactive programmes (Banks, 1995). In these cases, it is obvious that the task is an expression of a self-generated and shared will among persons who act, not because of pressures or duty, but because they wish to do things that they perceive as useful or desirable.

Another wrong conclusion that may be easily drawn from the schemata of relational coping is that tasks are somehow static phenomena that do not

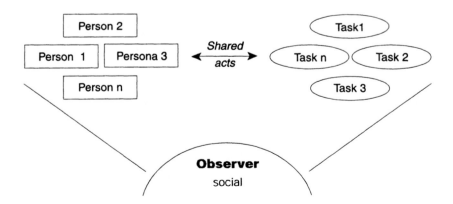

Fig. 1.12 Model of social coping, with the plurality of tasks emphasised.

change over time. On the contrary, tasks are processes; they are compound entities driven by a dynamism that is affected by the coping action but may even be independent of it – or in other words, independent of what the persons concerned do in response to them. Some tasks tend by their very nature to become more complex, others tend to simplify themselves. It is intuitive that the situations of elderly people tend in the long term to become more complicated, while those of minors or young families attenuate, or at any rate redefine themselves as time passes. In practice, it is difficult to determine to what extent a task changes by itself and to what extent it does so because of the action taken. Nevertheless, the distinction is useful.

7. I have thus far discussed networks which consist generically of 'persons'. Broadly speaking, this implies that the members of a social network are to be considered primarily as human beings. This specification may suggest a special reference to persons standing in primary relations like family members, relatives, friends, neighbours, colleagues, and so on. (We may define as 'primary' any structured social network that precedes the particular task at hand and persists beyond it).

In fact, however, the set of people held together by the social worker observer's view in a coping network may also comprise individuals who act upon the task almost exclusively on the basis of a formal role: for instance, the family doctor, a nurse, a clinical psychologist, the parish priest, and others. These practitioners deliver *in primis* specialized *services* which combine with the informal actions undertaken by non-specialists to form an *interwoven* or *mixed* (formal/informal) *network* (Litwark, 1985; Bulmer, 1987; Payne, 2000). However, consideration of a coping network must also include the professionals involved as well, those willing to think and learn from each other in order to determine how to best to deal with the global situation that requires care (which is what coping actually is). Therefore, professionals belong to a helping network when they leave their specialist (delivering) role to a greater or lesser extent and feel themselves part of multiple action.

A social worker who observes a coping network can see the action within it of those of his or her colleagues (working for his or her service or for others) who are already dealing with the problem. If the observer nonetheless sees a problem, this indicates that the set of professional actions, combined with that of the persons directly involved, is not sufficient. Consequently, a problem may still exist even when it has been perceived and addressed by the statutory system of formal social services delivery. It is therefore necessary to reconsider the idea that when professional intervention has begun – when, that is, experts adopting an evidencebased approach have moved in to take action – this by itself is enough to engender a solution, which may be taking a long time to arrive but sooner or later will. In fact, at this stage, the process is often stuck on the problem, because purposeful coping has not yet begun and sometimes this process seems to be hampered by the *self-referential* presence of professionals.

1.4.6. *Types of tasks in relational coping*

When we consider relational coping, as opposed to simple individual coping, it is more difficult to understand the nature of a task, given its association with a plurality of actors. In abstract terms, there are three logical possibilities (Table 1.1).

The simplest possibility is to conceive a network task as coincident with the task of a single Ego (the 'person 1' of the previous examples). The same challenge or need that prompts a person to act prompts others to do likewise. If the task is, for example, to ensure that Luigi 'eats regularly', when for some or other reason Luigi is unable to do so, this task may be the mental state that motivates, for instance, his wife or his two daughters or a cousin or home helpers, or all of them together, with diversified roles and intensities of action. If Luigi is partially able to cooperate – that is, if he is able to perceive the task and to respond in some way – then he too is part of the network. Thus Luigi's task and the network's task coincide: what Luigi feels that he should do (but is unable to) the other people in the network feel as well.

This, as said, is the classic pattern of social work in care situations. Persons other than the 'user' assume responsibility for his disabilities, taking on his tasks as if they were their own and thereby extending the range of action through a network. This illustrates very clearly a critical point in networking: although a social problem often consists of a person with a structural insufficiency of action (whatever its origin), this inadequate person is not the problem – either essentially (i.e. in his/her essence as an inadequate person) or in relation to what s/he does with regard to the problem. The inadequacy of a person engenders a relational dynamic (a networking process), and only if this dynamic in its turn becomes inadequate does a human (localized) problem become a *social* (diffused) one.

A second possibility is that the task may relate to the network as such, without being originated by any particular person (in social work: by a designated user). This conception of tasks as semi-collective is typical of networking coping. It is only when coping involves a plurality of interconnected actors that one can theoretically conceive of a category of tasks more general than the concrete task of an individual. In other words, the task jointly concerns everyone in the network.

Consider, for example, a father, a mother, two children and their family doctor. One of the children, Rodolfo, aged eighteen and attending high school, has for two years suffered severe mental problems. He never leaves the house, he is aggressive and unmanageable, he is a failure at school. In this case, the nature of the person is a challenge to the people around him. The task of coping with Rodolfo attaches to the network as a whole: it is not an Ego task. Indeed, Rodolfo does not perceive management of his bizarre behaviour as a task or a need: he is what he is, period. Ideally, dealing with Rodolfo's behaviour is a shared challenge, a set of responsibilities which engender stress, worry, hard work, wasted time, loss of self-esteem, and so on. Everyone connected with Rodolfo is affected by him and by his behaviour, which they perceive as a problem. Coping with everything that derives from his abnormality (however defined or experienced) is the *(semi) collective* task that I am talking about. If Rodolfo's parents (and perhaps his siblings/friends) find that they are unable to provide the care he needs and decide to join a self-help group (Silverman, 1980) for the parents of adoles-

TABLE 1.1
Types of networking tasks (summary of concepts)

1. *Coincident with individual tasks.* Tasks assumed by the network, consciously or otherwise, in order to compensate for tasks not performed by a particular person. For example, various people cooperate to take Adriano, a person with a physical handicap, out for walks. If the network fails to function, it is mainly Adriano who suffers.

2. *Coincident with the network.* Network tasks as such, i.e. shared by all members, actual or potential, of the network. A shared challenge or obligation which may originate in a person but is not of that person alone. The task is perceivable and can be entirely performed by the persons in the network. For example, in self-help mutual aid groups for the family carers of persons suffering from senile dementia, the task (to improve the quality of life of those caring families) is shared with all the members of the group. If the network fails to function, it is the network as a whole (and then all its members) that suffer.

3. *Extending beyond the network.* Tasks of a potential network which relate to collective projects whose repercussions on welfare extend beyond the boundaries of the network in question. For example, numerous school-age children in a city neighbourhood are at risk of delinquency. If a network of concerned citizens is not activated to deal with the problem, in the future it will be those children and more generally society (the community) as a collective entity larger than the agency network itself, that suffer.

cents in difficulty, then their task is shared by other families. A higher-order network is thus formed and is driven by a task of greater generality.

I said that the task consists of managing Rodolfo. 'Managing' is used here in the generic sense. It may also comprise a therapeutic sub-task, which can be defined as *modifying* Rodolfo's behaviour or restoring it to normality. In many cases, the two tasks (managing and changing, care and curing: that is to say, caring for the person 'as is', attempting to 'heal' him or her) are associated, perhaps confusedly, without the actors being aware of the fact. A specification is required, however. In the case of behaviour modification, the network cannot exclude the person who is directly involved, or put otherwise, the network cannot consider him to be a mere task or a mere target for action. The task pertains both to the network and to Rodolfo, and both of them must modify themselves (if this is possible).

Another type of task arises in cases where a phenomenon extends beyond the network of personal relationships that must or can deal with it. This is a shared task of the type we may call a 'community task'. Consider, for example, a neighbourhood in a large city where a large number of adolescents are at risk of delinquency, drug abuse, or similar. We agree that these adolescents roaming the streets and interacting on the basis of a shared culture constitute a task. But a task for whom? It may be a task for a hypothetical network of responsible persons which might just as well not exist, and then the problem might continue unabated. An observer of this extended coping may see a failure to activate unknown persons who, according to his or her detached point of view, should be involved (Morrison et al., 1997).

For example, are the director of education, the headmaster, the parish priest, the social worker, the members of a local voluntary association mobilizing themselves to help these young people? Are they taking appropriate joint action or are they merely doing something together? This network – which may or may not exist, which may or may not work – must undertake a task which does not directly concern its own welfare (that of the persons in the network) but rather the welfare of the community, the common well-being. That is to say, it is not an obligation for these people, nor is it a challenge for them, or a 'need' in the sense of something that they must necessarily satisfy lest their individual welfare suffer (as at point A_1 in Figure 1.1). Rather, it is a 'project' that they freely undertake. It is something subordinated to a shared perception and therefore to some a shared 'plan of action' (type A_2 in Figure 1.1) which, were it to exist, would tie these people together in a dynamic network. It is action that might even fail to occur without anyone noticing its absence (or only noticing the effects of its absence).

This awareness of the problem may also assign specific *responsibility* to one or other member of the network. In other words, it may be that one of these people – perhaps the patch social worker – is bound by official duty to do something for these adolescents. More frequently, however, action is left to these persons' good (and spontaneous) will. In any event, when legal responsibility is actually allocated (although this is rare in the case of community tasks), it is usually assigned, in accordance with the still dominant individualistic logic, to a single organization or to a single practitioner, but not to a network, which is an entirely different thing.

1.4.7. What 'causes' network inadequacy?

The greater complexity of network coping, where tasks and actors are differentiated and diffused, requires detailed analysis of how problems arise. To say that a problem is 'a network which fails to cope adequately with its task' encapsulates the idea but is too vague. By contrast, when we said earlier that a person was unable to cope adequately, matters were clearer. It was immediately possible to form a mental picture of this difficult coping: we could imagine either a complex task or a person lacking in some sort of ability, or better a task too complex for that particular person, which is a relation between the two entities. But when we consider a network, we must take pains to be clear.

The mechanisms that 'cause' a network to fail, thereby generating a social problem, are much more complicated than those that cause a person to fail. A person misfunctions or dysfunctions because of states of fact within or around him or her. These states of fact are immediately observable as unitary entities. By contrast, a network fails to function because of multiple states of fact, because of deficiencies scattered hither and thither, which can only be brought under observation through a creative act of perception able to interpret and bring out the whole.

A helping network may fail to function, and thereby give rise to a problem, for at least four reasons (which may overlap in concrete situations):

(a) *Because of quantitative inadequacy or a lack of differentiation.* The network has an insufficient number of components (insufficient relative to the tasks that it must perform).

(b) *Because of qualitative inadequacy.* The network does not possess the resources or the qualities required by the task. This point links with the previous one, because a lack of quality usually means that the network is in need of greater differentiation and extension.

(c) *Because of inadequate connectedness.* Although the components of the network are adequate in quantity/quality (according to the observer), they are not sufficiently interconnected. The network does not function as it should because its components do not interact with each other. They instead remain isolated to some extent. There is a consequent lack of those relations which produce the unity of action required by the task and distinctive of networks as such.

(d) *Because of inadequate perception.* The members of the network do not perceive the task as pertaining to them. Consequently, the networking as a task-driven dynamic does not exist. Only an external observer is able to conceptualize it, and then only by default from the missing link between task and action, as in the above example of the potentially delinquent adolescents. This is what we may call a problem 'of omission'.

Points (a) and (b) relate to a social problem that may arise when a network actually exists but does not suffice. To say that a network exists is to say that a set of persons interact to achieve a goal of which they are to a greater or lesser extent aware. When interaction takes place, all that is required to avert the onset of a problem is a (quantitatively) broader or more competent network. Consider the case of the family of Aldo, a building worker who lost his job when his firm went bankrupt. For some time, Aldo, his wife, his eldest daughter and his brother tried to find him another job. They explored every possibility and often discussed the problem together, but their circle of acquaintance yielded nothing. Their network was therefore inadequate to that particular task.

However, the majority of social problems arise because the quantitative/ qualitative resources of a group of people are not sufficiently mobilized or realized in dynamic interaction. That is to say, it is *connectedness* that is lacking (point (c)), and very often connectedness is deficient or lacking even when the task is clearly perceived (point (d)). It is evident that if there is no shared idea of the task, there can be no connectedness (which gives dynamism to the network), given that it is the task, as we know, that is the catalyst for the whole process.

Take the case of Alberto. An unmarried, middle-aged teacher, Alberto has lived with his sister, also unmarried, since the death of his mother. Ten months ago he lapsed into a profoundly depressive state. He tried a variety of antidepressants prescribed by specialists, and also spent time in a clinic, but there was no improvement in his condition. His doctor tried to help by giving encouragement and advice. Some of Alberto's colleagues visited him at home, but often found it impossible even to talk to him. Other people in the village asked the sister for information about Alberto but did not call on him. The parish priest talked to him from time to time, and almost forced him out of the house for walks or rides in his car. The sister took time off from work to look after him, and another sister pitched in to help her. In this case, therefore, there were numerous people aware that something had to be done, and they indeed did something. But each of them acted on their own account: the specialists, the doctor, the parish priest, Alberto's sisters, and his colleagues all acted in some degree of isolation.

It is connectedness that 'makes' a network. If linkages or multiple goal-oriented interactions are lacking, so too is the network as a dynamic. Even if there is an adequate network structure, even if relations exist – although these, it will be remembered, are mere possibilities of interaction – they may not be actualized in appropriate action. Alternatively, actions may be performed, but they are not linked together, as in Alberto's case. By 'connectedness' is meant exactly the process or dynamic of interaction among the persons in the network, obviously not any interactions whatever, but those which follow a certain logic or pattern determined by the task. Connectedness comes about when scattered elements are meaningfully linked together.

1.4.8. *Linking, networking and centralizing*

It is plain that connectedness is a process whose features should be carefully examined. First of all, as said, there may be connectedness without awareness of it. This is probably the most frequent eventuality in natural situations. When a task is perceived, it may set in motion a chain of interactions which, however, the persons concerned do not discern as such. Each interacting person sees his or her own behaviour (in part), and then the behaviour of the others with whom they come into contact. But they tend not to see the web of ongoing action and reaction. People are aware that they act as single individuals, that their behaviour evokes responses, but it is harder for them to realize that they are also part of a higher-level entity, even if it is they who have created it. Just as people find it difficult to discern interior features like mental disorders or motives, so they find it difficult to discern abstractions that transcend them. And thus it is for each individual in a network, with the consequence that we may state that every network displays deficits of self-observation.

A social network finds it difficult to see itself as such: it suffers from an intrinsic deficit of self-observation. This feature also entails that there may be connections, and that they may operate efficiently even if they are not deliberately oriented. Interactions take place as they should (if the process is efficacious). But they may also take place as if 'by magic', as if an invisible hand were directing the manifold actions, interweaving them to give them overall meaning. Each person does what s/he must do in relation to the others: it is pointless to ask oneself or the others why.

The network may exist unbeknown to itself, and it may function with no-one attending to it, or indeed knowing how to. Often, however, if we observe a network carefully, we find that one of its members works to ensure its connectedness so that individual actions link together. More than an invisible hand, though, this is often the hand of a concrete person who makes this connectedness possible and who therefore engages in some sort of networking. Once again, this 'patching' work may be performed unwittingly. We may call this unintentional connective work 'informal networking'. When a network is observed from outside, this natural networking function is easily identifiable: it is easy to see that actions are not randomly linked together but that someone is engaged in joining them, although this person is not aware of what he or she is doing. He or she has the impression of performing actions which are no different from others. But, in reality, networking is a 'super' action: it subsumes other actions in the precise sense that it is not a single item within the overall action but the thread that ties it together.

Let us look at an example. In the case of Alberto described in the previous section, although we said that the network lacked connectedness, it is obvious that in fact there is always some degree of linkage. In Alberto's case, it was his sister who provided the minimum of (inadequate) networking that nevertheless existed: when, for example, she referred the neurologist's findings to Alberto's doctor, or when she asked the parish priest to talk to him. These actions of hers were conceptually different from other, direct, actions performed by herself (when she tried to comfort her brother, for example) or by other persons in the network (when the priest tried to comfort him). These were actions oriented to networking, not to providing a specific caring act.

Connectedeness is a crucial feature of social networks, and in effect networking as a formal activity consists largely in making connectedness possible and in optimizing it. It should be pointed out, however, that the *intention* to connect cannot go beyond a certain limit: formal networking must always be kept rather bland, and space for flexible action should be left open. A natural helping network must always be able to 'move' and to adjust itself in accordance with its internal motives. Above all, action can never be imposed on a network by fiat. In that case it would become a system or an organization, where roles and competences are predefined and where action should proceed according to a centrally fixed plan.

A network can never comprise a rigid internal 'framework', although a certain amount of structuring is obviously necessary. The ideal balance between a network's rigidity and flexibility of action depends on the type of task being performed: as we shall see, the more a task is indeterminate, the more networking must depend on moment-by-moment observation, rather than being pre-determined from the outset. It makes sense to construct a system to achieve a goal only in the specific case when this goal is specific and recurrent: conditions which rarely arise in typical social work settings.

When a helping network fails because it does not see its task – when, that is, it is non-existent rather than inadequate – a deficiency of linkage may be the reason. A lack of shared perception may arise because no-one in the network is aware of, or affected by, a particular situation, which *could* be a task but is not one for the simple reason that nobody is aware of it. This collective agnosia may be caused because, for example, awareness of the task, although possessed by some persons in the network, does not spread, being confined to those persons because of the absence or inadequacy of interaction. We shall see in Chapter Eight that there are important strategies for social work which consist in enhancing awareness of shared problems through intentional networking.

A variant on inadequate linking arises in the particular case – particular but in fact very frequent – when this inadequacy is not due to non-existent or inadequate networking (because no-one is able to foster interaction) but to the existence within the network of a countervailing force, namely a centralizing hand, which concentrates action at a specific point, rather than allowing it to spread.

The abstract pattern of centralizing is depicted by Figure 1.13, which shows how a set of tasks are concentrated onto one particular member of the network, so that the network breaks down.

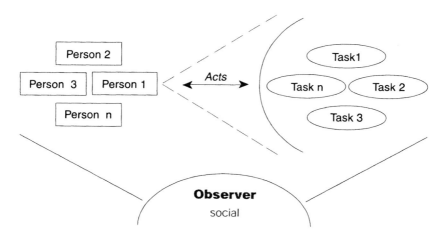

Fig. 1.13 Logical scheme of centralization.

Centralization is a process most evident when tasks are highly visible and cannot be postponed. Someone must attend to these tasks, and the habit forms (or a system is constructed) whereby that someone is a person, not a network. A concrete example is provided by the case of Maria (described in detail in the next section). Maria has to look after her rather maladjusted children, her difficult grandson, her sick husband, and other people besides. For various reasons to do with personality and circumstance, Maria acts as the family's main 'interceptor' of problems. This attitude is driven by positive feedback until, predictably, the system blows up. The more Maria intercepts problems, the more she must intercept them in the future, for two reasons. First because she learns skills from experience and succesful practice; second because the other potential interceptors – the other members of the network – in parallel unlearn these skills through lack of practice. A vicious circle is triggered: the more Maria does, the less the others are able to do; the less others do, the more Maria must do, and so on.

1.4.9. *Centralization, stress and crisis*

In a centralized set-up, the system collapses when the person who centralizes burns out. The delicate and longstanding mechanism which runs things breaks down when the pivotal person in the network is no longer able to perform his or her role properly. At this point the network is defenceless against the pressure of tasks, as well as being unable to learn. This is a crisis (Roberts, 1995; O'Hagan, 1987, etc.).

A crisis can be defined as an acute problem constituted by the rapid and unstoppable destructuring of a balanced coping system (Hott, 1995). The period of time that elapses between the onset of the destructuring dynamic and the finding of a new balance – at levels of systemic functioning that are lower, the same or even higher than previously – is the period of crisis, as shown by Figure 1.13 (which incidentally also shows that a crisis may be an *opportunity*, in that the destructuring may eventually settle down at higher levels of functioning than previously).

Whereas a problem arises because coping is inadequate, yet in equilibrium, a crisis is a revolution in that equilibrium, a revolution that may either be sudden or presaged by predicaments, most of which are difficult coping situations (i.e. problems). In a centralized system, the breakdown of the pivotal figure (individual crisis) throws the network as a whole into crisis. According to coping theory, the breakdown of the pivot – who may not necessarily be weak-minded: indeed, he or she may have been an exceptionally gifted coper – can be brought about by two causes: an increase in tasks, or a decline in personal energies/

resources, a decline which may make it appear subjectively that tasks have increased or aggravated when in fact they are the same as before.

One of the factors most likely to produce a progressive diminution of personal capacities is stress syndrome (Meichenbaum, 1985; Lehrer and Woolfolk, 1993; Aldwin, 1994). Stress is the activation of psycho-physical energies in response to stimuli (stressors) – what we have termed 'tasks'. In itself, stress is a good thing: it is a release of inner energy which enables the person to take control of the coping process. It will be remembered that coping is set in motion by a need for action which exceeds a person's immediate capacities/resources. It thus stimulates the forced production of physical or emotional energy. This energy must be constantly renewed, for if it is not, problems or crises will arise. The replacement of energy depends on two factors: the interval of time that elapses between stress episodes, i.e. the amount of time available for adequate repose (adequate with respect to the intensity of the event); and the perceived efficacy of the action elicited by the stressor. The more frequently psycho-physical tensions occur, and the less succssful they are, the more likely it becomes that as internal resources are progressively depleted, a 'void' will be created in the person, who at a certain point buckles under the strain.

The centralizing/stress/crisis dynamic is perceptively insidious, given the ease with which it deceives the observer. It over-exposes one particular person, so that attention is entirely focused upon him or her. The observer sees a person who (a) acts more than anyone else, (b) who then becomes overstressed, and (c) who then burns out. All of these are events which exhibit individual coping (Figure 1.2), and therefore a problem or crisis for that particular person. From a social point of view, the observer must focus not on *who* is most visible – not on the fragile activism of a particular person – but on aspects overshadowed by

TABLE 1.2

Summary of concepts

Linking	Interaction among the elements in a set. Relation among parts.
Networking	Action which increases the probability and efficacy of linkage (interaction among single elements). If the subject is unaware (or only slightly aware) of performing this connective action, it may also be called 'informal networking'.
Centralizing	Action which reduces the probability of linkage (even if the actor is unaware of it), so that response to the task is individualized.

whatever it is that occupies the foreground. In other words, the real problem – the one that lies beneath the surface – is not the person who centralizes and breaks down, nor his or her excess of activity, but rather the *complement* (the 'environment') to all this: the failure of a network to act in synergy. Whether the network is impeded in its operation by its centralization in one person, or whether it is impeded by centralization due to the passivity of the others – or, as more frequently happens, by both eventualities – what matters most for the observer is the network's inadequacy. Put more precisely: what matters is its *absence* during the more or less lengthy period of centralization and its *inadequacy* in the crisis phase, which begins when the centralizer withdraws and the potential network may finally act.

A noteworthy feature of centralizing is that it tends to replicate itself. When a centralized coping system enters crisis, its 'therapy' may be recourse not to the opposite – namely an interactional process – but rather to a similar scheme which is once again centred upon a single person. Attracted by the shock waves of the crisis, a new person is likely to put him/herself forward in the belief that s/he is able to resolve everything – that is, by centralizing once again. This may give rise to a curious paradox: the person who responds to the breakdown in centralization by proposing further centralization may be a professional practitioner. When an expert lacks self-control and acts impulsively, he or she often acts in exactly the same way as the client in crisis: namely by centralizing everything to him or herself. The expert considers it normal that, should he or she be asked by a client to take on the latter's problem, that problem henceforth becomes the expert's own. Breakdown is thus inevitable, for two reasons: firstly because this centralization impedes learning by the network; secondly because it leads directly to the expert's own stress and, perhaps, eventual crisis (Davies, 1997; Bernstein and Halaszyn, 1999).

To summarize: a network may be inadequate to a task because it does not comprise the necessary action, either because this action is non-existent, or because it is not activated for lack of stimulus by someone aware that action is lacking yet necessary. A second cause of inadequacy is the absence of connectedness among actions. It is evident that both possibilities occur in the majority of concrete cases. Social networks usually fail as a result of the joint effect of the two inadequacies mentioned: the quantitative/qualitative inadequacy of the network's components, and the inadequacy of the linkages among them. The importance of connectedness should be emphasised yet again, since one often finds the paradoxical situation of a component-rich network which fails to function owing to a lack of linkage. A typical example, at the policy level, is provided by the so-called 'network' of local health and community care services. In many cases, an adequate quantity of such services are delivered in a particular area of the country, but the efficiency of the network is weak: indeed, the network may be more inefficient, the more components it possesses. If connectedness is lacking, what appears on paper to be abundance may prove in actual fact to be poverty. For example, Pia, a housebound elderly woman looked after by the home care service, knows that all the services that she needs are available in her neighbourhood; however, her ability to effectively use the appropriate service at the right time is quite another matter.

1.5. An example of relational coping: a case study of Maria's family

In order to sum up the main concepts presented in this chapter, analysis follows of a concrete case dealt with by a social worker. For the moment, let us imagine this expert as the observer of the problem, engaged solely in making sense of what is happening. Discussion of what *should* be done to improve the situation will be postponed. The 'case' is as follows.

> Maria is sixty-seven years old. Her forceful personality enables her to impose her will and opinions on others. Maria has so far been able to cope, in her own way, with the numerous problems that afflict her family. Her eldest son, Stefano, has never held down a steady job and achieved economic independence, all the more so since his marriage three years ago.
>
> Her youngest daughter, Silvia, had a baby when she was still a teenager. Little Marco was placed in his grandparents' care, and Maria assumed every responsibility for his upbringing. Six years later Silvia got married. Since Maria regarded her son-in-law as unreliable, she preferred to keep Marco with her. And Silvia, who wanted to make a new life for herself, agreed to the arrangement.
>
> Marco thus continued to live with his grandparents, maintaining contact, albeit sporadically, with his mother. Everything proceeded smoothly for a number of years. However, as time passed, Maria found it increasingly difficult to cope with her grandson's aggressive behaviour, with his rejection of all rules and his failure at school. Marco is now twelve years old, and Maria feels tired. Arthritis restricts her movements and as if that were not enough, Remo, her husband, has recently suffered a stroke: he walks with difficulty, he only leaves the house if accompanied, his speech is impaired, and although he is still generally lucid, has moments of confusion. A neighbour has talked to Maria about applying for home help, but she is reluctant to have people around the house.
>
> Marco takes advantage of his grandmother's tiredness: he only comes home after suppertime, he does not do his homework, he skips lessons. Maria has

already been summoned to the school on several occasions. Then one evening Marco did not come home at all and stayed out all night. Enraged, Maria asked Silvia to take Marco back. Silvia refused because she was afraid of harming the relationship with her husband.

1.5.1. *For whom is this a problem and why?*

This, by hypothesis, is the idea gained by the social worker of Maria's situation from an interview conducted in her/his office. But to whom did the practictioner talk? Who was it that perceived what in his opinion constituted a problem? And, again in his opinion, who was mainly affected by the problem? There are numerous possibilities. The social worker may have talked to a member of the family – with Maria herself, for example, when she felt that she could no longer cope and decided to seek help – or with Silvia, worried about her son's future. Or the social worker may have talked to persons less directly concerned, but nevertheless involved in some way or other: Marco's teacher, perhaps, who after talking to Maria gained an idea of the family's problems and decided to report his worries to the social worker, having already collaborated with him on more difficult cases. Or a neighbour, or a Sunday school teacher, or other people besides.

Whatever the case may be, the social worker took on a problem perceived by others. It was not a problem ascertained by himself in person. Which means that Maria's network comprised perceptive resources with regard to its own difficulties. Moreover, her network also comprised the potential to signal the problem externally to the *expert* sector, in this case to the Social Services Department. Many problems exist in a natural state where those who suffer from them are not precisely aware of them (although they suffer from them). Even when this awareness exists, it is often not sufficient, or it is not sufficiently determined/organized, to stimulate a search for outside help. Many situations do not have internal eyes that perceive them; others do not have legs with which to go in search of help. This is a relatively early stage, what we may call the 'pre-problem' stage. Given that Mary's situation had attracted the attention of a statutory social worker, it had reached a more advanced stage of elaboration.

We must now establish whether the perception was truly of the network, or whether it was of one of its members. Generally, only one person is interviewed in the first assessment session by a social worker, and we may assume that this was so in the present case. However, we must be careful to determine whether this person was speaking for the other members of the network – with whom he or she had had sufficient intercourse – or whether he or she was acting only personally. If, for example, it was Marco's teacher that had taken the initiative of contacting the social services, it was obviously important for the social worker to ask whether or not the people most directly concerned (Maria, Silvia, Marco) knew that he had done so and were in agreement. Even if Maria herself, the person most directly concerned, had asked for the interview, the first thing to do was determine the degree of connection between her and the others involved (Seed, 1990).

Let us assume that Maria's network is adequately linked together as regards the perception of the problem: the majority of its members agreed that help must be looked for. The next logical step in the construction of a social problem is concurrence with this judgement by the social worker contacted by the network. If the expert agrees, the problem changes nature. It takes a jump forward and becomes a problem 'more than before', in the sense that it is now a problem *confirmed* by an external referent, by a previously uninvolved third party.

Hence a problem endorsed by an expert becomes 'even more' of a problem. It does so in a literal sense as well, by becoming more severe than previously. It is important to understand this point. In the logic of social construction, the larger the number of people who believe that a situation is a problem, the more, socially speaking, that problem exists. It is clear, however, that in order to assess whether this social 'consolidation' of a problem is useful or otherwise with respect to its solution, it is necessary to determine whether the problem exists or whether it does not (relatively speaking, obviously), and whether it may or may not be more amenable to solution if it is left relatively unfocused. These are all preliminary professional judgements of great sophistication which are often ignored. In any event, deciding whether or not a case should be taken on is an issue difficult to resolve *a priori*.

Let us assume that the social worker's interlocutor is Maria in person, and that during her interview Maria blames everything on Marco's behaviour, attributing all her family's difficulties to his changed personality. But let us also assume that Marco, like many adolescents, is in fact only going through a phase of temporary and manageable disorientation: he is, that is to say, a problem which 'is not'. If the social worker accepts the focal definition of the problem provided by Maria, and directs his action entirely at Marco, the boy's problem will certainly consolidate, but in a perverse sense (Boudon, 1984). Marco, with the weight of expert judgement upon him, and still subject to his grandmother's scolding, will feel even more stigmatized. His deviant identity, seen as a challenge or resistance against a label and social pressures which he does not accept, may be progressively reinforced in his mind. If a problem does not exist, but is nonetheless perceived and treated professionally, that problem is induced by the 'therapeutic' effort: it is a true iatrogenic effect (Illich, 1982).

On the other hand, Marco's deviant identity may not be a fiction but a concrete fact, perhaps influenced by dynamics more objective and dangerous than labelling: the impelling and largely uncontrollable influence of his peers, for example (Kierke, 1995; Cotterell, 1996). In this case, Maria's fears are entirely justified. And the social worker's endorsement of them, although it does not reduce the risk of stigmatization, takes the helping process and the possibility of changing the situation or managing it to a more evolved stage. The social worker's intervention may of course prove ineffectual, but this is not the point. In any event, the rule is as follows: if a problem cannot be resolved merely by ignoring it, the fact that it is perceived is always an advantage.

It is difficult for an expert worker to know beforehand whether a problem brought to him or her warrants formal consolidation, or whether s/he would do better to leave it alone or ignore it. Sometimes a social worker discovers with hindsight that taking on a case was a mistake; on other occasions, s/he realizes that not having done so was a mistake. It is difficult for the social worker alone to guess correctly. Sharing is the golden rule: the more the idea that a problem exists is shared, the more likely it is – likely, obviously, not certain – that the problem truly exists. If this were so in Maria's case – if there were broad concordance of perception, i.e. a broad basis of sharing – the social worker could more confidently endorse the problem presented to him by one or other member of the network. And his endorsement would close the circle of essential things to do *before* beginning the intervention proper.

Let us now imagine instead that it is an isolated person, on his or her own initiative, who contacts the social worker. In the course of the interview the social worker realizes that the idea that a problem exists – as well as the idea that it is so serious as to require expert help – is entirely restricted to the mind of the person before him (who is, let us say, the teacher). In this case, the social worker must accept *à la* Rogers the person who has sought him out, but he must also wait a while before accepting the problem. The expert must first network the assessment so that it becomes 'social'. He must be able to intuit immediately, if possible, and subsequently verify that the description given to him will not be rejected by the other persons involved. When the latter are informed that someone thinks that they have a problem, how will they react? Will they agree? If, for example, the social worker speaks to Maria and informs her that the teacher has told him about her problem, will she feel that she has been properly represented? If the social worker cannot be sure, he must somehow (in the manner he deems most appropriate) gather further information from other, independent sources and then make his assessment.

After the expert has investigated Maria's situation, he may be convinced that the problem exists even though the others involved are unaware of it, or even reject it. In this case matters become more difficult. But nevertheless, true help

– as opposed to forcefully imposed welfare measures – can only be based on a shared awareness. If this common sentiment does not exist, the social worker must first get to work on constructing it.

1.5.2. *What type of problem is it?*

Either before seeking out the social worker, or afterwards thanks to his/her patient networking, Maria's network realizes that something is wrong. Each of its members, however, may have a different idea of what is amiss. So what is the problem, exactly? If we re-read the above account of Maria's family – which is an account of a multi-problem family – it is evident that there is a plethora of problems, if we look for them analytically.

Each person in the network may perceive a different problem, and also attribute it to different causes, which are generally viewed as dysfuctions in one or other member of the family. Maria may think that the problem is Marco. Marco may think that Maria or his mother are the cause of the family's or his own difficulties. Remo, Maria's husband, may think that the problem is himself and his illness. Silvia, Marco's mother, may think that everything is due to the relationship with her husband, which prevents her from having Marco at home with her. And so on. The welfare specialists, too, precisely because they are specialists, if contacted by a member of the network will select one problem or other, whichever of them they feel best able to solve. The family doctor, on seeing Maria's stress and exhaustion, may give her a restorative or prescribe rest. A psychiatrist might suggest therapy for Marco, assuming his willingness to undergo it, or for Maria. The health visitor might concentrate on the invalid husband, Remo.

The social worker must instead think globally or ecologically. We have seen in theory that he must define the problem as 'the inability of Maria's *network* to cope with its tasks'. But what does this mean in practice? Generally, it means that Maria's network is unable to adapt to circumstances, to learn, to change, to gather new resources to meet new needs or to cope with new tasks. Its growth has failed to keep up with the growth, in number or complexity, of its tasks. When Marco was little and still manageable, before Remo had his stroke and when Maria was still in good health, the network functioned – that is, it got by without anyone inside or outside the family forming the impression of a problem. The social problem arose when the network's potential for action fell short of the tasks that it had to perform.

All this is generic. In order to understand matters thoroughly, we must proceed analytically. In the present case, the social worker must draw up a mental inventory of all the tasks and set them against all the persons concerned. This inventory is shown in Table 1.3.

The tasks listed in this Table are duties which must be fulfilled if the intrinsic 'factory' of family well-being is to function. Should the mechanism that constantly metabolizes all these tasks break down, the outward manifestations of its dysfunction – the various individual intractable symptoms – are immediately apparent. All the tasks must be fulfilled, although in principle there is no predefined way in which this must happen. There are no absolute constraints as to *who* should assume responsibility for them.

No one can say that the entire list of tasks should be assigned to one particular person. Saying that the *subject* that must attend to them is a social network is to say that everyone must take responsibility for them, and therefore no-one in particular. The 'subject' is dispersed hither and thither. In principle, there are no binding constraints that differentiate work tasks among the members of the family. But in practice these constraints always exist and – as we well know – mainly to the detriment of women (Lewis and Meredith, 1988; Dalley, 1996). In Maria's family these constraints are sharply defined. Rather than a flexible network, over the years a fixed relational system dominated by Maria has developed. Maria has centralized, the others have delegated, in a complementary macro-relation which has prevented the 'social' from acting. Action has been taken by Maria, not by 'a set of linked persons' (This situation is depicted in Figure 1.14).

Maria sees tasks and takes action. The others do not see these tasks; or if they see them, they do not act. Which prompts one to ask whether they fail to act because they do not want to or because they are unable to. Centralizing is a process of reciprocal learning in which one party (Maria) grows increasingly competent at coping (as long as the resources are available), while the other party – all the others in relation – develops a sense of inadequacy, or even a blindness of sorts that prevents them from acting. Even should the other persons in the network wish to act (but they do not), they probably do not know how to.

A centralized system like Maria's lacks, amongst other things, a culture of sharing or, more concretely, a division of labour. The idea of doing something – because of the learning process that everyone is subjected to – is 'all or nothing' in nature: either you give us all the task or you give us none of it. In Maria's case, all the task is too much, so that the others are discouraged or feel inadequate: Silvia feels unable to resume responsibility for her son Marco, after he has been entirely looked after by her mother. Silvia could (or should) do something. But, fearing that she will have to do everything, after for so long having done none of the things that her role as mother would prescribe, she retreats in alarm.

TABLE 1.3

Inventory of the tasks and the persons involved in Maria's case

List of functional tasks	List of persons in relation
Management/education of Marco (Maria's grandson) – relationships with school – making rules and enforcing them – encouraging and advising him – monitoring what he does – managing unforeseen situations	– Maria – Silvia (daughter) – Stefano (son) – Marco (grandson) – Remo (husband) – neighbour – teacher
Managing Remo (Maria's invalid husband) – looking after him (dressing/washing him) – taking him for walks (mobilizing him) – dealing with doctors and health workers (physiotherapist, etc.) – keeping him company – keeping check on him, etc.	
Household management – washing, cooking, ironing – balancing the family budget – doing the shopping – paying bills, etc.	

Centralizing is a pattern which usually *becomes* dysfunctional; it is not necessarily dysfunctional *ab origine*. Initially, when Maria's family was younger, the centripetal force acting upon Maria was perhaps a positive phenomenon. The fact that Mary attended to everything 'worked fine' from the point of view of the family system's functioning. Maria's capabilities probably made her feel that she was a good mother. She was efficient, and through learning-by-doing she grew ever more so. Everything went well, both in the functional sense, *vis-à-vis* the tasks performed and the benefit deriving therefrom to the family, and in the psychodynamic sense, *vis-à-vis* Maria's increasing strength of her personality and self-efficacy (Bandura, 1997). When things go well, learning takes place. Maria learnt how to centralize, induced to do so by positive aspects and not by the

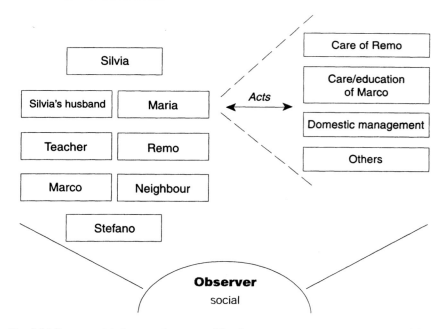

Fig. 1.14 Diagram of dysfunctional coping in Maria's situation, showing centralization on Maria.

negative latent ones that she was unable to see, like the more abstract non-learning of the others.

There is a process point at which centralization ceases to be adaptive. This point is determined by the individual ability of the centralizer to handle the tasks assigned to him or her. Beyond it, the force of tasks prevails. This is what happened to Maria, who began to find coping increasingly difficult. A typical stress situation thus arose, and the skein of psychological advantages slowly unravelled. Maria began to lose the confidence in herself which, presumably, she had so far accumulated. Her inner core, her sense of self-sufficiency, gradually dwindled. Two opposing factors now came into play: with time, Maria's tasks increased in number (she also had to look after the families of her children) and in complexity (with the onset of Marco's adolescence, in particular), while Maria psychologically and physically deteriorated (as she grew older). In the end she felt trapped and finally saw the hidden face of centralizing: the lack of collaboration. To her chagrin, Maria realized that she was on her own and could count on no-one to help her. She retaliated against the task and sought to get rid of it. She wanted to free herself of Marco by sending him back to his mother. But Silvia refused!

1.6. Summary and conclusions

A social problem arises when the shared or semi-collective capacity for action by a set of people linked together in a 'network' breaks down or is inadequate. A network is not an organic aggregate or a unitary whole in which everyone does the same thing or acts in predetermined fashion. This is a system. A network is instead the random and fragmentary union of a certain number – from 'more than two' to 'n' – of individuals who are mutually *sympathetic* (they share a common problem) and *synergetic* (they take joint action).

In social work, action acquires meaning with reference to one task or several: what in technical terms are 'coping tasks'. In everyday language, the term is associated with the activity of contending with complex contingencies which usually – and evidently – centre on the difficulties of individuals, difficulties which may then become tasks for the interconnected persons (relatives, friends, etc.). These difficulties, which must be dealt with, often spring from previous actions by the persons linked together. We should avoid confusion here. The networking approach does not concern itself with the process that has produced these difficulties – that is, pathogenic relations. Rather, it concerns itself with the interactive process that manages them in a prospective way. Managing means ensuring sufficient ecological quality despite the persistence of the *individual* difficulty (one may hope that this quality will, in the long term and indirectly, attenuate or even entirely eliminate the individual difficulty). The question to be asked is the following: 'What new 'ecology' must be produced – i.e. in what way must the social environment be reorganized – so that the existing problem can be managed or overcome?'.

Tasks may fall within the range of the actors' awareness (of all or some of them), or they may fall outside it. If the tasks are perceived, but not fulfilled, by those appointed to perform them, a problem eventually arises according to the meaning given to it by the actors concerned. If tasks are not perceived by their potential performers, and are therefore not fulfilled, a problem may arise according to the meaning given to it by external uninvolved observers (or better, ones not 'directly involved', given that observation is already a form of involvement).

In both cases, whether the inadequacy of action is realized by those affected by the problem or by observers makes no difference: the social problem requires something else for it to arise. Sometimes randomly and instantaneously, sometimes through deliberate action, these two distinct poles of perception intersect. When this happens, 'the light comes on'. The observer may agree with the actors, or the actors may agree with the observer: it is this concordance that creates a social problem in the strict technical sense, a problem ready to be addressed by formal means.

When the problem is formally taken up, the burden of care is no longer shouldered by the primary actors, namely the people directly involved and who have presumably already acted in the pre-formal phase as sole and inadequate copers. As soon as the expert observer decides to do something – rather than continuing simply to observe – to help the actors in difficulty, a higher unit of action is created, a joint relation between an already-active party (the network) and a second party which contributes specific skills and methods. This is the topic of the next chapter.

CHAPTER 2

The relational core of social work solutions
The joint working out of helping plans

2.1. Introduction

Social problems like those of Maria's family discussed in the previous chapter should not only be observed correctly; they should also be dealt with – that is, brought to a solution. The transformation of a problem into its opposite – namely a new situation felt to be satisfactory or normal (notwithstanding the ambiguity of the term) – is obviously a process more elaborate that its mere 'contemplation'.

Numerous concepts useful for exploring this more complicated terrain have already been introduced. Social problems, we have seen, *emerge* from social relations that 'are not there'. That is to say, they arise from a lack of combinations of *expected* actions, rather than from actual relations of pathogenic type. The same can be said of solutions, but by reversing the argument and thinking of solutions as 'successful' relational combinations. I place the word 'successful' in inverted commas for several reasons. Just as a social problem is not a static phenomenon, but rather a construct that constantly changes as regards both the tasks and the observers within and without the network, neither is its *solution* static. The solution of problems that concern the *humana conditio*, to use Elias's term, is never a clear and overt state of affairs, nor is it ever a final and definitive one (Elias, 1985). It is a reformulation of the unsatisfactory state of affairs that previously induced those concerned to say that 'there is a problem' and now to say that the problem 'no longer exists', or perhaps that a different problem exists. To paraphrase Popper (1994), who advises us that 'the knowledge starts from problems and ends with problems (so far as it ever ends)' we may more accurately say that social work intervention starts from a problem and concludes, if it concludes, with a new reformulated problem.

In social life, every 'solution' is a change or an improvement on the initial problem. However, it is always difficult for the observers to say what an improvement actually is, and whether an absolute improvement has taken place so that the problem has truly disappeared because a solution in the full sense of the term has been produced. Judging the *success* of combinations of actions (free interactions) over time is always an exercise in optimism which cannot rest on certain criteria. A social worker does not have a special sensor which measures increments of quality in social life situations and then at the appropriate moment emits a special signal to announce that the desired solution has been achieved. Fortunately, a sensor of this kind could never be invented. More than ever today, what matters is the practitioner's personal sensitivity and professional standards. It goes without saying that the worker's opinion or feeling that a solution has been produced must be shared, and the last word, even without espousing a strongly consumerist view, is indubitably that this sentiment lies with the individuals concerned: if they do not agree with the practitioner's optimism that 'everything's in order', they can always look for someone else or else go ahead on their own.

The social work solution process does not begin when the practitioner decides to become involved – when, that is, s/he decides to change his/her stance on the problem by shifting from the position of an observer to that of a problem-solver. Social workers should never forget that they graft their action onto a process that has already been set in motion, and perhaps a long time previously. Their own action is always preceded by that of the people directly involved in the problem, belonging to the prescientific world of dayly life, according to Husserl (1959). Social coping – defined as an attempt to manage or eliminate a living difficulty – is often a battle already begun elsewhere: who knows when, who knows by whom. Even when problems spring from unperceived tasks or duties, the people involved are by definition caught up in the management of the consequences arising from those problems.

In this chapter I shall seek to establish how important it is for professional social workers – and for what reasons – to engage smoothly with the social processes which, by definition, were at work long before they decided to act. In actual practice, if the undertaking is to succeed, the expert must know how to wait: s/he must not hastily apply the solutions that immediately spring to mind. Instead, in order for the expert to be able to wait and keep his/her impulsiveness in check, s/he must adopt an attitude that is easier to understand than it is to implement. I shall call this a 'relational attitude'.

This theme will be central to my argument. Before addressing it, however, I shall briefly discuss an idea that may bring some consolation to the impatient practitioner: namely that observation and intervention to some extent overlap. Even when practitioners are only observing, they are nevertheless making something happen. Vice versa, when they are acting, they are also observing.

2.2. Observation and intervention: two interconnected phases

I previously proposed a sharp distinction between observation and intervention. Indeed, separate chapters were devoted to these two macro dimensions of helping. This may have been useful for analytical purposes; yet, as with many of the conceptual distinctions drawn thus far, when we generalize this dichotomy, it immediately becomes nonsensical.

First of all, social workers never cease to be observers, however prolonged an intervention may be. It cannot be the case that practitioners observe for a certain period of time and then when they take action 'close their eyes', so to speak. A large part of social worker's action in the helping process – and especially when using the networking approach, as the next chapter will show in more detail – consists of monitoring or of some sort of supervision. The social worker watches ongoing action as it develops and provides feedback for those who – because they lie *within* the problem-solving process – may not see the overall picture and fail to grasp everything that is happening. We shall see that professional networking consists essentially in transmitting appropriate signals (feedback) to the persons involved on the basis of accurate observation and decodification of the interaction process.

Intervention *is* observation, therefore. But more than this, intervention also *produces* observation. Whenever action intended to changed the reality observed gets under way, the action will reflect back on observation (Donati, 1991). The movement and changes produced by the intervention yield new scenarios for the observer, who may find that this extra information enables him or her to see the problem differently from the way it appeared during the canonical phase of observation. Indeed, without the practical operations of action, pure observation can never be complete in itself. On the methodological level, this means that it does not make a great deal of sense to prolong observation beyond a certain point. Action may be effective even if it begins with only cursory observation.

Emblematic in this regard is the case of a small group of social workers (Folgheraiter 1992) who decided to make experimental use of the networking approach with so-called 'multi-problem' families. They set up a self-help/mutual-aid group but did not yet know exactly who it was for. This may have been 'putting the cart before the horse' but in the end it proved to be an advantage. The social workers' intention was simply to do something for famiües in need and to produce this vague 'something' that encouraged direct interaction among the families in accordance with the groupwork strategy (Doel and Sawdon, 1999). After some months, it became apparent that the group consisted almost entirely of families with marital problems and separation. It was thus easy to define the group *a posteriori* as a self-help group for 'broken families'. Once the news spread that a group of this kind existed, requests to join it increased immediately, and the group began to be vital. The moral of the story is that only when social workers begin tentatively to extend feelers towards the needs of the local community does the latter reciprocate and, so to speak, come out into the open. By taking action, the social workers were able to observe a problem in the community (the large number of families in crisis) which they had never previously noticed even though it was before their very eyes.

If observation is part of intervention, the reverse holds as well: intervention is part of observation. During the observation phase – that is, when the social worker is still forming an idea of the problem that s/he may or may not take on and therefore talks to one or more members of the group of people concerned – the practitioner is in actual fact already intervening. The expert's main function during this phase is undoubtedly to stand at the threshold and observe, deciding on his or her possible 'engagement', on whether or not to 'transform' the problem should s/he recognize it and take it on. But the observation, and the relation that should arise between the expert and those affected by the problem if this observation is to take place, have already begun to transform the problem regardless of the social worker's intentions. Even if we suppose that the social worker is only attending to the preliminaries of relatively detached observation/assessment, it does not matter: s/he immediately affects the problem as soon as the relation begins.

This is reminiscent of Heisenberg's famous 'uncertainty principle', which shook the foundations of modern physics. An experimenter cannot observe the positions of two electrons in an atom because as soon as s/he sets about doing so, the two electrons change their orbits. Of course, if observation is obtrusive in physics, it is even more so in the human domain.

In social work the concept is even easier to understand. Let us assume that a person goes to a social worker with a problem. This problem, as we have seen, is not that this person is unable to function; it is instead a *diffused* incapacity for action with the worry and distress connected with it. Let us also assume that the social worker invites the person to talk – also as the spokesman for others – initially only in order to understand what the matter is (i.e. to perform a preliminary assessment). While the person talks, the social worker, in accordance with his/her initial intentions, gains an idea of the events. But what happens to the person? Having to tell his/her story, s/he is forced to reorganize his/her thoughts. Perhaps by talking s/he may make sense of matters that previously s/he was unable to grasp; perhaps by seeing a calm expert who listens, s/he may feel that the problem can be coped with, or that s/he is in good hands; and so on. These are all small interior changes to thought or to more profound emotions or experiences, and they may pale into insignificance with respect to the problem as a whole, which in the end may require much more significant adjustments, both in the interviewed person and in others. Nevertheless some change to reality – which in actual fact should be part of the intervention phase – has taken place during observation. The intervention has already started with the first contact between the two interlocutors – as soon, indeed, as their relationship began.

The two phases of observation and intervention therefore naturally overlap, even when the professional strives to keep them separate. Often, however, it is the professional that causes confusion by superimposing them. One possibility is that s/he may linger too long on diagnosis in the belief that this is 'doing therapy'. The professional may dwell on the problem without moving on to concrete action, or s/he may do so only belatedly. Predominant in this case is a sort of intellectual curiosity which the professional feels that s/he must absolutely satisfy, perhaps prompted by the Enlightenment prejudice that it is always necessary to understand everything before acting. This attitude, however, is more common in psychotherapy, where diagnosis (the focusing on and understanding of the pathology, its type, etc.) effectively takes priority. In social work, by contrast, it is the opposite error that is more frequently committed. Due to the urgency and concreteness that often characterize social work provision, the practictioner tends to be impulsive (Meichenbaum, 1985): s/he may 'jump the gun' by intervening before s/he has gained sufficient knowledge of the situation – and above all before s/he has ascertained whether the problem reported by the interlocutor is socially based (that is, whether it is sufficiently shared or can potentially be shared).

2.3. The relational attitude of social workers and the helping relationship: beyond the directivity/non-directivity dilemma

What is a true *helping relationship* in social work, and what attitudes make it possible? Misunderstandings will be avoided in what follows if I immediately clarify this broad concept, which is often used inappropriately.

In general, by the term 'helping relationship' (Brammer, 1993) is meant the bond established between a person able to give help (the helper) and a person who needs that help (the helpee). In the particular case in which the latter actively seeks out help in an institutional setting – a Social Services Department or something similar – the image evoked is that of two people sitting opposite each other, of whom one is an *expert* and the other is a *client* (or a *user* or a *consumer)*. This common-sense view is adequate as long as we are talking about psychological helping – psychotherapy, for example – but it is ingenuous when we are talking about social work. In this case, the person who has a problem and consults an expert practitioner always and necessarily does so *also* as the representative of others, of his/her social base. From a networking point of view, the helping relationship arises between an expert and a network even when the practitioner finds him/herself interacting with individual people. But if this point is clear, there is something else that should be understood.

Let us concentrate on the intuitive definition of the helping relation given above. To proceed, we must delve into its interior and remove its most taken-for-granted meaning. What does the above definition express? Above all, the idea that it is *through* the bond established with the expert that the persons in difficulty receive the help that they need. The relationship is a helping relationship because the solution to a problem – i.e. the *help* – comes about because the person looking for it establishes a fortuitous relationship – and interacts for the time necessary – with the right person to give it to him or her.

Subsumed by this conception is a distinct intuition: that help is a 'gift' which the practitioner is able to give to the user. Obviously, it is a gift that the practitioner must first fabricate by immersing him/herself in a helping effort of greater or lesser complexity in the course of which s/he must first examine the problem and then come up with a solution. This taken-for-granted conception of professional help is ambivalent: it is right and wrong at the same time.

Every idea taken for granted has a basis in reality (as well as in banality). If an idea has become entrenched and is universally regarded as incontrovertible, then it contains an element of truth. In the case of the helping relationship, there is no disputing that the help is forthcoming *through* the personal contact between helper and helpee. If there were no direct linking between the two, what could ever happen? It is also certain that the expert practitioner plays a crucial role. If a person with a problem consults a professional and the problem disappears or noticeably attenuates some time after a satisfactory relationship has been established between the two, it would be ungenerous to maintain that the practitioner has nothing to do with this outcome, or only very little. Strictly speaking, this could only be thought in the limiting case of long-term therapy – psychoanalysis, for instance. In cases of this kind, the therapist's work may be diluted in the great flow of life, becoming infinitesimal and perhaps even questionable

(Shaw Anstrad, 1996). In these circumstances, if the problem is resolved, it would also be legitimate to envisage a different logical possibility: namely a spontaneous remission of the symptoms as documented by Eysenck's celebrated research in psychotherapy (Eysenck and Rachman, 1965). When the intervention instead has a well-defined (Budman and Gurman, 1988; Roberts, 1995; Hoyt, 1995; Feltham, 1997), and perhaps extremely adjacent beginning and end as in so-called 'single-session therapy' (Talmon, 1990), if success is achieved it is usual to give due credit to the expert.

The expert counts for a great deal in a formal helping relationship. However, it is quite a different matter to consider him/her as the creator of the help, the producer of the solution. Between the two things – counting for a great deal in a process and fabricating it – there is a difference. At the logical level, confusion between the two means presupposing that the helping relationship is *not* a relationship – which is the biggest contradiction.

According to the traditional meaning, the helping *relationship* is a personal bond necessary for the help to come about. This entails that the helper and helpee must know each other quite well, and develop a reciprocal *trust* relationship (Krasner and Joyce, 1995) so that the practitioner can act upon the other person. In this sense, the relationship has to do with help only in so far as it is a 'medium' between the two people. Thereafter, once the bridge has been built between them, it is only the practitioner that acts. It is he or she that gathers significant information on the problem from the clients so that a *diagnosis* can be made. Then, as soon as s/he has decodified and processed the information, it is again the practitioner who sets about transferring the solution from his/her mind to that of the person concerned *(treatment)*. This representation of the helping process reflects the Parsonian medico-professional model (Figure 2.1). It is ev-

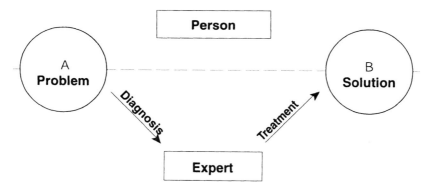

Fig. 2.1 Diagram of the helping relation according to the medical model, showing the single-directional phases of diagnosis and treatment.

ident that the entire process (diagnosis/treatment) is centred on the practitioner: s/he absorbs all the information required for the diagnosis and takes clinical decisions on the treatment required. Everything is focused on him or her, on his or her expert directivity. In this manner, the relationship is indeed the precondition for help, but – and this is the point – the helping is not a relationship.

When the interpersonal bond is viewed simply as a means to transfer the solution from the expert to the person concerned, a single-directional rather than relational (two-directional) idea of the helping process (Figure 2.2) comes to the fore. In this way, the reality of medicine, where the medical model may work well in principle, is confused with social reality, where use of this model becomes a rather serious error. Misled by the model, one fails to realize that in the social sphere – where the concern is with *action* rather than with *objective* internal states of people – helping always arises from the combination of *two* (or more) sources of action, distinct but merged, rather than from one alone.

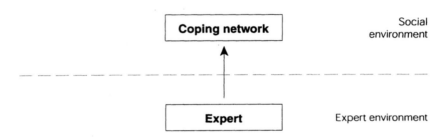

Fig. 2.2 Diagram of the helping relationship according to directive approach.

We must once again distinguish between relationship-as-bond and relationship-as-process. We may put the matter as follows: the establishment of a bond (type 1 relationship) between practitioner and user is simply the precondition for the activation of a type 2 relationship, a continuing process of interaction between them, not a unilateral transfer. The balancing of the two efforts may not always be perfect – in that one may have greater weight than the other – but nonetheless there is *duality* of action: inter-action, precisely.

No *social* work response can take place without the shuttling of action from one side to the other – both horizontally and dynamically. Helping *always* takes the form of a joint endeavour, or of an 'emergent effect', in the sense with which sociologists use the expression (Donati, 1991).

The foregoing points are summarized in Figure 2.3, where the two-headed arrow indicates the interaction between the expert sphere (scientific/technical sphere) and that of persons concerned (the common-sense sphere). Indeed, this arrow symbolizes, perhaps rather too subtly, a phenomenon of such importance in social work and generally in helping that only if it is fully understood, despite its deceptive simplicity, can one truly become an expert in this field. The more a practitioner understands the reality depicted by the two-headed arrow – namely that social work is a creative fusion of his/her action with that of others – the more efficacious his/her thought and action will become. All the methods and techniques of social work using the networking approach can be regarded as devices with which to put this golden rule into practice.

The relational stance also holds in reverse. It can be deduced from its consequences. If the result of a social worker's action is optimal, one can logically infer that it has been carried out in *practical* respect of that attitude. If the practitioner has been successful, s/he cannot have openly contradicted it. S/he will have certainly favoured the relationship even if s/he was unaware of doing so or did not wish to act in that manner.

Before returning to Figure 2.3 later in this chapter to examine its methodological implications, I must first clear up some potential misunderstandings. I shall proceed in reverse by first asking what the relational approach that enables-networking *is not*.

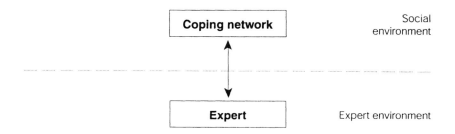

Fig. 2.3 Diagram of the helping relationship according to the relational (bilateral) approach.

2.3.1. Networking is not work on the network: again on differences with family therapy/systemic approach

A professional helper may seriously believe, although s/he would be mistaken to do so, that s/he is using a relational approach because s/he is in fact acting on relations. Considering that the object of his/her interest is not an individual but a (dysfunctional) system of persons standing in relation, s/he may be convinced that s/he has 'jumped the fence', and is working in a manner which is the reverse of the individualistic assumptions of the past (Neill and Krisken, 1989). This feeling of originality is distinctive, for example, of the systemic approach, which I have already discussed. There are numerous reasons to justify it but once again distinctions must be drawn. With respect to the idea of relationship, we may say that, generally speaking, the systemic approach has indeed attempted to jump the fence but still seems to be suspended in 'mid-air', unable to land on the other side.

We saw in the previous chapter – during discussion of how to observe a problem – that the systemic approach differs from the networking approach in that it perceives a problem as a *malfunctioning* of a fixed set of personal relations (social system) which usually provokes a malfunctioning in a single person (the so-called 'designated user'). It was said that the network method does not focus on the pathological essence of relations (that is, on structural disorders in basic human communication) but on their inadequacy with respect to a task – a task which in many cases may also be an inability to manage the person that has been malformed, so to speak, by those same relations.

Another and even clearer difference between the two approaches resides in their manner of conceptualizing (or 'feeling') the search for a solution. The systemic approach, by concentrating on a relational pathology and thereby implicitly presuming that the disorder is a technical matter to be dealt with technically, conceives the arrow in Figure 2.2 as having only one head: the one pointing away from the practitioner. The approach is heavily centred on the expert practitioner. Reasoning in terms of *pathology* and the *healing* of relations recalls the medical model – and therefore, paradoxically, a non-relational atti-tude – in extreme form. If the diagnosis/treatment of an individual pathology requires a certain amount of technical expertise which varies according to the type of pathology, symptoms, and so on, then the diagnosis and treatment of linkages pathology requires a necessarily higher level of technicality.

It is one thing to control and manipulate the (disturbed) essence of an indi-vidual person; it is another to control and manipulate the (disturbed) essence of the interaction among *numerous* interconnected individuals.

The bias towards the expert typical of systemic therapy is signalled by the fact that several practitioners are usually assigned to deal with a family system. For example, the session is conducted by two therapists, with another one watching from behind a one-way mirror. This typical systemic set-up directly reflects the approach's unidirectional and deterministic theoretical underpin-ning (the one-way mirror allows therapist to see the user but not the other way round!). Everything starts from the expert's side, to the point that if one practitioner is not enough, then a second and third may be called in, and perhaps others besides.

The situation with a throng of specialists on one side of the barricade and the persons in difficulty on the other, signals in itself that something is wrong. The *a priori* assumption is that excessive effort is required to produce and direct change. It is presumed that the situation must be forced to change in a manner contrary to its natural flow, when instead it should be guided back into its natural course.

2.3.1.1. The systemic approach and directive style in social work

Family therapy recalls the medical model, but this should not come as a surprise. We are dealing here with psychotherapy, and therefore with clinical matters where effort against the current is the norm, given that every intervention is intended to restructure what the person has become ('people processing' in Luhuman's espression) – or the extirpation of pathologies which connote the person (or, in the case in question, interpersonal relationships). More curious is the attempt to transfer the systemic approach to social work, where the concern is to develop the social action. The difference between the two views can be summed up as follows:

> In social work, networking means operating synergically 'with' systems, not trying to repair them one to one. It starts with their strengths, it does not diagnose and attack their weaknesses. It creates involvement, movements and autonomy of action in the social field; it does not isolate one system (the family) from others (other families, other interested parties, etc.) in order to skewer it with therapeutic manoeuvres and counter-manoeuvres in a therapy room. It creates care, maturation or development (and thereby also reduces or heals the 'pathology'), proceeding laterally to possible pathologies. It creates the premises for wellness, it does not bring it about directly. Social work fosters the development of the possible, not the authoritarian construction of the improbable (Folgheraiter, 1994, p. 187).

Let us take a step forward. Transposing the systemic model into social work does not always involve mistaking chalk for cheese: that is, carrying out one kind of therapy while thinking that one is carrying out another. This error occurs when a social worker encounters a family in difficulty (because of mental health-problems, for example) and sets about looking for interactional pathologies – dual bondings, paradoxes, denials, etc. – and seeks to eliminate them with some technique: paradoxical prescription of the symptom, for instance, or alliances. Such extreme confusion rarely occurs in social work. This is partly to do with the division of labour among human services, given that there may be colleagues specialized in such kind of intervention, and partly to do with good sense, since a social worker usually has more pressing matters to attend to.

It is more likely that even though social workers are well aware that they cannot and must not act as therapists, they will adopt a medical (non-relational) attitude even when they are doing exactly what they are supposed to do: help a network to cope with a task. Despite complying with the perception rules discussed in the previous chapter – and consequently observing a problem as purely relational one (and not as a pathology in relations) – they may devise the action but paradoxically forget the relation. They may act *on* relations using a unilateral directive style (of command/control type) which is especially distinctive – though sometimes packaged in the reverse form, i.e. as a paradoxical prescription – of the systemic approach (Haley, 1996).

The directive style resembles action by fiat or the top-down style of regulating behaviour typical of organizations. Obviously, a social worker who seeks to help a network to solve a problem, and who to do so must ensure that the actions of the various persons involved operate in harmony, can never behave like an office boss who gives orders to his subordinates and issues commands on what they must do.

No social worker would ever be so directive. They know very well that the clients with whom they interact are not subordinates. Experienced social workers also know that giving orders very often achieves the opposite effect to the one intended. However, if their deep-lying attitude is imbued with the idea that only they can produce the solution, it may happen that although social workers refrain from giving overt orders, they seek to manipulate the people with whom they are dealing, covertly trying to persuade them of the wisdom of their decisions. The intention is honourable, based as it is on the functionalist conviction that in this way a solution will be more rapidly and efficaciously forthcoming. Since the users came to the social worker in search of a solution and certainly do not know what it might be, and since the expert fulfils the role of the person that can provide one, it follows that even without imposing a solution, s/he will decisively push for one in particular.

In social work the directive style may arise indirectly, though not covertly, merely because practitioners have *objectives* in mind, without actually imposing them. Experts are directive (unidirectional) in their underlying attitudes even when they secretly hope that what they have envisaged will happen and fail to see the alternatives that might become available should they not act in that way. Agreed that I shall not give orders, the social worker may think; agreed also that I must not force decisions. Agreed above all that I must do nothing that the people involved might reject. Yet it is obvious that I must define objectives, and also that I must know beforehand what is to be done and why. Otherwise what role could I as an expert have?

To repeat: this covert authoritarian practitioner attitude is understandable but fallacious. Although practitioners may eschew excessively elementary or direct ways to handle social problems, because they are self-centred they still fail to grasp the relational idea. It is as if they have come as close as possible to the fence, but what they are looking for lies on the other side and they do not know it. These practitioners are well acquainted with the classic principle of self-determination (McDermott, 1975; Kapp, 1994), which closely resembles the relational attitude although it is not exactly the same thing. Guided by this principle, they know that no solution can be such unless the people involved concur, not only because this would be ethically wrong (Hugman and Smith, 1997; Banks, 1995) but also because it might not work. They sincerely grant the interested parties the right to *bargain* over, and even to *reject*, the solution that they propose. Which is admirable but not enough.

In social work, unlike other areas of helping like psychotherapy or social control procedures, practitioners do not usually show clients a solution in the truest sense of the word. If an expert devises a solution entirely on his/her own, it can never be a solution, not even in the fortunate circumstance that his/her interlocutors – because they are illiterate or because they are truly convinced – accept it. Logically, a solution which cuts out the social, or better which does not comprise within itself the social to which it is addressed, is null and void in both principle and practice. A solution of that kind could never be grafted onto a living base and be realized.

This constraint becomes more binding, the more numerous the category called here 'the people involved' or 'the social'. In a semi-collective dimension, when a certain number of (free) people standing in relation to one other are being dealt with, directivity slides out of control. For several reasons, but not only because it is difficult to ensure that all the people actually or potentially involved will – some to a greater, some to a lesser extent – do what the practitioner wants. This is a strategy which obviously requires effort to be invested in control, much more than is necessary in an *individual* dimension where the practitioner seeks to persuade only a single person to do what s/he has in mind. So much is obvious. But the key point is the one made earlier: since a solution to a complex human difficulty is such because the interested persons consider it to be such (i.e. a true solution from their point of view), and since it is through them that it is implemented, it must necessarily include their sensibility.

Experts are thus confronted by a twofold difficulty: on the one hand, they must control the action of many; on the other, they must mediate among the interests of many. In dealing with this dual constraint, the systemic approach is truly singular and should be thoroughly understood. It presupposes, as we know, that people act towards each other according to a *strict* systemic (deterministic) logic – that is, on the basis of structural constraints which determine the way in which relationships fit together. Exaggerating somewhat, one may say that the systemicists view the set of relationships concerned with a problem as like a Meccano set: that is, as comprising an array of pieces, each of which moves into place in a fixed order. The various actions gradually coalesce, so that after a certain period of time they assume fixed form on the basis of the static principle of homeostasis. The helping relationship in this particular guise is imagined by the expert as a challenge against a collective, mechanized counterpart. Though composed of numerous people, this opposite party is in fact monolithic, no matter how it is internally articulated. When a disturbance upsets the internal order of its elements, they begin to move with a knock-on effect in a direction dictated by the strict objective logic that ties them together. From the expert's point of view, the intervention must undo a crystallization of social ties – an already-realized relational homeostasis – and then accompany the change process when everything proceeds with cause-effect mechanisms that evade the intentionality of those involved.

2.3.2. Networking is not work by the network: differences with respect to users-centered approach

Let me now clear up a possible misunderstanding. The suspicion may have formed in the reader that what is being described here as the relational approach is the opposite of directivity. Does being relational in handling a social problem perhaps mean being 'non-directive' in the sense originally given to the term by Carl Rogers (Rogers and Kinget, 1969; Thorne, 1992; Farber et al., 1996; Barret-Lennard, 1998)?

Strictly speaking, a non-directive style adopted by an expert should mean that s/he does not 'direct' what happens in the helping process. The subject who directs is the interested party, who is assumed to be intrinsically able to do so. The expert makes it possible – technically 'ensures the conditions' – for this direction to come about. This approach is exactly the reverse of the directive attitude: in the latter case, the practitioner must do everything; in the former, s/he does no more than let it be done.

Just as directivity in the pure state does not exist in social work – practitioners cannot do everything, not even if they believe that they can – neither does non-directivity. Practitioners can never, not even if they really want to, let the others do everything. No matter how deeply-rooted the technical ideology which induces them to believe that they are acting in this way, the reality is necessarily different.

2.3.2.1. Carl Rogers' theory: from non-directivity to 'person-centred' approach

If practitioners truly do nothing – assuming that this is possible – we may ask what purpose is served by their presence in the helping process. When instead practitioners believe or say that they are doing nothing, although it is evident on the contrary that it is their action that matters, we may ask whether they are not being somewhat hypocritical, or whether they are being obtuse. Carl Rogers soon became aware of this paradox. He rejected the label 'non-directive' for his approach, calling it instead 'client-centred' or 'person-centred'. These expressions imply that the focus of the expert's action is no longer self-referential (self-regarding) but shifts to the other party. It is centred instead on the interlocutors with the problem, to whom the expert assigns a leading (though not exclusive) role in the help process, and pragmatically lets them perform it.

Given the importance of these concepts in social work, I shall dwell for a moment on a concrete example. I shall analyse a brief excerpt from a counselling interview which appears in Kahn and Cannel's (1957) well-known handbook. It shows the counsellor, an orthodox Rogersian, adopting an active client-centred approach, rather than a non-directive style. The example concerns a student who is looking for help because he feels psychologically in difficulties, and is unable to study.

> *Student:* I haven't written to my parents about this at all. In the past they haven't been of any help to me in this respect, and if I can keep it away from them as much as possible, I'll do so. But there's a slight matter of grades to explain, and they're not good, and I don't know how I'm going to explain without telling them about this (Meaning his upset emotional condition which, he has said, accounts for his problems). Would you advise me to tell them about it?
> *Counsellor:* Suppose you tell me a little more what you had thought about it
> *Student:* Well, I think I'm compelled to, because [...] [Pause]
> *Counsellor:* It's a situation you've really got to face.
> *Student:* Yes, there's no use getting around it, even if they can't take it the way they should, because I've already flunked may gym course. I just haven't come. I've just been negligent about it. Now, they'll know that you can't flunk in gym without being negligent about it. They'll ask why.
> *Counsellor:* It will be fairly hard for you to tell them.
> *Student:* Yes. Oh, I don't know if they're going to sort of condemn me. I think so, because that's what they've done in the past. They've said, 'It's your fault. You don't have enough will power, you're not interested'. That's the experience I've had in the past. I've been sort of telling them that I improved in this respect. I was – I was all right the first quarter. Well, I wasn't entirely all right, but I just got worse. [Pause]

Counsellor: You feel that they'll be unsympathetic and they'll condemn you for your failures.

Student: Well my - I'am pretty sure my father will. My mother might not. He hasn't been- he doesn't experience these things; he just doesn't know what it's like. 'Lack of ambition' is what he'd say. [Pause]

Counsellor: You feel that he could never understand you?

Student: No, I don't think he is – capable of that, because I don't get along with him, don't at all!

Counsellor: You dislike him a good deal?

Student: Yes, I-I did feel bitter toward him for a while and I've gone out of that stage, and now I don't feel bitter against him but I-I'm sort of ashamed. I think that that's it more than anything else, an experience of shame that he is my father. [Pause]

Counsellor: You feel he isn't much good.

Student: Well, he's putting me through school but [few unintelligible words] [...] I'm sorry to say, but that's my opinion about it. I think he had a lot to do in forming it, too.

Counsellor: This has been something on which you have felt pretty deeply for a long while.

Student: I have. [Long pause]

(R.L. Kahn and C.F. Cannell, 1957, pp. 73-75)

Space precludes prolonged analysis of this text, although such analysis would be interesting. As a whole it clearly demonstrates the potency of Rogers' insight that help does not lie outside the person, or the persons, who in the end must benefit from it: help lies within them, just as the problem does. The solution is mixed with the problem. Except that if the persons concerned feel that the problem is insoluble, this means that the problem obscures the solution: it overwhelms it and prevents access to it from outside. Indeed, in psychological counselling, as in the example, the solution may be simply the problem itself when brought into the open. The emotional troubles of the student were the feelings of confusion and guilt caused by his negative feelings towards his father: the student was unable to overcome this sense of guilt until he had externalized it by talking to somebody he trusted. His problem had to become the matter of discourse, the concrete *content* of the interview, for it to be dealt with. But such an embarrassing exploration is anything but easy, and one realizes how substantial the practitioner's contribution was to making it possible.

Behind his apparently passive stance, the counsellor was active. Behind his apparent non-directivity, he directed. He directed to the extent that he did not allow the student to channel the interview (their relationship) into the more customary course of the directive interview. When at the beginning the student asked: 'Would you advise me to tell them about it?', he metacommunicated approximately the following message: 'I've come to you so that you can give me the solution'. The counsellor actively and directly blocked this manoeuvre. By responding 'Suppose you tell me a little more what you had thought about it', he informed the student that help would never be offered; that henceforth the interview would be centred on the student, not on the counsellor, and that the student would be the one to decide.

The other point where the counsellor's firmness was evident was when he compelled the student to face up to reality, preventing him from skirting around unpleasant matters. When at the beginning of the interview, the student said that he felt forced to talk to his parents, and then left the reason why unsaid (although it was evident and obligatory), the counsellor prompted him by quickly and firmly saying: 'It's a situation you've really got to face.'

For the rest, the counsellor was active even when he remained passive. That is to say, he used a maieutic technique typical of counselling which consists in mirroring and reformulating what the interlocutor says or feels. This device enhanced the student's role in the helping process; it enabled him to be the protagonist in expounding the problem (who else could it be?); and it also allowed the flow of experience to emerge freely from his account, without interference by the counsellor. All this was made possible by the counsellor and his skilful deployment of the client-centred approach. If he had been directive – if he had given advice, asked questions, and so on – he would have thwarted his interlocutor's protagonism. If he had been non-directive – if, that is to say, he had not indicated any direction for the interview, allowing the student to go where he wanted – it would be impossible to say why the student had not already resolved the problem by himself.

2.3.2.2. The merits and shortcomings of Rogers' approach

Rogers' insight that help is centred on the person who benefits from it, rather than being centred on the person that provides it, is brilliant because it is counter-empirical. Experience and common sense induces us to believe that if people are unable to solve their problems and seek help, then help must perforce be given to them. If they are fortunate enough to find an expert who can solve their problems, what more can we ask for?

Carl Rogers freed psychotherapy, and social work even more so, from this platitude. The methodological error caused by banalities of this kind is subtle, but it should be clearly understood. It stems from the belief that help is the function of one single variable: the quality of the intervention. If, after intervention x, we obtain positive results, these depend – it is thought – solely on the expertise contained in that input. All the directive approaches – psychoanalysis, behaviourism, systems therapy, and others – are based on this unconscious conviction that gives rise to a curious phenomenon which we may call a 'hyper-perfectionism'. In the face of an intractable problem, the sensation arises that one's only recourse is to improve it even further. Whatever the level of perfection that one begins from, the presumption is that this perfection can be refined. A leap of quality in results (output) can only come from a leap of quality in the intervention (the expert input). This is a persuasive but insidious idea; it draws practitioners – and also, at a different level, policy-makers – into a vicious circle from which they are unable to escape.

It is difficult to thank Carl Rogers enough for having led the helping sciences out of this blind alley. He challenged the psychological culture of his time (the 1930s and thereafter), bogged down as it was in psychoanalysis and behaviourism. He shifted the focus of attention from the expert to his/her interlocutor, the person seeking help. He pointed out what was substantially a truism as widely ignored as it was banal: namely that since the recipients of help are subjects, by the logical rule of non-contradiction they cannot be *objects*. Since help-seekers are subjects, they have a role; they too are independent variables to the fullest extent. Since they are not objects, they are not inert materials to be shaped. It is therefore pointless to behave as if they are and act under that illusion.

Rogers had the courage to point out that the king had no clothes. He believed that all helping techniques were deluded. Since nobody realized this, he had to shout it out loud, and in his endeavour to attract attention, he inevitably and understandably overstated his case. Today, with the benefit of hindsight, as we comfortably exploit Rogers' insight, we notice a flaw in his approach. It appears structurally similar to the directive methods it opposed: it, too, is based on one single variable. It is unidirectional because it still presumes that the solutions to problems arise from only one of the parties involved, although this party is the opposite to the one previously envisaged. Solutions spring from dynamics entirely confined to the person – or the persons, given that we are now thinking in terms of networks – concerned with the difficulty (Figure 2.4).

It is easier to understand this point if we consider an extreme form of non-directivity – a form which, as we have seen, not even Rogers contemplated (or no longer contemplated after a certain point). If, in a helping relationship, the action is undertaken entirely by the client, who moves as and where s/he wishes and arrives where his/her efforts take him, then the *unidirectionality* of the action is clear. It is what 'vitally' (i.e. due to the effect of an intrinsic vital force) emerges from the client. The expert practitioner imparts the initial impetus and then does nothing except watch what happens.

But the same applies if we reason in terms less radical than absolute non-directivity – which, as said, is in any case impossible to achieve. Let us consider the approach centred on the person real and proper: that is, on a rather more active expert who unobtrusively guides the client (as the expert guided the student in the above example). Unidirectionality is present here as well, albeit in attenuated form. Consider a practitioner who imparts the initial impetus and sets up the relationship. But then, rather than let matters take their course, s/he continues to create the *conditions* (Egan, 1990; Farber, Brink and Rasking, 1996) so that the vitalism of the persons concerned may persist throughout the process – and also directs it as is *appropriate*, not as s/he wishes. This practitioner seemingly works on a more realistic and sensible basis. Indeed, there is already a relationship in the true sense of the word, because there is already a clear sepa-

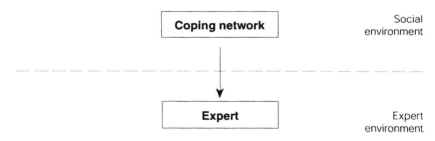

Fig. 2.4 Diagram of the non-directive or person (network) centred approach.

ration between the parties. However, if the expert is convinced that all s/he need do is allow the resources of the people concerned to emerge, then s/he is still working within a unidirectional framework. S/he has a *maieutic* view of the helping relationship, as we have seen, but it is important to grasp the limitations of this kind of relationship.

Maieutics is the art of midwifery. It is obvious, however, that a baby is born from only one of the parties. The midwife attends to the baby during birth but she does not give him of her own substance, so to speak. She facilitates the birth and alleviates suffering, but what the baby actually is does not depend upon her. The relationship between the mother and the midwife has to do with the birth – that is, with the emergence of what is within – not with the essence of the baby. In the helping relationship, a typically Rogersian person-centred approach enables a solution to emerge but it does not contribute *elements of itself* to it.

It is important to be clear on this point. Bringing out all the self-help resources contained even latently in every problem situation is a basic social work strategy, in the sense that it is the first thing to do and must *always* be done. A social worker who systematically violated this principle would be reprimanded, because preceding the activity of his/her interlocutors with his/her activism would impede it or distort it. Often, the simple strategy of 'bringing out what is there' is enough, and nothing further is required. It may be so in counselling, where the help by definition consists in the catalysing of inner psychic resources. And it is sometimes so in social work as well, although here matters are more complex.

It is frequently the case in social work that a problem may remain unsolved even when all the internal resources of the person concerned have been activated. It could be objected, of course, that everything depends on the point of view, and in particular on how the boundaries of the reality within which one presumes to have worked have been defined. In practice it is always difficult to define the precise confines of the container from which what is within is to be brought out. Brought out from what? In the case of an individual person, we already know that these confines are narrow. The networking approach came to the fore when it was realized that drawing out the potential of a single person is often reductive. The focus consequently shifted to the network, and here the reverse problem arose: a network does not have boundaries. If, for example, we think of the resources of a particular family – father, mother and two children – rather than of the resources of only one of its members, the field is indubitably more extensive, and it is more likely that a solution will be found. But there is obviously nothing to guarantee this outcome. If this informal network proves inadequate, it is always possible to consider an even larger one which includes it – the family's network of kin and friends, for example – and so on. But, however extensive the informal system, and however much it interweaves with the formal one, no one can say that these ever larger entities comprise the solution that is being looked for. Obviously, the more extensive the network, the more it will contain the creative resources required for a solution; but this is not to say that it will always contain the solution (The network may also comprise unacceptable pressures or actions which the social worker regards as anything but solutions).

In short: whenever intervention by an expert is necessary, the solution is *worked out jointly*. It is neither fabricated according to the welfare conception of which Gouldner (1970) calls 'bureaucratic-industrial', nor is it discovered. A social worker cannot be conceived – nor can s/he conceive him/herself – either as *homo faber*, a fabricator of whatever s/he needs, or as a new Socrates who elicits what s/he needs ready-made. If there is something to be learnt from the discussion thus far it is that a solution (a) is not to be found ready-made in the circle of interested people and (b) nor is it to be found ready-made in the head of the practitioner: *it is jointly worked out in the course of time through synergy of all the parts involved.*

2.4. The helping relationship as a reciprocal improvement in the capacity for action

I have shown what the relational approach is *not:* it is neither a directive attitude nor a non-directive one. It is neither one nor the other of these opposing styles; not even when they are diluted into their less radical versions: the practitioner-centred and person-centred approaches (for a synthesis of these concepts, see Table 2.1).

Now if an entity is neither one thing nor everything that is 'other' than that thing – it is neither 'a' nor 'non-a' – then one may ask what else it can possibly be. In logical terms, one can argue by inclusion rather than by exclusion. One may say that it is *both* things ('a' *and* 'non-a') combined. The relational approach is therefore both directive and non-directive at the same time: it is a blend of the two and simultaneously neither of them. The two-headed arrow in Figure 2.3. is a synthesis of the unidirectional arrows of directivity from the practitioner to the interested parties, and of non-directivity from the interested parties to the practitioner. Both flows are simultaneously in operation. What this depicts is the style of action by a social worker who fully knows and feels that help (the solution) is a *relationship*. All this has the precise significance, now hopefully clear, that a solution is built from bricks provided by both sides of the relationship.

2.4.1. *The relational attitude as sentiment: 'knowing how to be'*

The relational attitude is a deep-lying sentiment within the practitioner towards his/her interlocutors and towards him/herself. Even before that, remembering the A.A. lesson, it is a feeling of respect for the problem and for its intrinsic force (McCrady and Miller, 1993). The relational practitioner should be free from the subtle sense of hubris which s/he might harbour as a professional: by definition, every expert should be self-assured and confident of his or her ability to control events (Bandura, 1997). In truth, the presumption of an ability to transform everything or to solve every problem lies even more deeply, well below the crust of professionalism. It is the mental clothing of modernity; it is the attitude typical of the particular species of mankind bred in the era of technology (Jonas, 1974). Although these pressures are applied from all quarters, experts who want to work with the social style should be able to resist them. They should be inoculated against the endemic virus that is an excess of manipulative self-confidence. They should be aware that every social problem has its own intrinsic logic. At the beginning, when the problem is first perceived and when joint effort to deal with

TABLE 2.1

Non-relational approaches to social work solutions (summary of concepts)

Non-directive	The practitioner relates to his/her real and potential interlocutors on the assumption that everything they do is by definition functional to the helping process.
Person-centred	The practitioner relates to his/her real and potential interlocutors on the assumption that they must be supported to a certain extent so that the solution that resides *within* them emerges and becomes operational.
Practitioner-centred	The practitioner relates to his/her real and potential interlocutors on the assumption that they must collaborate – or be enabled to collaborate – so that the solution that resides within him/herself can be applied.
Directive	The practitioner relates to his/her real and potential interlocutors on the assumption that they must do what s/he says.

it starts, ignorant of its possible solutions are both the interested parties (otherwise they would have already dealt with it) and the practitioner him/herself (otherwise s/he could have immediately have revealed that logic and resolved the problem).

To be precise, I am not distinguishing between easy and difficult problems, between routine ones where a certain amount of hubris might be justified, and weighty ones with respect to which every expert sees that s/he must be humble. In regard to *any* social problem – that is, any problem which has to do with coping – the relational attitude should arouse a twofold awareness of weakness and strength in the expert. Likewise it should signal the strength and weakness of those involved with the problem. The practitioner should know that *none* of those who share the problem possesses the key to its solution. Even if we assume that the problem is objectively simple, its solution does not exist at the beginning and must be jointly worked out.

The relational attitude is an inner strength of practitioners which enables them (a) to accept their weakness and their sense of limitation as a fertile environment within which a solution can be found, and (b) to perceive and accept, as a further facilitating factor the strength of the persons concerned mixed with (or concealed beneath) their declared weakness.

For experts, accepting their weakness, being skilled, specialized, and so on, requires inner strength. Equal strength is required to recognize the strength of interlocutors in difficulty, who often have their official condition stamped on their foreheads. I am not just saying this as a matter of course. In order to feel sentiments of this kind, absolutely integral psychological strength is required.

Many social workers are able to accept that they do not already possess a ready-made key to the solution. They are also able to accept that they must construct the solution piece by piece, with a great deal of patience and taking their time. However, they find it much more difficult to accept the fact that they cannot construct the solution without the help of others, without transcending the confines of their own professionalism, because this apparently limits their role as experts. It is not easy for them to accept the notion that transcending professionalism – taking action in the knowledge that it is insufficient, and yet without discouragement but seeking to go *beyond* it – is the best way to reinforce such professionalism.

A practitioner is relational if s/he does not feel the unconscious need to nourish his or her personality by exploiting the intrinsic power structure of the helping relationship that places the expert in a higher status position than his/her interlocutors (Genevay and Katz, 1990). Social workers without self-confidence may unconsciously rely on this aspect of their role, exploiting its advantages for the purpose of self-therapy (Köning, 1997). Their self-esteem may be boosted by the submissive or trusting attitudes of their clients, who grant them a higher technical status. This interactive imbalance to the social worker's advantage may be gratifying but it is fraught with risks. The more experts make their image depend on their presumed ability to solve the problems of others and seek to impress their interlocutors with the exercise of their exclusive abilities, the more they risk triggering a chain reaction of frustrations in themselves or in others. Let us imagine an expert with this technological cast of mind. When s/he feels growing insecurity due to the inevitable disappointment in practice of his/her technological expectations, what will s/he do? S/he will try to deal with it by adopting exactly the same attitude as before. That is to say, s/he will try to prevent failures in the future by insisting even more that s/he alone is able to deal with problems according to his/her self-referential parameters. S/he is therefore trapped in a blind alley.

The relational attitude is a feeling of *self-confidence* which enables an expert to accept, and indeed to cultivate, an essential *uncertainty* in the work setting. This firmly-held sense of ambivalence prevents the expert from assuming attitudes which are methodologically incompatible with effective action. A confident practitioner who knows from the outset what s/he must do, and who envisages no alternatives, is an expert in thrall to his or her self-confidence and therefore unable to handle complexity. An effective social worker must be confident in the sense that s/he 'hopes' that a certain outcome will come to pass but is not 'certain' that it will. S/he is 'confident' in the profound sense of the word defined by Hans Jonas as not being a prey to fear ('a fear which dissuades from action') but instead possessing the 'courage of responsibility'.

> Have we not overemphasized the threat of technology and underplayed its promise? Only the voice of warning and caution has been heard, not that of an inspiring task. A heuristic of fear, so one will say, has its points, but only in counterbalance to a heuristic of hope, which has hitherto lighted mankind's path. (Jonas, 1974, p. 203)

The determination to proceed with caution despite being aware that there are dangers and difficulties ahead (and the determination is fed by precisely this awareness) is what I am talking about here.

When the relational attitude is anchored in an appropriate psychological base, it may be deployed operationally. When experts are not preoccupied with their own well-being, they are able to act upon problems exactly *as those problems require*, and not as prompted by the covert interests of their personality. Note that a psychological stance of this kind may also come about unconsciously. Practitioners do not need to have precise knowledge of this rule. They may act as if they know that complex solutions require synergy, and therefore openness and trust, even when they do not actually think about such matters. It is for this reason that I insist here upon *sentiment*, although this is an ineffable phenomenon about which one should instead refrain from talking. Sentiment, indeed, can act as the compass which directs all action.

In the history of the helping professions, authentic relational action came before intellectual understanding of its nature and necessity. There are countless numbers of social workers who although they have trained in the one-sidedness of the helping process, prove to be outstanding in practice because they have acted relationally. While their trainers sought to imbue them with perhaps mistaken positivist ideas – some of them indeed presuppositional in the literal sense that they presupposed too much of the fledgling expert, imagining him/ her with a hypertrophic Ego – the trainees did not feel the psychological need to take these ideas on board and subsequently acted unconsciously in a manner contrary to them. Without realizing, they adopted a relational humble attitude, as Kierkegaard has taught to us:

> All true caring starts with humiliation. The helper must be humble in his attitude towards the person he wants to help. He must understand that

helping is not dominating, but serving. Caring implies patience as well as acceptance of not being tight and of not understanding what the other person understands (Kierkegaard, 1849; quoted in Hobbs, 1987: XV)

Tacit insubordination of the trainees towards the trainers: only this explains such a surprising contrast between abstract theory taught and the practice actually performed by the practictionerrs. It is the only explanation, in fact, unless someone comes up with a convincing explanation as to why superb unilateral attitudes in social work might be appropriate.

2.4.1.1. The feelings of users when they consult an expert: are they relational-oriented?

Experts often find it difficult to assume the correct operational stance because they are misled by their interlocutors. I have talked thus far of the relational attitude as an attribute of the expert. It must now be said that the persons involved in the helping process may have a similar attitude: that is, they may be aware of the roles played by both sides in the helping relationship. However, it should be pointed out immediately this does not often happen. Usually, experts have no idea of joint action, and even less so do their interlocutors.

When people consult a professional practitioner, they do so because they feel that they cannot cope on their own. When they realize that at a certain address, in a certain street, they can find a social service – a counselling centre, a social work unit, or similar – and decide to go there, this is because they hope to find the right person to help them. This faith is justified (if they found the wrong person, something would indeed be wrong), but they usually do not realize that finding the right person is not everything: it is only the first step.

Users place themselves in the hands of an expert on the basis of some sort of trust relationship. They normally do not know – and do not wish to know – that the expert that they have decided to consult has only limited powers. By force of habit they transfer to the social worker the behaviour they adopt in other professional fields, when they take their problems to an interior designer, for instance, or to a doctor or a lawyer. Giddens's theory that modernity has failed because the professional expertises believed to be certain are not exhaustive (Giddens, 1990) is too sociological a notion for ordinary people; it applies mainly to the social professions. But in social work, if the idea of the relative impotence of the professions is not clear to the expert practitioner, it is even less clear to his or her clients.

The behaviour of a non-relational expert is often reinforced by non-relational 'clients'. A practitioner who wishes to believe that s/he is self-sufficient has no difficulty in finding users who want to believe the same thing, namely that the expert is really as capable as s/he implies. In this case, we have a synergy of self-deception. Who should break the circuit? The answer is obvious: the person who possesses the greater intentionality – that is, the practitioner. It is the practitioner that must educate the others into a positive synergy, and to do so s/he must first overcome the initial countervailing force that is him/herself. When the client sits down opposite the expert and implies that s/he is expecting a solution, the expert must make it clear, not that s/he will not provide this solution, but that it must be worked out together. If the practitioner states this firmly and clearly, the client will soon learn. We may say of the relational attitude what Pericles said about a good policy: few are able to produce one, but everybody is able to recognize one.

The expert must often begin by combating the anti-relational stance not of an individual user but of a group. An example is provided by self-help/mutual support groups (Steinberg, 1997). When an expert sets about creating a group of this kind – which if it does not have a relational attitude is not this type of group but one of another kind, a therapeutic group for example (Hurvitz, 1974) – the preliminary phase involves the learning of this logic by the members of the group. Especially when the facilitator is a highly-skilled specialist – a psychiatrist, for example – the following situation often arises. The members of the group agree to talk to each other about their problems, but they expect that when these preliminaries have been concluded, the real therapy will begin. Their expectation is that the expert will soon start to talk and then draw his/her conclusions and issue his/her prescriptions; in short, do what they expect. Indicative of the attitude is the fact that as soon as the expert shows signs of wanting to say something, the group immediately falls silent so that it can hear properly, whereas previously its members only listened to each other distractedly. If a mutual support group is to work, its members must always overcome this phase; and they will be able to do so more rapidly if they are assisted by the practitioner. Who, moreover, must close his/her ears against what is, at base, pleasing adulation.

If a user does not assimilate the meaning of the relation after long interaction with a helping professional, the danger arises that he or she will adopt the attitude opposite to acritical trust and seek to discredit the practitioner. S/he may think that, because results are not yet forthcoming, the expert has not lived up to the expectations placed in him/her and is consequently worthless. The user must therefore look for a more capable expert; or alternatively s/he must deal with the problem him/herself. It is difficult for the user to realize that it is his or her expectations that are at fault. S/he will instead believe that s/he has unluckily ended up with an inept practitioner and seek to discredit him/her. There are increasing numbers of people who believe that the experts working for the statutory social services are useless because they have failed to keep their promises. It is a comparatively short step from exclusive investment in an expert to exclusive investment in oneself. The so-called self-help movements now widespread in all the industrialized societies (Gersuny and Rosengren, 1973; Riessman and Carroll, 1995; Wann, 1995) were born in open antagonism to the expertise of the welfare state (as if to say: 'Forget those theories! Forget those techniques! Learn how to do it from us!').

2.4.2. The relational attitude: knowing 'how to do'

It is of paramount importance that the expert should adopt an appropriate 'emotional' stance towards the problem and towards his or her interlocutors. Then, obviously, if this stance underpins a set of well-oriented concepts, so much the better. An expert must act deliberately and appropriately, if possibile, without investing mistaken hopes in back-to-front results. That is to say, s/he must not expect badly thought-out action to somehow yield positive results.

At the cognitive level, the relational attitude is substantiated in the twofold principle that every expert should know very well: namely that his or her presence in the problem situation will *improve* the other party. And here we are on safe ground: the prototypical traditional expert is well acquainted with this notion. But, conversely, the clients will in their turn *improve* the expert; they will improve him or her generally as a person or practitioner, but they will also specifically improve his or her technical ability to deal with the actual problem.

An expert who believes that s/he is solely a care *giver* and need never be a care *receiver* will never be able to learn (Casement, 1989). S/he generously dispenses help but will never accept it. When an expert interacts, in the exact sense of the word, his/her interlocutors enrich him/her with the resources essential for effective action (or to be precise, capacity for action) throughout the entire helping process. There is nothing romantic about this: it is a plain technical fact. The expert's interlocutors will open up and allow him or her – but once again it is the expert that must not shut down the interlocutors by concentrating the entire process on him/herself – to penetrate to the subjective meaning of the problem, and also to the subjective meaning of what will or should be its solution. This information flow should be towards the practitioner, improving his or her expert capacity to handle the situation. Without this constant flow of information from his/her traditional counterpart, the practitioner will not know precisely what to do, apart from resorting to some or other predefined measure.

The idea that in social work the expert should learn from his/her interlocutors is largely intuitive. However, to understand the idea more thoroughly, we must examine it in even more abstract form, as follows: every worker can/must learn from the products of the work that s/he does, even when, as often happens in social work, it has nothing to do with people. Popper writes:

> According to the theory of self-expression, the quality of the work we do depends upon how good we are. It depends only on our talents, on our psychological, and, perhaps, on our physiological states. I regard this as a false, vicious, and depressing theory. [...] there is no such simple relationship. There is, on the contrary, a give-and-take interaction between a person and his work. You can do your work, and, thereby, grow through your work so as to do better work- and grow again through *that* better work, and so on. (Popper, 1994, p. 140)

Besides the idea that the social worker's job is to improve his/her interlocutors, we must see how the latter can reciprocally improve the practitioner's ability to do his/her job so that s/he can then improve the interlocutors, and so on. I shall now examine this notion on the premise that the circular process of improvement just described is both *structural* and *dynamic*.

2.4.2.1. Reciprocal structural improvement: coupling experiential resources/abilities with technical-methodological ones

I said earlier that a practictioner must dispassionately accept a twofold reciprocal ambivalence of social work reality: namely that in the face of a problem s/he is weak despite his/her strength and his/her interlocutors are strong despite their weakness. Though acceptance of this notion is essentially emotive, the danger arises that the intellect will be blocked by this apparent paradox. The obstacle, however, can be overcome by a not very difficult insight. If this reciprocal ambivalence is suitably 'cross-connected', the strengths of the interlocutors are able to off-set or improve the weaknesses of the expert, while at the same time the strengths of the expert are able to off-set or improve the weaknesses of the interlocutors (see Figure 2.5).

If we regard the expert/clients pairing as a unit, we find that the structural imbalance in each of its components is redressed. The strengths of the two entities are joined together to form a new relational unitary *structure*. As we have seen, it sometimes happens that although the expert and the interested parties stand in a relation, they both go their own ways. As a result, it is likely that the weakness of each will eventually cause them to stumble. It is as if they have one leg to give them impetus but they do not have another one to give them balance. Conversely, if they are structured together, one party acts as a crutch for the other as they approach the problem.

The image of the crutch helps maintain a modest attitude. After the expert and the parties involved have been joined together, it is not that they become miracle-workers. Even when the *structure* of the action has undergone the formidable step of being joined together, it is still inadequate. Even though its strengths have been combined, they are still only relative strengths. They must develop throughout the helping process, and even then the maximum possible may not be achieved. Nevertheless, significant progress will have been made: two props rather than one.

The (inadequate) strengths of the practitioner and the (inadequate) strengths of the interested parties are essentially different. This difference is partly due to their positions *vis-à-vis* the problem, and partly due to their respective endowments of cognitive-instrumental resources to cope with it. The peculiarity of the expert's position was discussed in the previous chapter. The practitioner occupies a *distanced* (which does not mean 'detached') position from which s/he can first observe the problem and then perhaps transform it from outside. Also discussed was the technical-scientific armoury in the practitioner's mind which enables him/her to draw specific meanings from what s/he observes. The practitioner sees partly different things compared to the interested parties, and s/he interprets them differently. Obviously, the practitioner also has material resources or instruments different from those already present in the natural situation. Taken together, this array of resources can be called *expert skills (or technical-methodological skills)*.

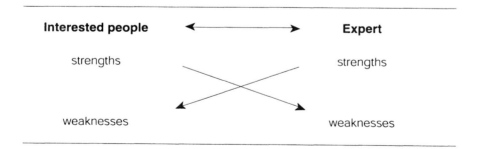

Fig. 2.5 Diagram of the dual crosswise ambivalence in the helping relationship.

Interested parties with different experiences of the events that concern them are involved to various extents in the situation. Each of them is 'within' the situation and from this insider position acts as a 'participant observer'. Involvement is the fuel that drives motivation, or in other words, it is something that constantly provides motive for action. Having experienced the entire trajectory of the problem situation (or portions of it) from within, the client possesses the immediate (but always partial) meaning of what happened (in the past), of what is happening (now) and of what may happen (in the future). S/he possesses memory and also something more: a set of skills developed through learning (Clark, 1991; Hobbs, 1992; Schopler, 1995). These are abilities gained from, or grounded in, experience of what has already happened in the situation. They may therefore be called *experiential skills.*

The expert social worker contributes the *objective* meaning of the situation. This meaning may derive from the filtering of reality through his/her technical and theoretical concepts – or in other words, through his/her logical-analytical knowledge (in the left hemisphere of the brain). Or it may derive also from the *experience* of the practitioner, who has already met similar situations and may therefore compare the situation now being observed against previous ones. The expert filters the observed data through his/her reference schemata, which are objective in the Popperian sense that they are not just the outcome of contingent experience (Popper, 1994).

The people involved contribute the *subjective* meaning of the situation: the sentiments, views and partial knowledge of those who are directly affected by the problem to varying extents, who live it from within as it unfolds. This feeling-from-within (or subjectivity) is, as Husserl puts it, an 'enigma' for the positive sciences (Husserl, 1959). But it is a feeling that professional social workers cannot ignore even though it lies outside them.

The practitioner's strengths are like the two sides of the proverbial coin in that they are perfectly specular to his/her weaknesses. The same applies to the interested parties. For each of them, the exclusiveness of his or her point of view, interpretations and instruments are a distinct resource but also a structural constraint. Possession of a point of view or a conceptual interpretative grid enables them to construct what Schütz (1972) calls 'finite provinces of meanings': categories irreducible to any others. They take possession of the mind and tend to erase meanings that do not fall within their compass.

The most potent and invasive mental categories in the helping relationship are those of the expert. If they are exercised without the necessary caution, the expert may find him/herself trapped in a blind alley. The more s/he appropriates reality by sifting it through his mental categories, the less intuitive contact s/he has with it. Accordingly, we may say that the expert grows weaker as s/he grows stronger, and vice versa. The more s/he cleaves to the methodological dimension (for example, if s/he seeks to improve only by the standard means of increasingly specialized training courses), the more the expert will weaken in another dimension, the directly experiential one, which will prove more elusive the more his/her mind is concerned with other codes. Whilst weakness derives from strength, in order to gain strength one must make oneself weaker, which is a paradox similar to the 'double bind' (Sluzky and Ramson, 1976).

Is there a way out of this dilemma for practitioners? Only if they head down the road of relationship. If they look for the solution self-referentially – that is, only within themselves – they will never escape. In social work, experts have an impelling logical necessity to go beyond themselves. They should not be worried by the discovery that an increase in strength along the technical-scientific axis has the converse effect of greater weakness along the one of intuitive feeling. The missing component can be found outside themselves. With the correct attitude, they can acquire what they lack structurally and incorporate it into their action, *but they cannot do so on their own.* The rider in italics will be explained in the next section.

2.4.2.2. Dynamic reciprocal improvement: joint learning/development

Described thus far has been the best initial configuration for an effective helping relationship: the two parties in the relationship – the expert and the network of people concerned with a problem – may indeed have specific identities, but they must nevertheless be regarded as jointly and equally involved. We have imagined the objective dimension of methodology and the subjective one of experience as statically separate. Were social work a process comprising two independent realities complementary to each other, we would have to say that reciprocal improvement comes about in so far as each reality *compensates* for the other: it does not improve it, that is to say, but acts as its external prop. Like a crutch, it makes up for what the other lacks. This is the idea of 'partnership' formulated by Litwak (1985), which is a good step forward but is still not a fully relational notion. In reality, the improvement may also be intrinsic and dynamic, in the sense that each party is able to induce the other to grow through progressive interaction.

When the configuration is such that each party is able to act, then everything is ready for true *social* work 'intervention' to begin, meant as reciprocal learning among the parties. According to Barnes,

> [Social work] is not just a question of applying professional knowledge, but also of learning from the knowledge of those they are assessing, become 'expert in the problem solving process rather than expert in problem solving as such'. (Barnes, 1996, p. 140)

Literally, 'intervention' means 'action taken from outside in order to change a situation'. Matters are different in social work: the change is brought about internally to the unit comprising the two parties in interaction. Admittedly, each party taken individually is external to the other and therefore intervenes in the other; but taken together they constitute a whole cemented by their interaction. Each party is able to modify itself and in so doing modifies the other party. Thus generated is a self-feeding process, a dynamic which will continue as long as the action receives the fuel it requires – fuel which, in concrete terms, consists of jointly-held skills, motives, energies, etc. – and does not flag. Interaction between two linked parties engenders change, and it is learning.

When reciprocal learning between a provider and a recipient effectively takes place, the stereotypical roles of the person who gives help and the person who receives it disappear. It is this feature that crucially distinguishes a relational intervention from others that are only apparently such. Barnes makes the point very clearly:

> While community care policy is founded on a trust in the capacity of family carers to provide a major source of support to older people and the other users of community care services, that trust is not always evident in willingness on the part of individual service providers to learn from their experience of providing support. Nor is there much evidence that disabled people, those with mental health problems or learning difficultues are trusted to be able to determine their own needs. (Barnes, 1996, p. 149)

In a process of reciprocal learning, the two parties – the one relying on codes of technical competence, the other on direct experience – not only complement each other (the one is the crutch for the other) but they come into contact and co-penetrate. However, here the argument requires some distinctions to be drawn.

A joint learning process between two parties interacting in a stable relationship can be imagined in two only apparently similar ways:

(a) as a process in which party A enriches the shared action with what is distinctive of itself (A) and thereby causes party B to grow in what is specific to it (to B);

(b) as a process in which party A contributes what is distinctive to it to the shared action and thereby causes party B to grow in features that belong not to B but to A.

Beyond the tangle of words, the difference between these two patterns has analytical importance and warrants brief clarification. More concretely: in version (a) – where A alters B in what is distinctive of B – the methodological component, which provides objectivity, improves the experiential component in its subjective sense. For example, a user suffering from anxiety is able to confide in a calm and reassuring practitioner able to reformulate his feelings in appropriate words. The user improves his emotional experience and feels more serene about his situation. The subjectivity of the user is filtered through the objectivity of the practitioner's skills and is thereby improved (as subjectivity).

In version (b) – A modifies B in what is distinctive of A – the methodological component, which provides objectivity, improves the objective content of the experiential component, which is extraneous to it and instead pertains to the expert interlocutor. For example: the family of a chronic psychiatric patient consults the staff of a mental health service. These practitioners adopt, let us say, an integrated psycho-educational approach (Fallon, 1988) which involves creation of a setting in which the practitioners teach specific stress-or crisis-management skills to the family. The intention is to help the family by transferring cognitive inputs (i.e. technical-methodological skills) to it which instead pertain exclusively to the expert practitioner.

In short, the objectivity of the expert may make the partner either more experiential or less experiential – that is, either more him/herself or less him/herself.

The same thing happens in reverse, when we consider the action of the experiential component on the expert one. For example, in professional counselling an empathic expert may draw information from the user's reactions to his/her proposals or advice, which thereafter guide his/her action. S/he may become more flexible or more incisive, but whatever the case may be his/her expert action becomes more appropriate. In this case, the objectivity of the expert is filtered through the subjectivity of the user and then returns to him/her, reinforcing his/her objectivity and thus making the expert more him/herself. Vice versa, when the practitioner is receptive to the subjectivity of users, some of this receptivity may remain within him/her. The experience of the other party may become his/her own experience, their sensitivity his/her sensitivity, and so on, which is *sharing* in the fullest sense. In this case, objectivity filters through subjectivity and does not return; or better, it does return but in different form.

To sum up, one partner may progressively improve the other in the two ways just described: by improving the other in what s/he already is, or by improving the other by making the other similar to him/herself. In the former case the growth comes about in a single dimension; in the second it comes about in a different category. Both these processes develop, often subliminally, in every helping relationship. Nevertheless, it is obvious that they are different processes, and also that they have different degrees of 'dangerousness'. The first pattern (A changes B in what is distinctive of B) is more transparent and is always beneficial, even when it comprises a high level of intensity. The second one (A modifies B in what is distinctive of A) tends to produce confusion and muddle: although in small doses it may be beneficial, it becomes damaging to both parties if pushed beyond certain limits.

Various examples can be provided to illustrate this point. One of them concerns what is known as 'counter-transfer'(Maroda, 1991; Genevay and Katz, 1990; Dalenberg, 2000). In the helping relationship, when the expert comes into contact with the situation of a user, it may happen that the situation triggers some unconscious association with similar situations in the expert's life. Within the framework used here, we may say that the user's subjectivity triggers an *analogous* subjectivity in the practitioner, and that this latter subjectivity overlaps with the former.

A book by Genevay and Katz (1990) which deals with the most difficult situations of care for the elderly provides, amongst many others, the following example. A social worker is negotiating with the family of an elderly man over their greater involvement in his care. The social worker herself has an elderly mother who lives with her older sister, and for various reasons she rarely sees her. The two situations – the practitioner's interlocutors who should help more, and the practitioner herself who should do likewise – may merge.

The emotions triggered in the practitioner are the reflection within him/her of those of the user. The one subjectivity invades the other, and interferences may ensue. If the expert is unable to keep his/her experiential reaction under control – that is, if s/he is unable to impose the constraints of his/her objectivity upon it – then the richness of the difference is lost. No longer do we have an expert party who encounters and enlivens an experiential party, and vice versa. Instead, there is an undifferentiated subjectivity that encroaches upon and destructures professional objectivity. When subjectivity is insufficient, it cannot improve by enriching itself solely with further subjectivity, because there is the obvious risk that what increases will be its insufficiency.

Further light is shed on the effects of an overlap between the practitioner's and the user's experience by the following description by Amodeo of an ex-alcoholic therapist who is treating an alcoholic patient.

> The therapist who was a heavy user of drugs and quit without assistance may become impatient and angry with clients who are using compulsively and are unable to cut down or quit on their own. Similarly, therapists in recovery often suffer from overidentification with chemically dependent clients and

become exceedingly directive and controlling in their interventions. The first hand experience of the devastating effects of the condition may make it almost impossible for them to work dispassionately with clients while being haunted by the specter of the client's repeated failures at controlled drinking, continued physical and emotional deterioration, refusal of treatment and, possibly, death, which the recovering person sees as highly preventable because of his own personal experience (Amodeo, in Stephanie Brown, 1995, pp. 105-106)

Some degree of co-penetration between the two sides is inevitable, and may be a factor of reciprocal improvement. Objectivity may be injected with subjectivity, and subjectivity with objectivity, but the two processes should not become blurred. An expert dealing with a case of child fostering, or one of family breakdown consequent on divorce, may be more sensitive if s/he too has been a foster child or comes from a broken home. However, it should be pointed out that this greater sensitivity will give rise to an effective improvement in the expert's action only if it boosts his *professional* capacity, and not just his/her generic humanity. This subjectivity should be absorbed by the expert through the filters of his/her distinctive objectivity and processed in keeping with that logic.

Relevant here is Rogers' classic distinction between sympathy and empathy (or better, empathic understanding). In every helping relationship, especially when the practitioner does not have direct experience of the situation confronting him or her, s/he must be able to immerse him/herself in its subjectivity. Without this co-penetration, the helping relationship cannot come into being. But the barrier must remain intact. The user's feelings should penetrate the expert, but they should not affect only his/her sentiments by evoking an analogous experience, as happens in the case of sympathy. Rogers uses the term 'empathic *understanding*' to emphasise that the predominant domain is the rational one of methodology, not the emotional one of experience. The practitioner should not empathise 'integrally' – that is, be directly affected by the feelings of the client. After giving the latter a chance to express his/her feelings, the expert practitioner must understand these feelings and then relay them back in rational rather than emotional form (Hough, 1996).

The same applies to the expertise that may be injected by the technical-methodological component into the experiential one. As said, there is a growing tendency for social services practitioners to instruct clients: an example of this trend could be found in the increasing self-help literature or bibliotherapy (Santroch, Minnett and Campbell, 1994). Here too, everything goes well for a while, but then a damaging breakdown of the boundaries may occur.

An example is provided by situations in which the social workers believe that it is a good idea to interact with a group of voluntary carers, and immediately set about organizing a course of 'technical' training for them. It is important that voluntary workers, like other involved subjects, should acquire skills as well as some elementary technical expertise. However, care should be taken to ensure that these well-intentioned efforts do not subvert or dilute the non-professional specificity of the original attitudes and skills that everyone possesses (Illich, 1977). When experts decide that it is advisable or necessary to interact with voluntary carers, it is the latter in and of themselves that they need, not a surrogate for themselves.

If intentionality or rationalization is increased beyond a certain threshold, it may destroy the immediate and intuitive sense of the caring act. Oriental wisdom understands this dilemma very well:

> But compassion has no result. A is suffering, he says to X: 'Please help me to get out of my suffering' If X really has compassion his words have no result. Something happens, but there is no result [...] Does compassion have a result? When there is a result there is cause. When compassion has a cause then you are longer compassionate. (Krishnamurti, 1981, p. 253)

2.5. The principle of indeterminism in social work

> 'I do not know. But I know that I do not know'. The difference that Socrates posits between himself and others is precisely this: the others do not know that they do not know, whereas he knows that he does not know [...] This is a prosaic truth – in that it consists simply in knowing that one does not know – but it is also a valuable one, because it induces us to search for that true knowledge which we now know that we do not possess (Severino, 1994, p. 73)

Traditional social work approaches take a static view of the expert. They envisage a person who remains what s/he is while seeking to change others. By contrast, the relational approach is dynamic. It describes a practitioner who changes in the helping process because s/he must necessarily learn his/her job while doing it. His/her professional expertise ensures that s/he constantly learns anew, not that s/he has already learnt everything at the beginning.

Given that professional social workers deal with problems – and given that a problem is something which for the moment evades understanding – they are by definition ignorant, just as those in whose service they place themselves are ignorant. But if social workers know that they do not know, from this apparently banal truth they draw strength – like Socrates, when he was told by the Oracle that he was the wisest of all the Greeks because he knew that he did not know. It is hoped that this initial mutual ignorance (about what to do so that the situation changes for the better) can be remedied by a process of joint learning which will last as long as is necessary. Ongoing reciprocal learning guided by an expert who knows that it is necessary: this may be an apt definition of the helping process.

Initial ignorance is a crucial component of problem solving in social work. And it is so for every sort of social problem, not just for those classifiable as complex or complicated. It is doubly crucial, in fact. Firstly because it concerns a problem which, if there is no initial ignorance of its presumable solvers is of course not a problem. Secondly because what it is intended to change is a future social reality: an interweaving of prospective actions that have yet to happen. A more extreme cocktail of ignorance conditions would be hard to find.

The social intervention being discussed here – a change of reality with a view to bringing about that future event which is help or replenished well-being – lies within the realm of indeterminism. This seems worrying. We may ask, with some alarm, how we can possibly construct precise methodological arguments when the cornerstone itself of modern thought – determinism – is called into question. How is it possible to define meaningful rules of efficacy/efficiency for professional social workers when there is no absolute predictability of cause and effect? And yet indeterminism can be viewed as not entirely negative, as a limitation on positivist thought in the social sciences (and professions). If determinism is unable to explain the reality to come, this does not mean that we are compelled to grope in the dark; it only means that we must dispense with this mode of thought.

2.5.1. Negative indeterminism: initially 'there is no solution'

Indeterminism entails that it is logically impossible for an observer to make accurate predictions – on the basis of scientific theories or calculations, or the like – as to how a certain state of affairs $(x0)$ at a certain time $(t0)$ will have changed into a different state of affairs $(x1)$ at a subsequent time $(t1)$. If the observer seeks to envisage a certain trajectory of change, and at the end of that trajectory sees a question mark, this is indeterminism. If indeterminism holds, the observer is free to imagine whatever s/he wishes; and reality is likewise free to do whatever it wishes. A practitioner who draws up a precise but abstract plan exerts control only over that plan. S/he can conceive it as s/he wants, but s/he has no control over its outcomes. If I endeavour to change reality (that is to say, if I intervene in reality), the principle of indeterminism states that I cannot know exactly what I will achieve: state of affairs *a* will not necessarily turn into state of affairs *b*.

Indeterminism entails unpredictability and low *ex-ante* control over action. In point of fact, however, indeterminism does not entail the utter unpredictability of events, or an absolute breakdown in cause/effect relations, but rather the impossibility of predicting *with certainty*. The calculations we can make are still valid, but only to some extent. And the fact that our initial calculations do not automatically lead to the outcome expected is due not so much to the difficulty of calculation as to the fact that the indeterminism principle states that reality is inherently impossible to calculate with complete accuracy.

2.5.1.1. Beyond the doctrine of perverse effects

It is important to understand this point clearly. If we assert that reality is so complex that it is easy to make mistaken plans, and if these plans are more adequate or more 'global' (i.e. able to comprise several aspects of reality) so that complete control can be achieved, then strictly speaking it is incorrect to talk about indeterminism, since indeterminism is intrinsic to the social reality, and not a simple *ex post facto* evidence of human fallibility.

When expected outcomes are not achieved because a plan is intrinsically flawed, we are within the paradigm of *perverse effects* (Boudon, 198?; Hirschman, 199?) which is itself comprised within the logic of determinism. The practitioner takes aim at the target as best s/he can, but the arrow follows an unforeseen trajectory. The outcome is different from the one expected, but there was an objective nonetheless, and it could have been achieved had we acted more adroitly. We may call the unexpected outcome of an action, or an outcome which occurs *together with* the one expected, an 'unwanted unintentional effect'. Many effects that come about despite our intentions may turn out to be pleasant surprises. When this happens, we have what can be called 'good effects'. Conversely, 'perverse effects' are the unintentional, unwanted outcomes considered damaging or undesirable by the agent, or by neutral observers. An example is provided by the harmful side-effects of numerous drugs, for instance the antibiotics that kill the intestinal flora. A 'paradoxical effect' is a perverse effect which is exactly the opposite of the one expected, an example being a well-intentioned campaign against drug-taking which arouses curiosity in drugs or romanticizes addiction, and so on.

The theory of perverse effects does not give the lie to determinism; instead, it teaches that determinism is, so to speak, a serious matter. It tells us that we cannot ingenuously suppose that it is only necessary to plan our actions for the results to come. Things are not that simple. We should bear in mind that reality has such complex facets and interconnections that it often precludes a certain accuracy of prediction. To achieve a specific outcome, total accuracy is necessary with respect to the contingency that requires it. Determinism assures us that it is possible to envisage an exact intervention to match every given circumstance; if then in practice the result is not forthcoming, or not yet, that is another matter. The result *may* come, and this is the essential consideration.

It is another matter to say that we have left determinism for a different paradigm. If we say that an initial plan, however constructed, and therefore even the best plan possible, *may or may not* (we do not know) achieve the goal, we are talking about a logical form of indeterminism, a characteristic of reality rather than a testimonial to human fallibility. Indeterminacy of this kind is displayed by schemes in which the input may trigger not a single predictable reaction, nor an even complex chain of preordained reactions, but a range of equally strong reactions. Each link in the chain opens up a range of unpredictable possibilities, so that it is impossible to make *a priori* pronouncements. Instead we must follow the process link by link, following it as it unfolds, but also in prudent awareness that we cannot acquire certainty, only a greater amount of probability.

It is part of the expertise of a practitioner to know whether s/he is working with a reality that lies inside or outside the logical field of determinism. The principle of indeterminism also holds for physical reality, both macroscopic and subatomic, as Ceruti explains:

> Contemporary physical sciences know that we can not make any exact prediction about the prospective behavior of many deterministic dynamic systems [...]. The ambition to predict and control the physical system's future course, already tackled by discovery of indeterminism in the quantistic microcosm, today it is seen in a sceptical way also as the conventional deterministic macrocosm is concerned. (Ceruti, 1995, pp. 12-13)

However, for the Newtonian physical world, in which the human mind is used to operate, we can maintain the intuitive idea that certainties exist, even incontrovertible ones, like the apparent conquests of science and technology show us. Our entire world, even that of everyday life, is anchored in the iron-clad principle of determinism. If it failed to hold, life would seem ungovernable, and perhaps everything would already have collapsed on top of us. However, we should be very careful to draw ingenuous generalizations.

There are realities *sui generis* in the world of nature (and in human affairs) which regulate themselves according to other codes. If we approach them using the compass of determinism, then that compass immediately goes awry. In fact, something even worse happens. The compass does not visibly go wrong – in that case we would notice it and throw the compass away – instead, it *seems* to function. It gives information which is wrong yet plausible and therefore deceives us with greater and more insidious effect.

2.5.1.2. From social policies to social work, or from the general to the particular: a crescendo of complexity

We know that determinism does hold for human affairs because when the input (a 'cause' of some kind) *invests* in a human being, the *subjectivity* of the presumed object that we intend to transform, interposes itself between the input and the output and creates potential 'incoherence'. Husserl would say that people are not mere '*de facto* men' – that is, beings like the objective facts that happen externally to them, and which they then perceive as the subjects which apprehend them in immediate experience. The positive human sciences, psychology above all, have tried to study these '*de facto* beings' and yet Husserl has shown that they are in crisis (Husserl, 1959).

We must now take a step forward and distinguish between *collective* and *individual* human realities, because each of these categories reveals different degrees of structural complexity and therefore different levels of indeterminism. It should be immediately pointed out, however, that complexity grows in the opposite direction to what we might intuitively think: it grows, as Boudon (1984) has explained, in the direction of the particular. This point requires clarification.

Broadly speaking, by 'social intervention' is meant both universalistic intervention in society as a whole and particularist intervention in some or other network of people in a situation. In the former case we are in the domain of *social policy*, in the latter we are in that of *social work*. At both these operational levels, those who plan action – whether policy-makers or front-line workers – must know that linear *ex-ante* planning has broad margins of uncertainty, as we have seen. Whether the intention is to plan a new policy to support large single-income families in a given geographical area (Italian or Welsh families, for example), or whether the concern is with the specific situation of a large single-income family, the Smiths or the Robinsons for example, it is impossible to escape the law of the imponderable. When standard measures are planned for concrete situations, disappointments, perverse effects, etc., are inevitable. However, the likelihood of success increases in ratio to the number of people targeted by a measure. If I address a problem specific to the Smith or Robinson family, and if I have only a standard *a priori* measure available, this measure has a more or less zero probability of success; whereas if I address a collective problem shared by all the x number of families concerned, the probability of success increases proportionally to their number.

The more a social problem is generalized, the more it becomes in some way objectivized – if we can use this term, considering that we are talking about people. When people are lumped together into a statistical corpus, situations can be purged of their particular variations – the specificity of each – and their shared essence can be examined and affected by standard provisions. This process of grasping the core effectively reduces the complexity: the more the level of generalization increases, the more complexity decreases. It is not an error to consider a collective intervention to be standardized, or, in other words, as a measure that should work well enough for everyone, or the greatest number. The expected result is a statistical datum, so that a wide range of outcomes can be credited with success. For example, a family policy which receives a 30% approval rating may be considered a success, irrespective of the remaining larger portion of the target group that has not responded, and which on the basis of cost/benefit analysis would be deemed a failure. When action is taken to help the Smith family, however, anything less than one-hundred-per-cent success is unacceptable: either the Smith family responds as envisaged by the plan or the undertaking is a failure. Standardized intervention must, in fact, function as if it were individualized, which is improbable. This is why Boudon (1984) argues that the understanding – one might say the manipulation, too – of *particular* realities is 'infinitely complex'. In this respect fieldworkers are less fortunate than policy-makers, so much so that they require a distinct methodology.

2.5.2. 'Good' indeterminism: there may be several solutions

The principle of (negative) indeterminism tells us that a solution may not be forthcoming despite the good intentions and ability of the practitioner. Therefore it is as if that solution does not exist; as if an archer were aiming at a target that does not exist. The conventional methodology of social work does not take account of this eventuality. It envisages a practitioner who (a) works out on paper the best possible plan with which to achieve a pre-established outcome; (b) implements the plan; (c) checks on what has happened. This model takes for granted a premise that is invalid in social work: namely that the target exists.

In social work, the model of linear *ex-ante* planning does not run into difficulties solely because application of the plan may escape intentional control, with the consequence that there is no necessary correspondence between the initial state of affairs (the theoretical solution) and the outcome (the actual solution achieved). There is a more radical difficulty involved, namely that the expected outcomes do not exist at the beginning. They arise while the action is in progress. They must not only be brought gradually into the open – using the so-called incrementalist method – but also negotiated or created relationally while doing so. If they are apparent at the beginning of the process, they reside only in the unilateral imagination of the planner and then fade like a mirage. In truth, I have said that an *ex-ante* strategy may work – but only to some extent and constantly subject to criticism – in social policy programmes which, despite their greater quantitative size, leave some margin of manoeuvre. But for the micro-programmes of social work, this model is inadequate.

The principle of indeterminism invalidates the classical methodology of social work which bases itself on determinism. And yet the principle is also of help to us because it lays the basis for an alternative methodology. When applied to specific situations, the principle of indeterminism reveals an unexpected quality.

Positive indeterminism operates as follows: every specific (non-generalizable) social problem admits to a plurality of solutions, all of which are equally possible at the moment when the intervention gets under way. There is indeterminacy, therefore – a certain solution does not exist – not because there are no solutions available, but conversely, because there are numerous ones. We have indeterminism when 'the problem show us insufficient data and admits noumerous solutions' (Lalande, 1926).

This is different from saying that it is impossible to know the sole existing solution with certainty. If we had only this notion to hand, we would be entirely unsure what to do. At the beginning we cannot know the solution – indeed, strictly speaking, there is no solution at all – and yet we have the higher – order certainty that there are numerous viable, albeit unknown, options which can be discovered or even *created* in the course of the action. We can only see solutions *ex-post*, but they are created or emerge *in itinere*, and there may be many of them. Indeed, we may even hypothesise a direct correlation between the complexity of the individual situation and the number of possible acceptable outcomes: the more substantial and ramified the social problem, the more roads open up before us.

2.5.2.1. Social work: the metaphor of the 'adventurous journey'

Why should a social worker be discouraged because s/he does not initially have a target to aim at? S/he is not an archer shooting an arrow, who quite rightly wants to know where s/he should aim. The social worker can begin without knowing precisely where s/he will end up. S/he must have a sense of purpose – that is, s/he must know that s/he should move in a certain direction – but s/he does not need to know precisely *where* s/he must arrive, even less *how*. S/he will find out the best direction to take along the way, and in the end, if everything has gone well, this best direction will become clear to him/her. The road will be well signposted and will lead in the right direction. 'Road' is perhaps not the appropriate word, given that the journey is not well defined: it would be more accurate to talk of a route. In social work, to use Machado's expression, we make the road while walking. While walking we always obtain two results together: we come closer to a goal, and we construct the road behind us.

Social work is like an 'adventurous journey' in the course of which we must constantly take decisions, with the risk of making mistakes and then having to correct them, continually feeling our way ahead (Hall and Hall, 1996). It is not an easy journey, nor is it one marked out by the guidebook. On the other hand, what really matters for social workers – as it did for the pioneers as they set off for the American West – is not the certainty of where one is going but the achievement of good arriving.

The expert social worker must equip him/herself, in his/her small way, with a practical epistemology like the one recommended by Karl Popper in his celebrated work *The Open Society and its Enemies*. Ralf Dahrendorf sums up Popper's argument as follows:

> Popper's message is simple and yet profound. We live in a world of uncertainty; we try and we error. No one knows quite what the right way forward is, and those who claim to know may well be wrong. Such uncertainty is hard to bear. Throughout history, the dream of certainty has accompanied the reality of uncertainty. (Dahrendorf, 1988, pp. 86-87)

Popper was obviously referring to political action, but the analogy with the particular kind of small-scale politics that is social work is clear. Throughout the social history of mankind, the 'dream of certainty' – which culminated in the welfare state and its laudable endeavour to establish certain rights, certain benefits, and so on – 'has accompanied the reality of uncertainty'. Further analogies emerge as Dahrendorf continues:

> Great philosophers have fostered this dream. Plato painted the picture of a state run by philosophers-kings, in which those who know have to say. Hegel, and Marx after him, claimed to speak on behalf of history when they pronounced that what is reasonable either is already real or will be that after the proletarian revolution. But these are false prophets. They cannot know what you and I cannot know. The real world is one in which there are always several views, and there is conflict and change. (Dahrendorf, 1988, pp. 86-87)

Are social workers false prophets? Or are they led astray by false prophets? We must answer 'yes', for we realize that they are bluffing when they imply that they know 'what you and I cannot know'; when they lead us to believe that they know exactly where they are going when the 'journey' of social work begins; when they forge ahead without constructing the map jointly with the interlocutors travelling with them.

2.5.2.2. Indeterminism and the prevalence of subjective meaning

In social work, the practitioner metaphorically embarks on a journey, but it is not his or her journey. This is the fundamental reason for indeterminism, and it should be clearly understood.

The expert is a guide who accompanies people who by deliberate choice, or by chance, or perhaps by some bureaucratic constraint, entrust themselves to him/her on a journey of uncertain outcome. S/he is a guide *sui generis*: not an expert on the place of arrival and the route, but an expert reader of the signposts which point out the way. Before him/her lie a wide variety of different paths, some of which may be deceptive or misleading (as the doctrine of perverse effects teaches). His/her task is to help the travellers read the signs and understand which of the many acceptable routes is the one best suited to the contingent situation. But 'best suited' for whom?

By now there is one thing that we know very well: reading the signs along the way requires that the expert's skills be coupled with those of the people involved. With this synergy of different intelligences, it is more likely that the decisions required at every crossroads will be pondered more carefully, and that they will be more efficacious as a consequence. And if the two intelligences are not enough, by interacting they will induce each other to grow in a virtuous circle of learning. This is what I have called the 'joint working out of the solution'.

As for recognition of the goal, the theoretical balance between the expert and the others must be reconsidered to some extent. Who is it that decides that the point of arrival is the right one? It is a decision, or often simply a feeling, which pertains principally to the interested parties. Obviously, the expert will have a say in the matter by, for example, assuming the critical role of the devil's advocate to help the others consider the weaknesses in their optimism. But in the end it is the interested persons that decide. After all, the journey is theirs and the expert only accompanies them.

If we ask why, in social work, technology cannot operate solely according to its canons and objective logical structures, the answer is as follows: because the ultimate meaning of what the intervention intends to achieve does not belong to the possessor of that technology. Technical self-referentiality breaks down at a certain point because the solution must be a complex action that is meaningful to those who undertake it. This rule necessarily applies in helping, and therefore in all social work activities undertaken in the best interests of the users. But of course it does not apply, or applies to a lesser extent, in those social work activities where operators must perform functions of social control, and in clinical practice too. In these cases, it is more often the specialist who makes the diagnosis and also decides whether the treatment has been successful, and therefore whether it can finish, according to objective parameters to which only s/he has access. The client may assist the specialist, but the decision, based on technical considerations, is taken by the expert alone. The opposite happens in social work, where the technical decision as to whether a situation has improved, or is now acceptable, usually cannot stand alone.

It is therefore evident that indeterminism in social work is not a matter to be taken lightly. The expert who fixed on the solution right from the start would be foolish, not only because the solutions are many, and the most suitable one can only be discovered *in situ*, but also because s/he is unable to grasp the ultimate meaning of what the solution is. This meaning exists on a different plane. The solution, like the problem, inheres not in physical things but in the social, in the converging minds of human beings involved. This social – that is, these human beings standing on an equal footing – also comprises the expert, since s/he has been summoned by them to involve him/herself in their network. But even with the addition of the expert, the social remains at base the same; all that has happened is that it has been enriched. And it is the social that possesses the meaning of the solution.

The primacy of the subjective meaning of every helping solution should be emphasised for a further reason. In reality, the idea that social work is a journey and that the solution is the point of arrival – the destination – of that journey is not entirely accurate. In many cases, the journey does not end with the solution; it instead continues. The solution worked out with the help of the expert is more properly described at the point at which the travellers strike off on their own. Social work often means travelling some distance together with the intention of finding a further, safer road; it does not mean arriving at a point of stasis. The goal is the beginning of a new road, which the interested parties follow by themselves after thanking the expert and saying goodbye to him or her. In social work the true journey is the continuity of life. Consequently, it is essential that the interested parties should be sure that the new route plotted with the expert is the right one. The expert, too, must be convinced that it is, for s/he carries some of the responsibility; but the conviction of his/her interlocutors takes priority, and should there be any argument, it is overriding.

2.5.3. 'Aims' and 'goals' in social work

One point to clear up as regards indeterminism is the following: if helping is never the more or less haphazard application of a solution already possessed by an expert, but rather its progressive elaboration, we may ask whether the expert must always proceed by groping in the dark. What does it mean never to have a clear idea of the goal at the outset? Is there nothing that can help the expert to find his/her way?

To answer these questions, we must draw a distinction between an *aim*, which a practitioner may have clearly in mind from the start and pursue with determination, and a specific *goal*, which s/he should eschew if it comes to him/her too early in the helping process. In other words, the practitioner must keep what pertains to the methodological structure of the helping process (and is proper to him/her) distinct from what pertains to the content of that process (which is extraneous to him/her).

Indeterminism concerns the *goals* rather than the *aims* of helping action. By 'aim' is meant a broad orientation of action, a cardinal point which indicates a general direction ('go towards the North', 'go towards the South') without fixing a specific destination. By 'goal' is meant a specific orientation of action, the exact specification of where to go or what to do, or how to do it. A goal may be subsumed by an aim and therefore be coherent with it: in which case it is one stage in its accomplishment.

It is easy to grasp the semantic difference between the two terms. But it may prove more difficult to keep them distinct in practice. Aims and concrete goals arrange themselves along a general-to-specific continuum with the ideal aim at one end and the ideal goal at the other. It is midway along this continuum that discrimination becomes difficult. It is easy to distinguish between an extremely general aim and an ultra-specific goal; less so between a more specific aim and a more general goal. Are they not the same thing? Confusion can be avoided by following this rule: the practitioner should proceed cautiously and never go too far along the continuum from the general to the specific. S/he should take as his/her aims those options that are so general that there is no doubt that they are opportune. If there is any doubt, s/he should treat them as if they were goals, and consequently negotiate them with his/her interlocutors.

The example that follows relates to Table 2.2, which plots the possible logical paths of action to help Mario, a sick elderly man who lives in his own home. An extremely general aim of the helping process – one which is even redundant or tautological – is to 'improve' the situation or to 'resolve the problem'. An expert enters into interaction with a problem, operationally speaking, only if s/he is motivated by this intention. We should not be misled by the obviousness of this statement: the analysis conducted in the previous chapter of types of observation and problem-definition introduced the possibility that a practitioner does not see or does not endorse a problem exactly as it is presented to him/her. At times, non-intervention may be a deliberate technical decision. Here I assume that the expert decides that s/he must do something to improve Mario's situation. This decision establishes what constitutes an aim insofar as it is so general I deliberately said 'do something to improve', nothing more definite or exact, in order to emphasise that the range of options available comprises anything that may in some way or other lead to an improvement. This general intention to improve is superordinate to all preconstituted theoretical orientations – that is, to the type of school or type of methodology to which the expert adheres (psychoanalytical, behaviourist, systemic, etc.). Henceforth the aims will instead relate to some or other methodological orientation and develop in accordance with it. I shall now concentrate on those aims which, if they are formulated appropriately by the practitioner, direct the helping process towards the networking approach.

Consider, for example, the following practical decision taken by a social worker: 'In order to improve Mario's situation, something should be done to strengthen his helping network, because at the moment it is inadequate to the task'. From the network perspective, this aim, too, is extremely general and almost platitudinous. Nevertheless, it is more specific than when the social worker merely said: 'Something should be done to improve the situation'. All this may still seem banal, but care is required. This general option – so general that it is pursued almost unthinkingly or automatically – it is the passageway through which one enters or leaves the *social* domain in the helping process. If the social worker instead says, again with the same general intent to improve the situation: 'At this point we should remove the task from the social network', s/he will veer in the opposite direction. With an option of this kind in mind, the practitioner sets about acting upon the problem from the traditional welfarist point of view, which hardly comprises the concepts of social action. In this case, s/he performs the following drastic reduction: my task is exactly that of the social network. And this would be to confuse the formal task with the natural one. In other words, s/he substitutes for the primary agents, so that s/he or some other agency takes on the problem in their place. It is as if s/he says to the interested parties: 'You've failed, you can't do it, step aside: from now on I'm taking over'.

Strengthening a preexisting social network so that it can handle a task, instead of being overwhelmed by it, is an aim that every social worker has the right to pursue and if necessary, with due caution, to impose. It may happen that the expert and the interested parties agree (a) that there is a problem and (b) that something should be done to improve the situation; but thereafter (c) their points of view diverge. The interested parties believe that the situation will

TABLE 2.2

Flow chart of a hypothetical helping process.

The upper column plots a traditional form of action; the lower one a network approach

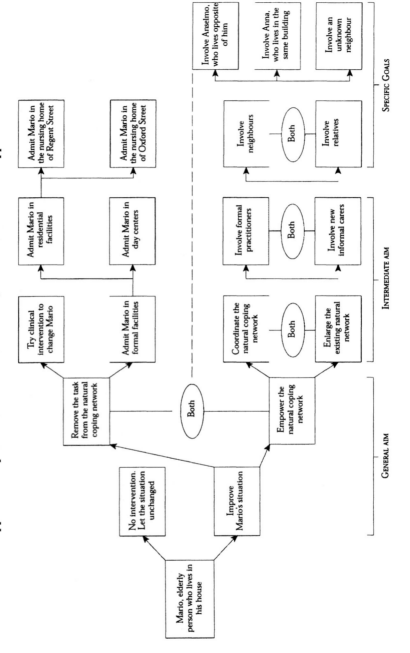

improve if they are relieved of a task which they can no longer cope with. The classic example is the one in which the family of an elderly man are no longer able to look after him and ask for him to be admitted to a nursing home. Or again, in the case of Maria discussed in the previous chapter, the family may ask for Marco to be placed in a boarding school or referred to a specialist for treatment. This perception of an aim as the removal of a task stems almost entirely from the typical standpoint adopted by the persons involved: they view their task as unmanageable, and they also believe, justifiably from their point of view, that if they were relieved of that task, the problem would disappear. But the practitioner cannot accept this aim in the first instance – not even to comply with that otherwise imperative and beneficial principle of sharing. When the interested parties ask to be relieved of a task, the operator must *oppose* the aim of his/her interlocutors until the evidence shows that strengthening the network is impossible in those circumstances, and that there is nothing else to do but remove the task from them.

While specific goals must necessarily be negotiated with the interested parties, general aims may not be, and not solely in the case where they are so obvious that they do not require any explicit agreement. Indeed, within certain limits, it may even be necessary for the social worker to force the situation so that these aims are accepted. Aims are methodological options which relate to the social worker's stock of expert skills. They fall within the ambit of that objectivity which the professional must inject into the situation from outside in order for his/her involvement in it to be meaningful. This point can be verified by inspection of the interview in section 3.2.1, and specifically by looking at the counsellor's first move, when he does *not* grant the student's request.

To continue with the example, I shall now consider other aims subsumed by that of strengthening the network (which is the overarching aim of the network approach). Once the social worker has decided to move in that direction, s/he must set about 'extending the network' (general aim 1) or coordinating it better (general aim 2) or both (general aim 3), and so on. It is evident that decisions of such an eminently methodological nature can only be taken by the practitioner. S/he may discuss them with the interested parties and ask for their opinion. But on the other hand s/he may equally decide not to seek their opinions, for various reasons: if s/he thinks that such abstract issues will not be understood, which is likely, or that the outcome of the discussion will be misleading or inconclusive, or for other considerations of propriety or pertinence.

Goals, or whatever one wishes to call the increasingly specific options that open up from this point onwards, and which form the tangible *content* of intervention, are an entirely different matter. When the focus moves from the 'values framework' of the helping process (aims) to its operational substance – that is, when decisions must be taken as regards the concrete solution to be arrived at – the practitioner has no choice: s/he must enter into a relationship.

Continuing with the example may clarify the point. When the general aim 'extending the helping network of the interested parties' has been established, how does the social worker proceed? How can s/he give concreteness to this abstract intention? For example, s/he could take the decision (still following Table 2.2) to 'involve the other people in the informal network', or to 'involve practitioners or voluntary carers from the formal services', or both. These are obviously rather general goals, for which reason we may call them 'intermediate goals'. It is evident that the practitioner must seek agreement with his/her decision to involve someone or other in the network (and not just for the sake of courtesy, obviously). The practitioner may say his/her piece, explaining why this decision is opportune, but the user or the other interested parties must necessarily be part of the decision (that is, they must help to formulate it, not just agree to it).

The practitioner, therefore, must not establish what is specifically to be done on his/her own. And as the goals grow more and more specific, more and more inteaction or negotiation becomes necessary. For example, once the social worker has decided to involve the informal network, s/he must then decide whether to involve family members, or relatives, or neighbours, or others. The practitioner may contribute to these decisions, s/he may provide advice and support, but it is not s/he that takes them. This rule will apply even more forcefully when the moment comes to penetrate more deeply into concrete reality, for example when it must be decided whether Mario's neighbour Anselmo, who lives in the flat

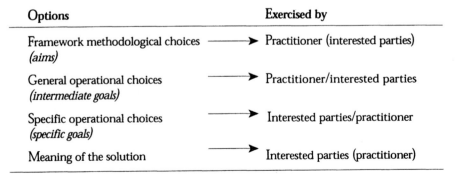

Options	Exercised by
Framework methodological choices (aims)	⟶ Practitioner (interested parties)
General operational choices (intermediate goals)	⟶ Practitioner/interested parties
Specific operational choices (specific goals)	⟶ Interested parties/practitioner
Meaning of the solution	⟶ Interested parties (practitioner)

Fig. 2.6 The relational balance between the expert and the interested people at each stage of the helping networking process.

downstairs, or his neighbour Annamaria, who lives in the block of flats across the road, should be involved. How can the operator choose on his/her own? If s/he did, she would confuse quite distinct levels of action. Because of fundamental confusions of this kind – in abstract, by confusing methodology with tangible content; in concrete, by deciding that Anselmo, the neighbour who lives downstairs, should do precisely this or that – a great deal of so-called network care has failed in the past and will fail in the future.

2.5.4. *The opposite of indeterminism: the strategy of delivering standardized services*

A methodology of social work is compatible with the law of indeterminism when it allows action to follow the route on its own. It is as if the outcome makes itself be achieved by the action plan. The 'social' solution attracts the intervention to itself (or rather, the *possible* intervention). The outcome is not a target accomplished by virtue of an accurate pre-vision; it is instead a shrewd – rather than 'opportunistic' *à la* Luhmann – process of navigation.

The social worker who conceives intervention in this way takes action to ensure that matters proceed in a certain way. As said, s/he lets the intervention unfold, s/he allows it to determine its direction according to the circumstances and not according to his/her force of will. The social worker is both present and absent. S/he monitors progress, she controls things and is carried along by them, navigating in the flow of relationships.

The idea of social work as a journey whose direction only becomes clear at its end is both simple and complex. It is simple because this is always what happens when social work is efficacious (with respect to the interested parties), and there are thousands of instances of efficacious social work interventions, and there will be thousands more in the future. But if we look at it from another point of view, it becomes clear that this approach is much more frequently ignored than it is practised. Why is this so?

2.5.4.1. About needs-led and services-led approaches

An indeterminate approach – that is, one which is flexible, hypothetical, recursive, in a word 'network-based' – is the only possible approach in conditions of complexity. Knowing that social problems are made irredeemably complex by their very nature – because they presuppose a plurality of actors, situations, sensibilities, and outcomes, and many other factors besides – entails that a social worker is *obliged* to operate in the acceptance of uncertainty and unpredictability. In other words, s/he is forced to be a networker. This reasoning is correct on paper. In practice, of course, if this principle is to work, the expert must comply with a specific psychological condition: s/he must take account of complexity and be genuinely determined to contend with it.

One can learn either to dominate complexity or to evade it. Social workers and the organizations for which they work may take up either option. Some of them learn to navigate through complexity, others let it pass over their heads. Available to social practitioners – and especially to social workers with the statutory responsibilities of the welfare state – is an approach to problems which is diametrically opposed to networking: the delivery of 'standard provisions' (Davies and Challis, 1986).

The mechanism is as follows: the social worker has access to a set of already structured and, usually, well-organized services. S/he is able to decide, for example, on access to a day centre, to residential care, to home help, to an economic benefit, to subsidized housing, to meals on wheels, to therapy or to counselling sessions, and to an infinity of other provisions. When the provisions are made available by the agency for which the practitioner works, s/he has a formidable opportunity to provide help regardless of complexity: all s/he has to do is restrict his/her action to deciding which of the provisions available is best suited (or least ill-suited) to the specific situation at hand. Elsewhere (Folgheraiter, 1994) I have described this process as follows:

> The predominant logic of public social services planning is to emphasise the *supply* of services rather than the 'reception' of demand. The intention is always to set up new services, to differentiate them, so that the range available is as broad as possible. Thereafter, *one* response is made to each individual demand by choosing, from among these options, a provision which is pre-established and largely the same for everybody. In other words, the procedure is not to 'address' the need as it presents itself with the set of necessary responses, but rather to choose that 'bit' of need which is best suited to the service available.(Folgheraiter, 1994, p. 100)

The expert thus regards him/herself as the 'gatekeeper' to the various services delivered by his/her agency. S/he must ensure that the abstract mechanism of entitlement (access to social citizenship) functions properly, so that already rationed public provisions reach the citizens who have the right to them, or who need them. This work may have its difficulties, obviously, and it may be useful in numerous circumstances, but it is limited in its scope. It does not fully take up the challenge of complexity.

The social worker makes a 'services-led' assessment (Davies, 1992; Payne, 1995) as it is now commonly called. His/her action is indeterminate to the smallest degree represented by the number of standard provisions available. If the social worker can choose among, say, three services, the degree of indeterminacy is three: when the intervention begins, the doubt is whether the 'solution' will be the one, the other, or the other. By contrast, we may say that the certainty exists at the outset, that the solution will be one or other of those three services, or that there will be no solution at all. In practice, therefore, the indeterminacy is practically nil, and as consequence, if the argument so far is correct, there is (almost) nil probability that the inverted commas can be removed from 'solution' so that it becomes effectively such.

A slight variant of the 'standard provisions' approach arises when the social worker is operating in a more open field – that is to say, when s/he is able to mobilize services that do not pertain solely to the agency for which s/he works, but to other ones as well, which have contracts with his/her agency or more simply collaborate with it. This today is the most frequent case, and it is also the more realistic one, given that a single agency, however large and ramified, is unable to deal with social problems on its own. This strategy of bundling several provisions together by a statutoty practitioner is reminiscent of the British variant of case management (Payne, 1999). This contains an element of networking, in the sense that the social worker (the case manager) is able to acquire additional resources by going outside his/her agency (in a market or welfare mix regime) and interacting with other ones. However, it should be clear that the purpose of this minimum of networking is only to refine the coarse method of standardization to some extent. Consequently, in complex cases it only serves to delay the probable failure, in that it only postpones the moment when the social worker must turn to a non-preconstituted approach: namely networking in the fullest sense of the word.

There is no networking if it is thought that the solution consists in choosing among a set of pre-established options, and assembling them. No matter how broad the range of options from which the plural solution is selected, if the already-organized service (or services) is the independent variable, and if the social worker's job is only to exercise his/her discretion in allocating a single pre-established provision in a care package tailored to the needs of the individual client, then this strategy is different from, or even contrary to, the networking method.

As we shall see in more detail below, the networking approach is something quite different. The independent variable is the problem, not the solution. The practitioner's work consists in encouraging the gradual 'condensation' around the problem of a set of free *actions* which may also comprise some standardized provision. In the end this action will lead to a composite solution which is the more imponderable at the outset, the more multiform it is at the end. His/her work is not to select a single provision from a more or less broad range of options, but rather to deploy multiple *ad hoc* responses, woven together in various ways, even unpredictably or unwittingly, and activated by the uniqueness of the specific situation. A mosaic of actions, not a package of provisions, therefore: a complex of initiatives to match the complexity of the situation (Gubrium, 1991).

However, a specification is in order. All social services, of whatever type or level, are complex organizations, and they must necessarily standardize and rationalize (in Weber's sense) their procedures if they not to be at the mercy of events. But here I am saying that it is the final *outcome* (the comprehensive solution) which cannot be standardized, not the organizational scaffolding that supports it, or the single punctual provision that is part of it. When the function of an agency is not to deliver provisions but to manage problems *in toto* – and therefore has to concern itself with the overall coherence of measures – that agency could rethink its strategies and make a leap of quality. It could shed its nature as a traditional organization – with its constraints, controls and procedures – and while still centralizing and rationalizing its underlying functions (administrative, secretarial, etc.) create sufficient freedom for the advanced stages of the helping process to unfold. A margin of freedom is crucial in the 'hot zone' of interaction between the organization and life, between the statutory care system (of which social assistance is part) and the real problems of people in flesh and blood. This means in concrete terms enough freedom for those who by definition operate in this zone of interaction, the so-called 'frontline workers'. I say this even though the recent advance of so-called 'managed care' (Winegar and Bistline, 1994; Corcoran and Vandiver, 1996) designed to standardize and to subject social workers to close control by managers is pushing in the opposite direction.

2.6. Toward relational empowerment

The method of standardized service delivery is widely used, and always has been. This has been partly for cultural factors, because there was a time when this method seemed to be the most appropriate, and partly for practical ones, because it seemed to be the easiest and least demanding defence against complexity. But there is a more profound reason, one ideological in nature, which is gaining consensus in many countries, not only Britain or North America, and is responsible not for the fact that the standardization method has imposed itself but for the fact that it may persist in the future.

This is a reason which is intriguing in its ambivalence: it has both some foundation as well as some illogicality, depending on how one looks at it. And precisely because it has been accepted and rejected at the same time, it warrants closer analysis. The idea is the fulcrum of neo-liberalist thought in social policy, and it runs as follows: methods with a low threshold of complexity – for example standardized services delivery, but also, if possible, even simpler strategies – are necessary and opportune. Providing minimal public services are not a surrogate for better responses which cannot be given and to which impossibility we would do well to resign ourselves; it is exactly the right strategy. In the face of complexity, the argument goes, the level of complexity of the investment of statutory resources (financial, professional, etc.) *must* be kept low and stricty controlled by rational procedures. This theory, therefore, is not simply realistic – that is, it is not based solely on the idea that it is impossible to do anything, or on a desire or need to curb public spending – it is 'honourable', because its theoretical intention is not to impede the action of the persons concerned, conceived as consumers within the general context of a care market.

The most effective strategy available to policy-makers, therefore, is a certain tendency towards *inaction* or if not, towards action that can be closely controlled *a priori*. Complexity cannot be challenged openly and intentionally by professional practitioners and the statutory services; this is instead the primary task of the interested parties.

The non-paternalistic idea that social workers must not deal proactively with problems by individualizing a global response but are instead required merely to deliver rationed and standardized provisions when asked to do so by their clients (at most using case management to provide a minimum of advice on the choice or purchase of services), who are then left to get on with it, if they can, introduces the notion of 'empowerment' (Adams, 1996a; Payne, 1995; Parsloe, 1996): a general notion in human sciences which helps us gain more thorough understanding of what network-based social work is.

Empowerment is a process which from the point of view of those who possess it *(self-empowerment)* signifies the 'feeling that one has power' or 'that one is able to act' (Barber, 1991). From the point of view of those who facilitate it in their interlocutors – social workers, for example, or policy-makers – it is 'a strategic attitude which increases the likelihood that people will feel themselves 'in power' to act', or conversely 'the technical ability to prevent people from feeling that they are powerless'.

Empowerment is a sentiment or a psychological state (the conviction held by the actor that s/he can or must act) as well as a welfare strategy of re-balance of power (a way to interact with the actor so that this conviction is not undermined). This notion is of crucial importance in social work. One may argue in the manner of the 'conservatives' that the action of the interested parties is paramount. Or one may argue in relational terms that the action of the interested parties is important. Whatever the case may be, the significance of empowerment is beyond question. If one believes that a person's action is valuable, the fact that this person feels self-efficacy, that it is within his/her power to act, is an indispensable psychological variable for social action (Bandura, 1997).

Unfortunately, the idea of empowerment, like the previous one of indeterminism, also lends itself to ambiguous, not to say conflicting, interpretations and operational options (Brown, 1995). On the one hand, following the proponents of *laissez-faire* in social policy domain, it may lead to the belief that holistic social work strategies like networking, or other strategies with high formal involvement, are pointless or even counter-productive. On the other hand, it may prompt the belief that 'global' perception and action is essential in social work, albeit in policy contexts of high or very high fragmentation. This point is developed in the next sections.

2.6.1. Empowerment as a 'passive' strategy: investing subjects with total responsibility for action

The very existence of social services, as well as the traditional method of delivering services and help, may weaken or annul the empowerment of the recipients of such help. With respect to the good intentions of the welfare state (Thane, 1996), this is a perverse effect – or even a paradoxical effect – of colossal proportions. To weaken empowerment is to produce the reverse of help. If helping is enabling people to act, then making them feel that they are unable to act at the same time as one is helping them is the exact opposite of what one should do.

When confronted by a superior competence, a person with inferior competence may feel even more inferior: s/he may feel inadequate and introject the conviction that it is better not to act, given that the person with superior competence is already at work. This mechanism may operate unconsciously. An example follows. If Massimo, a parent trying to cope with a difficult son, knows that he alone (or perhaps together with his wife) can/must do something, he will take action: he will do his best. This action may not be perfect, but no matter; it need only be *almost* perfect, to put it à la Bettelheim. If Massimo knows where to find a psychologist – at the local health unit or family advisory bureau, for example – he may think that it better to consult this specialist because he is unable to handle the situation. If the psychologist in his turn thinks that one of his colleagues – his supervisor, for example – is better able to deal with cases of this kind, he may feel inferior to this colleague and leave it to him or her to act. And so on: one could go further up a hierarchical scale of this kind.

The examples abound, and not just at the individual level. Empowerment can also be evidenced (and is perhaps best known) in its collective dimension (Netting et al., 1998) when the sense of power is shared by groups of people (users and carers, for exemple) or an entire community of citizens *(community empowerment)*, both for radical/antioppressive/antidiscriminatory purposes (Thompson, 1993) and for caring self advocacy ones (Craig and Mayo, 1995; Barnes, 1997). It is well known that the creation of residential facilities (Carrier and Tomlison, 1996) in a particular locality – therapeutic communities for drug addicts, for example, rest homes for the elderly, day centres for the handicapped, etc. – although these are useful for the general achievements in social care, they may unfortunately disempower and/or deresponsibilize not only those directly concerned (the users, their family members, etc.) but also the surrounding community. When there is an official service that assumes responsibility for problems – under the logic of modernity with all its Parsonian specialisms – the local community can relax as if from a sense of relief that it no longer need concern itself with problems. People with the problems (users and carers) and those who are extraneous to them but nevertheless close – for example people living in the same neighbourhood or village as drug addicts, the elderly, the handicapped and their families – are told that they are not entitled to intervene because a service has taken over the problem, and that they should consequently keep their distance. The message conveyed is that when the people directly involved with a social problem are unable to cope with it, the specialized agencies take over. A void opens up between them and the community, which withdraws because it feels that it does not have to do anything, or that it is unable to do anything, or that even if it did do something it would make no difference.

A more specialized competence tends to squeeze out the other less expert ones and tends to dominate the field. The direct and invasive exercise of this competence undermines the primordial ingenuity and the sense of efficacy of those who also possess that competence, though to a lesser extent. The divide between high and low competence widens even further. I shall not dwell on this topic, given that it relates to the pioneering well known theories of Ivan Illich (1977; 1982). In order to come rapidly to the point, I shall only ask one question. Given that this secondary effect of cultural disempowerment (Illich talks about the *expropriation* of folk skills) truly exists (there seems to be no doubt on the matter), what can be done to obviate it? The answer that immediately comes to mind, and which has become a political issue, is to dismantle or at least scale down the institutions of the national welfare states (Esping Andersen, 1996). Given the drastic nature of this proposal, one must carefully enquire whether it is the correct answer or the only one possible.

Does justified concern for empowerment entail that only this passive strategy is feasible? Is it truly enough only to *remove* public services and do without welfare institutions, or to rely on them to a lesser extent, because everything is going well? One's first impression is that leaving frail people to get on with it – throwing them in the deep end so that they learn to swim – is a high-risk strategy which only occasionally works. More often, people thrown in at the deep end do not have enough time to learn anything at all.

2.6.2. *Empowerment as a relational strategy: the reciprocal boosting of the capacity for action*

The argument developed here is that the empowerment of individuals, groups and communities may be weakened by the existence of services only in one particular circumstance: when they can effectively do without those services. The perverse effect is triggered when the help is excessive: the persons concerned are able to act, but they are prevented from doing so because there is an official service that acts in their stead. Only under this logical condition – which incidentally often holds in practice – does the strict neo-liberalist conception of welfare make sense. But when people are left to navigate by themselves through the network of new care markets, and may become lost, then matters are quite different.

As Prior (1993, p. 11) points out, it is doubtful whether the theoretical user imagined by *laissez-faire* policy-makers actually exists. He or she would be

> The theoretical citizen cherished by the Conservative government is not a member of any pressure group but rather a heroic lone consumer with time, money and information to back up his or her individual choices. This paragon sounds suspiciously middle class-and relatively rare. (Prior, 1993, p. 11)

More directly, Prior says

> [...] One significant aspect of serious mental illness as it is assessed in the late twentieth century, is the perceived inability of mentally ill persons to manipulate a symbolic order successfully, or at lest, with any rational plan. And this observation alone should generate suspicions about the potential of people who are mentally ill to integrate themselves as consumers into mainstream social life [...]. Rather than entering in to the social worlds of the economically active, ex patients in the community tend to live in the subworld of the disabled and the handicapped and the sick-a subworld in which contacts with mainstream life are, at best, fleeting and superficial. (Prior, 1993, p. 178)

Wistow and his collegues wonders whether it is correct to liken social care to any other market good (Wistow et al., 1996). They reply that personal welfare is a commodity *sui generis* which cannot be bought in the market like bread and milk at the corner shop. It is a commodity which not only often requires assistance in its purchase but equally often cannot be purchased at all: care must at least in part be home-made, so to speak. From the networking point of view, we may use the expression 'problem-solving assistance'– as distinct from standardized service provision on request – for this across-the-board assistance which helps the citizen-consumer to make the best use of scattered services and of the environmental opportunities around him/her that s/he is unable see, or does not know how to exploit.

Empowerment must be framed within an *active* logic. Rather than advocating the mere delivery of services on request, or indeed questioning the very existence of those services, discussion should centre on how the more complex forms of problem-solving assistance should be conceived and provided when they become necessary. Is it possible to devise a complex type of help that does not collide with empowerment – that is, with the action of the interested parties? This is the point at issue.

The above distinction between empowerment as a feeling and as an operational strategy now proves useful. Empowerment of the former type (as a sense of individual self-efficacy) may be weakened if the work of social services and experts contradicts empowerment of the latter type; that is to say, if they act not in order to support possible action but to do the work themselves. The interested parties' feeling of self-efficacy if the experts are unable to handle empowerment as a technical strategy, or in other words, if they do not know how to act without obstructing their interlocutors.

Active empowerment strategies require practitioners to involve themselves in the helping relationship in such a way that they do not just avert the perverse effect of deresponsibilization but, on the contrary, increase their clients' sense of personal capacity. This goes beyond the fundamental 'principle of subsidiarity' to the effect that the expert – and more general those in a position of 'superior' levels of competence or responsibility – should not act if the clients, i.e. the 'inferior' levels, are already able to do so. The notion of relational empowerment is more advanced than this: it states that even when the expert must necessarily take action because there truly is a need for it, s/he should only do so in a manner that still involves the interested parties, without his/her being misled by their declared inability to act.

Relational empowerment is a method with which the expert can persuade people in difficulties, or those close to them, that they can do more to help themselves than they could if they were in the following two situations: (a) left to fend for themselves, in which case it is more probable that they will be overwhelmed by their difficulties; (b) helped in the wrong way by methods which prevent them from acting and exclude them from the solution. I shall now develop this latter point.

2.6.2.1. The damaging effects of directive attitudes on self-empowerment: some examples from counselling settings

I explained at the beginning of this chapter that directive strategies often fail because they presume that the expert is certain to succeed without the help of the parties concerned. This attitude has never been adequately problematized in traditional casework. It arises from the fact that the typical users of social services often display a low capacity for action (Barber, 1991). This apparent inability triggers some sort of reflex action intended to compensate for it by means of direct empowerment, but which unfortunately reduces it even further.

Directivity is the enemy of empowerment. A capacity for action entirely centred on one of the parties – the expert – confounds the helping relationship's dynamics. And this is so not only for functional reasons because it materially interferes with the users' actions, which otherwise might be extremely valuable, but for psychological ones as well, if the expert feels that only s/he is capable of taking action and saps his/her interlocutors belief in their own abilities. The expert, in short, steals power from the persons whom s/he should be giving it to.

The psychological process of stealing the sense that one possesses power or a role is an extremely subtle one. It is almost imperceptible but it may have formidable unconscious effects on both the person who does the stealing and those that s/he steals from. Both parties may be unaware of what is happening but nevertheless profoundly marked by it.

This reciprocal muddling of the empowerment dynamic can be evidenced by concrete examples, which I take from Mucchielli's (1983) classical book on counselling. Following Rogers, Mucchielli singles out five intuitive (spontaneous) types of directive attitudes apparent in counselling interviews:

Judgement: the judgmental attitude, transmission of a point of view determined by the practitioner's personal morality.

Interpretation: an attitude which distorts the interlocutor's thoughts or provides explanations or indicates their causes.

Support: the affective, supportive, sympathetic attitude which minimizes the problem.

Investigation: the attitude of searching for further information.

Solution: the attitude of actively searching for a *solution to the problem* and immediately proposing one.

The form that these various attitudes take in concrete situations is illustrated by Table 2.3, where the social worker 'responds' to a mother worried by the behaviour of her small daughter.

All the social worker's responses have an explicit sense given by their immediate meaning, as well as an implicit one which must be brought to the surface.

TABLE 2.3

Examples of directive attitudes and their harmful effects on empowerment

A mother talking about her six-year-old daughter

This child is fundamentally bad. She's constantly naughty, and punishing her has no effect. She doesn't even cry. She constantly defies us and it's getting worse. My husband and I are worried about her future: she's a delinquent in the making...

	The expert's explicit statements	*Their implicit meaning*
Judgement	• You pay too much attention to the child's naughtiness: this may be counter-productive.	It is in my power (not yours) to see the error of your ways.
Interpretation	• There must be a hidden reason for your hostility towards your daughter. It is obviously a reaction to some sort of disappointment.	It is in my power (not yours) to understand what is happening.
Support	• Children of this age are often awkward. You shouldn't dramatize things, everything will sort itself out with puberty.	It is in my power (not yours) to understand that the problem does not actually exist.
Investigation	• Tell me, are there any other children at home?	It is in my power to ask for all the information necessary for me (not you) to understand the situation.
Solution	• Have you thought of taking her to a play group?	It is in my power (not yours) to know what to do.

When examined carefully, all his answers say more or less the same thing beneath the explicit information that they convey: 'It is my responsibility to understand your situation and to give the advice or the support that you need. This is my job and I am very good at it'. More drastically, Miller and Rollnick (1991) suggest that directive responses of this kind implicitly communicate: 'Listen to me! I know better than you do.'

'I can and must act,' the social worker implicitly declares, 'the power to act is mine'. When an expert says these things to him/herself, no harm is done. But when s/he utters them in an interactive situation with another person, then their latent sense has a symmetrical implication. As well as 'I have the power to act' they imply 'and therefore you do not'. They convey the following message: 'You cannot and must not act in this situation where I already can and must act'. In other words again, the interlocutor is informed that she is bereft of power. In a helping context, communicating this message is rarely advisable. Its harmful effects on action are obvious, as well as the more specific damage caused to self-esteem. The implication is that having power is a zero-sum game – if it is mine, then it cannot be yours, and vice versa – rather than a shared or relational commodity, something that becomes more mine if it is also more yours, and viceversa.

In formal counselling situations, when the expert is seated on one side of a desk in a public agency statutorily obliged to give help, the structure itself of the arrangement may already undermine the sense of self-efficacy. The person seated on the other side of the desk may feel that s/he is there to receive help provided by others, who alone are deemed competent to furnish it. Unfortunately, the structural distortion induced by the formal setting cannot be eliminated; it can only be attenuated to some extent. What the practitioner can do (what is in his/her power to do, to use the present terminology) is control his/her helping attitudes and utterances so that, although they occur in an institutional setting which necessarily issues latent messages to the contrary, they accept and therefore reinforce the user's capacity for action.

2.6.2.2. The boosting effects of empowerment through the relational attitude: the example of the reformulation technique

We know that a fully relational attitude can produce these effects, and that the technique able to bring them about is the reformulation procedure. Let us again consider Mucchielli's example, but this time as regards two responses or 'reformulations' which are not centred on the practitioner (Table 2.4).

Mucchielli, following Rogers, calls the first reformulation 'reflection' because it takes what the interlocutor has said and repeats it back to him/her in the most

TABLE 2.4

Examples of relational attitudes in counselling and their beneficial effects on empowerment

A mother talking about her six-year-old daughter

This child is fundamentally bad. She's constantly naughty, and punishing her has no effect. She doesn't even cry. She constantly defies us and it's getting worse. My husband and I are worried about her future: she's a delinquent in the making...

	Statements	*Their implicit meaning*
Reformulation 1 (reflection)	Your daughter's current behaviour makes you think that she has a deviant personality and that this will compromise her future.	You have the power to bring out and explore your daughter's problem *jointly with me.* The assumption is that you will then be empowered to *act* upon the problem outside this room, with or without my help.
Reformulation 2 (explicitation)	You have found that the more you scold her and punish her, the more she defies you.	

exact form compatible with the need for brevity. The second response Mucchielli calls 'delucidation' to indicate that it is an attempt to clarify the essence of what has been said without distorting it. In order not to imply didactic intent by the practitioner, this latter type of reformulation might better be called an 'explicitation', an attempt to bring out, or even to infer, the implicit content of the person's statement. When compared against the categories introduced above, it is apparent that the 'reflection' reformulation is more centred on the person, while the 'explicitation' reformulation is more relational in the sense that it is centred midway between the person and the counsellor.

Both procedures are efficacious as regards empowerment. In neither case does the practitioner convey a desire or decision to take action by himself. The practitioner allows the person to stay with her problem and with herself. He does not, as in the directive responses above, jump in with 'I know better than you do!'. The practitioner skilfully introduces an active empowerment strategy: that is to say, he both leaves intact and boosts his interlocutor's sense of self-efficacy. His message refers primarily to the here and now of the immediate context of the counselling interview. The expert works to ensure that the interlocutor is actively engaged in managing her problem, but then, if he is to be consistent, he must hand the initiative over to her, granting her the freedom to explore the problem.

By means of reformulation, the expert communicates, covertly but clearly, 'I believe that you can do it', both during the interview and subsequently when the interlocutor must take effective action. In point of fact, he communicates something more subtle. In the case of the explicitating reformulation especially, he goes further and says 'You and I together, *we can* do it.' The implicit message is that the capacity for action resides in the relationship between them, not in him (the expert) nor in her (the user), but in both of them together. In conformity with the relational approach, the expert communicates: 'I must not act on my own, nor must you act on your own: we must act jointly'. Only in a non-directive attitude taken to the extreme – for example, when a counsellor merely nods his/her head to signal 'Yes, go on' and does nothing more – only in this case does the relational model of reciprocal empowerment falter. The reformulation technique always envisages the presence of the practitioner: that s/he should be involved is beyond question.

2.6.3. *Empowerment and building trust in the helping relationship*

Let us consider a person invested with relational empowerment in a professional helping relationship. The expert informs this person that s/he is giving him the power to act, not simply that s/he will do nothing, and that he will have to manage on his own. This approach may have beneficial effects on the psyche and therefore on the helping dynamic. Every strengthening of the sense of self-efficacy in the interlocutor reinforces his/her self-esteem. When we are called upon to help, when we are told that there is room for us in joint action, when our contribution is solicited, our self-esteem is bolstered. Beneath the statement 'I believe that you can do it' lies the even more important message 'I believe that you are worthy'. This message is also conveyed – perhaps even more forcefully, in fact – if before we met the interlocutor that we now deem worthy, we were convinced that s/he was not. If a person believes that s/he is inadequate, or that it is not his/her responsibility to act but someone deems them adequate and asks them to join in (but without misconceiving or denying their objective difficulties), they may feel a beneficial psychic contradiction.

The surprise of a user when s/he feels accepted and respected as an actor – at the same time as his/her case is taken on because of his/her evident inability to be such – usually leads to the building and strengthening of a trust relationship, and therefore to *involvement* in the helping relationship (Fine and Glasser, 1996; Barnes, 1996). Users normally have ambivalent feelings towards themselves, and the same goes for their significant others. Beneath their sense of impotence there always smoulders an awareness or a vague feeling that they should or could do something; that without their involvement or initiative, however marginal, nothing positive will be achieved. If the expert is not sensitive to this sentiment in his/her interlocutors – which, as said, is often the last resort for their residual self-esteem – then they may undergo a process of gradual psychological aliena-tion: they feel a distance growing between themselves and those who want to help them.

If the practitioner instead respects this vague feeling of potential empower-ment, the interlocutors may immediately sense that things are about to change. They will feel the weight as well as the lightness of the expert, which is exactly what their ambivalence requires. Here too, one realizes the importance of the relationship in helping work. If the expert merely communicates 'I think you can do it, so get on with it', his/her interlocutors will still be aware of the other side of their situation, namely their feeling of inadequacy. They will therefore con-clude that they have been misunderstood and will devalue the operator exactly as they would if s/he communicated the reverse to them, namely that s/he believed them incapable. Only the 'joint' message to the effect that 'You and I can do it together' is meaningful and respects the interlocutors' ambivalence. When users realize that a practitioner has responded to both sides of their con-flicting attitudes towards themselves, they will unconsciously feel that the 'ex-pert' is, at last, truly an expert.

A true expert is able to detach him/herself from the paradigm of 'I' (as in 'I'll do it', the code of directivity) and also from that of 'you' (as in 'you do it, it'll do you good', the code of non-directivity). S/he obeys the relational code of *we*, as in 'we'll do it together'). The interlocutors will thus have greater trust in both the practitioner and themselves, and trust is the primordial force that drives the helping process and engenders every therapeutic change (Barnes, 1996).

2.7. Relational empowerment in networking practice: the main cognitive obstacles and their removal

A practitioner must be extremely sensitive to his/her interlocutor's feeling of self-efficacy when they stand in a two-way relationship, and even more so when s/he is working within the one to many relationships typical of networking. Em-powerment is the basis of networking because, as we have seen, it is an endeavour to give or restore capacity for action to the social, i.e. a set of interconnected persons. Compared with traditional counselling, where the expert must activate a sense of adequacy in an individual client, in networking the expert must constructively interact with the potential empowerment of numerous persons in some way connected (or connectable) with the user or, in more abstract but proper terms, with the task being poorly coped with. This is an indefinite and diffused empowerment, which requires greater sensitivity and attention on the part of the practitioner, like a juggler keeping numerous balls in the air simultaneously. If an expert decides to use the networking approach, the first requirement is that the persons constituting the network must feel, or be enabled to feel, a sufficient sense of *shared* power with respect to the task. If, owing to the social worker's action, the network as a whole or each individual within it does not feel capable of acting, or does not feel obliged to act, or more simply feels able to achieve less than is within their potential, then the networking action exists only in the intentions of the expert.

Numerous obstacles may hamper the practitioner in fulfilment of the delicate task of enhancing the empowerment of others. The psychological obstacle raised by the expert's determination to 'do it on his/her own' was discussed at the beginning of this chapter. But when the expert is free from deep-lying hindrances of this kind, other more 'superficial' obstacles, of a cognitive rather than psychodynamic nature, may arise, and they are just as insidious.

2.7.1. *Perfectionism versus the search for adequacy*

One of these obstacles is the practitioner's perfectionism. Take, for example, a sensible expert convinced that his/her action should be principally in the service of the others in the network, and also aware that, if the others do the work, this does not mean that s/he is incompetent. S/he may nevertheless be hampered by the belief that the users must undertake the action as well as s/he would have done. This expert is therefore unaware of the limits to expert action. S/he rightly thinks that others are able to act (which is a major step forward) but is then obstructed (and obstructs the others) by insisting on too high standards.

The expert must accept that the others will do things differently. Not only must s/he accept this, but above all s/he must *hope* that it will happen. If the others did the same things in the same way, this would eliminate the richness of differentiation and therefore, indeed, the network. The existence of a network requires more than the involvement of a certain number of people; it is also necessary for each of these people to act in a specific way. The expert should be so well aware of this that s/he is willing to relinquish his/her traditional quality standards in order that it can happen.

When faced by a task, if an expert is to do social work properly, s/he must always ask him/herself the following crucial question: who could *adequately* (which is different from perfectly) act in my place? In fact, this question should be broken down into at least four specific queries: (a) who could do *better* than me?; a question which subsumes (b) who could do *as well as* me? It is evident that if the expert is fortunate enough to find interlocutors able to achieve at least his/ her own quality of action – albeit in a different way – s/he should let them act, or better give them support in acting. However, if the expert finds no-one of this calibre, rather than halt the process, s/he should lower his/her standards and ask (c) who can do almost as well as me with my help?, or finally (d) who could not do nearly as well as me but would still perform acceptably? If the answer to even the last question is 'no-one', then the expert can – or *must* – take action on his/ her own.

In order to comply with the rule of empowerment, when a social worker addresses a task, s/he must not only avoid this last, extreme option – of acting on his/her own account directly and immediately – although this is difficult; s/ he must also ask all of the above questions in order (from a to d) and explore the situation thoroughly. Only after ascertaining that the answer to each of them is 'no-one' can s/he accept the evidence and decide to act in the first person. Obviously, thorough exploration of the four possibilities – which in substance means exploring the so-called 'network potential' – is not just a question of patience and a correct methodological approach to empowerment. Sometimes there are important factors that impede implementation of this rule.

This point should be clearly understood: the strategy of empowerment, and by extension the entire strategy of networking, cannot be applied mechanically. Like every professional strategy, networking presupposes sensitivity and the exercise of discretion. There are situations in which a practitioner cannot linger even for a moment to verify whether there are partners with whom s/he can act jointly. S/he must immediately take unilateral decisions and assume full responsibility for them, as in the classic examples of emergency or crisis (cases of abuse or violence, for instance). The same applies to *control* measures where, as we saw in the previous chapter, the expert may make an assessment which conflicts with that of the interlocutors and therefore may by-pass them and act alone. These are extreme cases, however, at the limits of (truly) social intervention. Social work requires that the social must be activated and involved whenever possible, except in cases where the practitioner makes a different and motivated decision. In any event, when a practitioner breaches the rule of empowerment, it is one thing if s/he does so in the awareness of what s/he is doing and why, and quite another if s/he breaches the rule without realizing it and for no reason. In the former case we have mature professionalism, in the latter error.

2.7.2. *The reparative approach versus the developmental one*

Another erroneous belief by an expert that may hamper or thwart his good networking intentions, is that s/he must 'fabricate' the sense of psychological self-efficacy – or more generally the will to act – when these are absent. This attitude is the reverse of the previous one, which tended not to require or not to stimulate action because trust was lacking. In this case, the practitioner instead thinks that someone in the network should act, although s/he is failing to do so or is unable to do so, and is willing to invest a great deal so that the action which s/he envisages takes place.

I have already dwelt on the need to reject the reparative approach to pathologies. It is by now clear that those who engage in networking cannot concern themselves with individual dysfunctions or with dysfunctional relationships (conflicts, mind-games, etc.); nor, consequently, can they conceive their action as a therapy for such abnormalities. We also know that network-based social work starts from realization that the network's action is inadequate; or in other words, from realization that some or other person is not doing something or other that they should, but without investigating and treating the underlying reasons for this inaction. But then – and this should be stressed – after concentrating on inadequacy while observing and assessing the problem (operations which are obligatory, otherwise the problem would not be apparent), the social worker must adjust his/her focus when examining the solution. A cognitive shift is required to the other side of the coin: from the inadequacy of action to its residual adequacy. The social worker must look at positive aspects, although it is obviously the negative ones that justify and solicit expert action. S/he should look at the capacity for action that nevertheless exists, not the capacity that has gone, so to speak. Put simply, s/he must see the glass as half-full, rather than half-empty.

Acting according to the logic of empowerment means eschewing any curiosity as to who is responsible for the problem or as to why it has arisen. The social worker must instead ask him/herself which of the persons concerned are willing and able to cooperate in dealing with it. S/he must presume that what is now an inadequate capacity for action can be 'developed': a word that only makes sense here if we think of the enhancement of existing capacity/willingness (enabling). Obviously there must be a basis for this development: capacity or willingness cannot be created from nothing through the technical transformation of their opposites, namely *in*capacity and *un*willingness. Alchemies of this kind never work. Social work enhances strengths, and grows with them, it does not eliminate weaknesses. Problems are resolved because the weaknesses that constitute it are compressed and reduced by the growth of their complement. In social work weaknesses are like the black holes of astronomy: they swallow up the practition-er's energy and cause his/her work to implode. Strengths are the foundation, the basis for growth.

A social worker who focuses on the inadequacy or unwillingness of the members of the network, and decides to change or transform them with direct technical treatment, finds networking an uphill struggle. In practice, indeed, it is as if s/he were not networking at all. S/he contradicts empowerment at the very moment when his/her good intentions bring it to the maximum (i.e. create it artificially). The strategy of enhancing the power to act is such because it pre-sumes, sustains and encourages a growing pre-existing capacity for action. It may judiciously try to force this growth, but it must never force it too far, otherwise the endeavour will collapse onto itself.

On the practical level, this criticism of the reparative strategy on empower-ment is more moral than technical in nature. When a practitioner engages in networking, the greatest risk is not that s/he will improperly focus on the persons who objectively lack the ability to act and invest in techniques enabling them to overcome that handicap. An example might be a social worker who, on seeing that the husband of a woman in a wheel chair is unable to understand how she feels, decides to treat his insensitivity by clinical means. Few social workers would have the time or the desire to undertake an operation of this kind. Once it has been realized that such measures are difficult with official users, it becomes obvious that they are inappropriate for the unknowing members of a network. The most frequent risk is that the expert will focus on persons who (in his/her opinion) are perfectly able to act, but are *unwilling to do so*: for example when a social worker decides that a particular relative of a man just released from prison should look after him, give him work, and so on, but the relative refuses. It is here that the moral sticking-point may arise: the social worker may persuade him/ herself that the person deemed most suitable is wrong not to do what is required. S/he may consequently apply pressure and invest energy in the moral conversion of the reluctant relative. The social worker thus decides by fiat what the network should be: that is, who the interlocutors should be, what they should do, and so on. Acting in this way is like pushing a car with the brakes on. In practice it is a waste of effort, but in theory the matter is more serious: focusing on and treating the inaction of a particular person is to fall back on an approach centred on individual deficits, and this is a strategy at odds with the concept of devel-opment.

Often, the subject that resists the social worker's intentions is not a physical person but the community in which the expert works. For example, it may happen that a team from the drug addiction service decides to mount a drugs awareness campaign in a neighbourhood where it is needed because, according to the social workers, 'Here everyone keeps to themselves, they're not interested in the community'. The team has decided to sensitize the local community and regards its campaign as action against its insensitivity. The campaign is indispensable – the team declares – to prepare the ground for networking projects or initiatives to prevent drug taking, involve young people, and so on. But rather than starting with the few members of the community *willing* to involve themselves – in the hope that the network will then develop by acquiring more and more members – the team decides to treat all those who are unwilling to join: which is the sign of a reparative mentality which paradoxically emerges even within a proactive approach.

2.7.3. *The lax or delegating approach versus monitoring and support*

Working on empowerment means assuming that a capacity for action exists until proof to the contrary is forthcoming. This entails that the action should be monitored and supported by the expert, and therefore that interaction should continue even after the collaborators have been recruited. By contrast, however, it is often believed that networking consists of recruiting people who undertake to provide help on the bidding of the expert, and then everything stops. This is delegating; it is not the building of a network.

It is possible to imagine two very different situations: (a) the expert recruits collaborators who then act on their own account; (b) the expert recruits collaborators and then works together with them, each party with its own competence. We may say that only the latter practitioner knows what networking is and fully practises it. The former has only a vague idea of networking: he begins well but then abruptly stops.

An example is provided by the relationship that a particular service establishes with foster families. Let us suppose that the local social services consider the family to be a resource for the temporary care of people in difficulties (minors, the disabled people, etc.) – a better resource than residential facilities. So far, so good. The problem is what will happen next. Will situation (a) above prevail, namely the search for self-sufficient collaborators, or situation (b), namely the search for linked interlocutors? The experts organizing the scheme can either take it for granted that the families, once recruited and selected, and once the fostering has begun, will go ahead on their own, or they can assume that fostering is always a joint endeavour involving numerous actors.

Experts often restrict themselves, improperly, to the role of official controllers or administrative officers; a role which is formal and distant. Rather, they should act as guides, carefully monitoring events and providing help, both technical and practical, when difficulties arise. This monitoring and helping can be performed through the network, not directly by the social worker. If, for example, a scheme provides for periodic mutual support meetings attended by the families involved, so that they can help each other and be helped in their turn by the expert, the latter in fact is monitoring a self monitoring group process, and helping a self-help process, which is precisely the nature of networking.

Organizing an effective support structure in which roles are shared, while the social worker seeks the collaboration of volunteers, is much more worthwhile than repeated exhortations or moral pressure (that is, a reparative approach). Even the best sensitization campaigns, if they are based solely on appeals to the sense of duty, may be unconvincing – even for families who already very willing to join a fostering scheme – if they are not accompanied by concrete support measures. Empowerment is extremely sensitive to the non-verbal, to doing rather than saying.

Perfectionism itself may be a symptom of a lax or delegatory approach by professionals. Schemes to recruit foster families often have careful initial selection procedures and then, for the families chosen, specific training courses. The idea that the volunteers must be nothing but perfect probably arises from an unconscious decision to delegate in the near future: that is to say, once the families have joined the scheme, they should be left to get on with it. Lacking is the conviction that voluntary work is a learning experience whereby everyone can learn from errors and help each other.

2.8. Summary

In this chapter I have tried to sow doubts concerning the adequacy of a rather ingenuous method – but nevertheless widely-used because it is based on solid intuitive basis – of dealing with social problems. I refer to the directive approach, also known as deterministic/linear. Every social problem, it is believed, has its solver, who acts unilaterally. But this never actually happens, not even when the official solver – the professional practitioner – exists.

I have also questioned another well-known professional 'style', the reverse of the directive approach and based on Rogers' idea that the focus should be on the person seeking help. Although this approach is much more refined and fruitful than the previous one, it too tends to be unilateral, in that it envisages a marked and constant over-emphasis on the user.

The overall argument of this chapter is that the helping relationship must above all be an authentic relationship. It must effectively involve the penetration of meaningful action by both poles of the helping process. On the one hand stands the *expert* pole, in possession of technical-methodological skills and able to inject rationality and objectivity into the situation; on the other, the *experiential* pole, by which is meant the person or persons involved in various ways and to various extents in the problem, and who therefore contributes essential intuitive knowledge to its solution.

When the helping process is relational, so that action is undertaken by all those involved, it is free to unfold: it organizes itself and makes its own way according to a variety of inputs and contingent necessities. Acceptance of relationality by the expert signifies his/her willingness to be influenced by, and learn from, his/her interlocutors. And it also signifies that s/he facilitates their capacity for expression, enhancing their ability to propose and take action by means of the helping strategy known as empowerment.

When reciprocal capacity for action is maximum, the helping process becomes *indeterminate*: in other words, it can move in any one of several directions, because the possibilities are not controlled by only one agent. The question thus arises as to how an expert can perform a constructive role when caught in a double bind: that of ensuring the indeterminism of the action (that is, not being directive) but not abandoning it to its own devices (as a non-directive practitioner would do). This dilemma can be resolved by introducing the notion of 'relational guidance', which I analyse in the next chapter.

CHAPTER 3

Relational guidance and networking
Methodological outline

3.1. Introduction

Networking is deliberate action by one or several social workers which takes the form of *a relationship* – in practice, joint action – with *a network* of people, i.e. with other pre-existing or potential relationships. It thus improves the quality and capacity for action of both the expert and the network, as they seek indeterminate *ad hoc* solutions – or, in other words, as they undertake courses of action unknown to them at the outset.

If we reason in terms of empowerment, we may define networking as the activity of a social worker who does not endeavour to centre upon him/herself the task of the persons with whom s/he has come into contact (the task for which s/he has assumed responsibility). The practitioner lets the task stay with the others, and if possible involves further persons, or other colleagues, assuming until proved wrong that all of them are competent. Thereafter s/he does not withdraw but delegates.

S/he continues to contribute in two ways: (a) by doing something specific like any other member of the coping network, and (b) by assuming a supervisory role in which s/he provides guidance for the network as a whole, what we may call 'relational guidance' (Wilke, 1987; Donati, 1991). Obviously, in the light of what has been said about relational attitude in helping, this is *'frail'* guidance which does no more than is necessary to enable the network (and therefore the practitioner him/herself) to fulfil the task at hand.

3.2. Networking is a relationship 'at work' with other relations

What has just been said is illustrated by Figure 3.1. It will be remembered that in Figure 1.9 – which was the core of Chapter 1 – the expert was in the position of an observer. S/he deduced the existence of a problem from the inadequacy of action shown by the persons effectively involved in a *shared* task, or one which

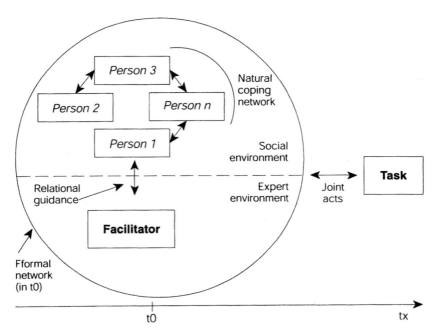

Fig. 3.1 Diagram of a possible initial configuration (at time t0) of a joint coping process. Point t0 marks the moment when the expert and the natural coping network meet.

they should have perceived as shared. In the figure above the expert has moved a step forward and is now engaging with the natural relationships that previously s/he merely observed. With this manoeuvre, meaningful action on the task expands into joint action by an 'expert plus network'.

The task thus becomes a 'common good'. As well as being shared by the members of the network (actually or potentially, in the eyes of the observer), it is also shared by the expert, who Donati describes as pursuing a

[...] strategy of social action which is not geared to charitable aid for the vulnerable in the sense of 'giving them something', but instead involves them in a project for their common good. (Donati, 1991, p. 166)

The idea of joint action directed towards a shared goal is depicted in the diagram by the single arrow linking the plurality of actions to the common task. This idea is the fulcrum of networking. It dismantles the insidious traditional idea of professional 'taking charge' and counters the equally insidious temptation to delegate everything to non-experts. It tells us that when formal intervention begins, neither the network nor the expert shirks the task, just as neither the expert nor the network monopolizes the action. The expert may assume responsibility for the problem situation, but the network is still involved. If the network is still involved, this is not to imply that the expert has nothing to do or has no role to perform.

This mixed responsibility is crucial. The crisis of welfare institutions in Western societies – which is perhaps emblematic of the more general crisis of modernity (Vattimo, 1988; Giddens, 1990; Bertens, 1996; Smart, 1999) – has laid bare their inability to resolve the dilemma of involvement/detachment with regard to the societal difficulties that they are required to resolve. The attitude is that of either/or rather than that of both/and. It is taken for granted that *one or other* of the main spheres of care should be involved in problems: either the *experiential* sphere, as long as problems remain unobserved in the everyday world beyond the reach of the care institutions, or the *institutional* sphere when they emerge so forcefully that they demand formal intervention. The logic is always one or the other, *separately and distinctly.* Technical services are conceived as *replacing* or *substituting* the natural care of persons concerned. The latter are ready to take on the problem again when and if the statutory care is withdrawn, although they still hope to find another welfare organization willing to take on the unresolved problem, and so on. Each of these spheres – the experiential 'sphere 1' and the professional 'sphere 2' – is poised between doing everything and doing nothing, between appropriation and delegation. Relational theory permits us to imagine – to use Popper's celebrated metaphor – a comprehensive 'sphere 3' produced by the conjunction of spheres 1 and 2 (Popper, 1994) and which subsumes exactly the idea of 'common good'.

The upshot of this interactional view is that a solution is a dynamic process. This means that joint action is by definition inadequate at time t0 when the problem is first formally acknowledged. Moreover, it is very unlikely to become adequate subsequently, when the expert engages with the difficult situation (by implementing the guidance relation). Consequently, the joint coping network should be allowed to grow – it should be allowed to develop a dynamic – for an indeterminate period of time until the task is coped with adequately (which does not always mean optimally).

The key concepts are guidance and growth. But what must the expert do to ensure that the network, of which s/he is also part, is able to grow? And what exactly is this reciprocal growth of the network and the expert? These questions can be answered if we first analyse the concept of the 'natural helping network'.

3.2.1. *The natural helping network: a glance at its structure*

The idea of networking as 'a relationship at work with other relationships' prompts the question as to what these 'other relationships' are. In social work, the current expressions used are 'natural helping network or 'natural coping network' (Collins and Pancoast, 1976; Froland et al., 1981). Generally speaking, the natural network is the social reality that confronts the external observer. In formal interventions, it is everyone that the social worker sees when s/he first observes the people directly involved in coping with a welfare task.

Defined as 'natural' are those social relationships which already existed in the coping situation: that is, *before* the social worker deliberately began to provide guidance. They are 'spontaneous' relationships in the sense that they are not conditioned by anyone as such (when they are, i.e. when a social worker deliberately alters the form of a network, they are no longer natural but 'formal' or 'contrived'). In my definition here, natural helping relationships may be *primary* in the sense that they existed not only (a) before the practitioner's intervention but also (b) before the onset of the problem, or they may be the *secondary* relations which arise spontaneously as a consequence of the problem. Both primary and secondary natural relationships may be *informal* (the typical relationships of everyday life) or *formal* (those performing a specific helping role). Let me give an example.

Daniela, a district social worker, has been asked to take on the case of a family consisting of a father, mother and three children no longer able to cope. For three years the mother has suffered recurrent mental breakdowns, and the family is on the brink of collapse. When the woman's illness first became apparent, a change took place in her helping network. Of the woman's numerous relatives, acquaintances, friends and neighbours, broad social network comprising those that the social worker found involved in her care were, besides her immediate family, a sister and a nephew, the woman from the corner shop who was also her friend, the neighbour who lived opposite, the parish priest, and the family doctor.

This was the woman's *primary* natural helping network: the one which by definition existed before the onset of the problem.

> After the woman's first breakdown, the family consulted the family doctor, who arranged to have her admitted to hospital. She was 'helped' in particular by a psychiatrist and by a nurse who has continued to look after her since she returned home. The psychiatric service has also referred the family to a voluntary worker at the local association, who lends a hand from time to time. The woman attends a day hospital, where she is monitored by professional social educators, and where she has met two other patients and their families.

This is the woman's *secondary* helping network. It, too, is composed of formal relations with the psychiatrist, the nurse, and the social educators, for example, and of informal ones with the other patients and their family members.

With the onset of a problem – which may be sudden, as in this example, or gradual – the network always begins a process of unconditioned adjustment. This shift reveals a more circumscribed *helping* network 'within' the broader *social* one – i.e. the everyday relationships that are already in being. In stressful circumstances, social relationships at large undergo some sort of Darwinian process which selects the persons able to commit themselves more decisively to management of the new task: those, that is, who remain in the situation and 'cope' with it. I say 'remain in the situation' because the onset of serious problems may alienate those other persons who, although they belong to the social network, are unwilling or unable to involve themselves in the caring process. This may also happen because the inner nucleus of the helping network, the family for example, closes ranks against outsiders. On the other hand, however, the spontaneous shift in the network may also lead to its extension. In the above example, it brings the network into contact with the domain of mental health services and professionals, both specialist and voluntary, and from this spring various second-level relationships which merge with the pre-existing network or to some extent supplement it.

This 'cluster' of coping actions constitutes what is usually taken to be the natural helping network. However, it is necessary at this point to draw a technical distinction between loosely-connected static networks and tightly-linked dynamic ones. The latter are networks which are deemed to be such also by the persons who constitute them: the network exists in the mind of the network itself. The former are networks deemed to be such either by a single member of the network or by an external observer.

3.2.1.1. Natural coping networks with little or no linkage

Consider the following situation. A young teacher, Daria, lives alone in the city to which she moved two years ago. Because of her withdrawn and difficult personality, she has no friends apart from a colleague who drops in to see her from time to time, and then with no great enthusiasm. She has contacts with her mother at home and with a brother. She has been on sick leave for three months because she suffers from severe depression. She sometimes sees her doctor – for medical certificates and some words of encouragement – and a psychiatrist for private therapy. Every so often she receives a telephone call from home or a visit or telephone call from her colleague.

What helping network is this? It is a network in which each of the various persons involved performs a function, but there is no direct connection among them. It is devoid of integration, either behavioral or cognitive. I shall not discuss whether or not this network is 'adequate' to its task (that of supporting Daria). I merely point out that the network is fragmented and held together by its single node (Daria). There is some sort of common action only from the point of view of the latter, who may merge the distinct actions together in her mind. The plural action may also be perceived by an external observer who reconstructs the contributions made by the various individual carers and sees an abstract connection among them arising from the fact that they are all concerned with Daria. Internally to Daria's network, however, there is no vantage point (apart from Daria herself) from which the caring action can be viewed it in its entirety. The neuropsychiatrist is only aware of what he does: he does not know about, or ignores, the network's other components. The same applies to Daria's mother, her doctor and her colleague. Each of them acts independently and only perceives what he or she does in relation to Daria, but the fact that all of them can in some way be linked to one particular task means that we can, in logical terms, consider them to be a network.

An external observer will see that the task of 'supporting Daria at a difficult time' is divided among four individuals, two 'formal' and two 'informal'. Each of these elements reacts to the task – that is, its relationship with Daria – according to its competency and feelings. The action of each may be influenced by the other components of the network, but it is so only indirectly via Daria. For example, if the neuropsychiatrist prescribes the wrong drug, a possible consequence may be that Daria's mother must spend longer on the phone consoling her, and the doctor may perhaps have to write a certificate extending her sick leave.

This is a network with very weak cross-connections: it is a loosely-linked helping network such as that depicted by Figure 3.2. The diagram shows that the people involved never actually get together – neither two of them nor three of

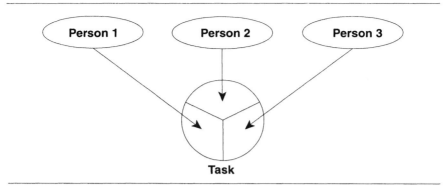

Fig. 3.2 Coping network with no linkages among acting persons.

them, nor all of them together – to talk about the situation and to devise shared strategies. There is no output by relational creativity. The actions of the people involved are not linked, nor are they altered by the influence of direct interactions. They only change in response to the task and to its evolution over time. It is, therefore, a 'fragmented' network. Nonetheless we should continue to call it a 'network', for the people involved are linked with the task, and therefore with the person that embodies it (Daria). Obviously, this structural fragmentation hampers innovation in the coping network and impedes the emergence of shared solutions or adjustments.

From a practical point of view, however, a fragmented network may be an efficient one. It is efficient if the single portions of the task are all covered by individual actions or initiatives. But it is obviously not efficient when – and this often happens – this 'patchwork' does not comprise all the parts of the task, or when individual actions overlap. A network of this kind is more likely to be efficient when the task does not change over time, so that the various, separately acting, individuals are able to take precise measure of their areas of competence and thus grow into something akin to a 'system'. At moments of crisis, when the situation unexpectedly changes, this type of network has narrow margins for learning. Each of its members must change; yet his/her change responds only to his/her own logic, so that it is often insufficient or dysfunctional with respect to the overall logic of the situation.

3.2.1.2. Natural networks with total linkage

In actual fact, entirely fragmented networks like the one depicted in Figure 3.2 are relatively rare. The diagram shows an ideal type, a situation more theoretical than real. Equally ideal-typical is a natural network with total linkage of the kind shown in Figure 3.3. In this case, every action by every individual is traversed and modified by reciprocal contacts or interactions with the other members of the network. All of them are directly connected together, and this gives rise to shared understanding and joint action: a set of social outputs where the whole is greater than the sum of its parts.

The idea of joint or shared action springing from integrative processes within a natural network will become more useful if we draw some distinctions. In particular, we must separate out the two basic components of action: the covert (cognitive/emotional) component and the overt operational one, or the concrete behaviour which 'executes' that part (White, 1995). The former 'inner' component comprises mental processes ranging from, for example, the production of the action's meaning to the more specific acts of assessment or decision-making. The emotions and thoughts of the various subjects involved can be linked together and enhanced by interactions. This fusion does not apply to the behavioural component of action: this consists of concrete acts (motor activities) which remain detached from each other because they pertain to each individual as such. When they are combined, from the point of view of their overall impact on the external environment, should they be synchronized or coordinated for some reason, one is able to see a joint action – although it would be accurate to say that what is joint is the output. Only if we think of something akin to a tug-of-war can we grasp this idea of numerous individual actions effectively reduced to just one.

The actions directed at the task by each member of the network are always physically distinct. All that one can say is that an external observer sees some sort of synchrony among them, although it is dispersed in space/time dimensions. By contrast, the intellectual activity of decision-making (deciding, weighing the alternatives, etc.) may become a truly shared process, so that when the subsequent actions are taken, they are the fruit of genuine interaction. The cognitive substrate of the individual actions, and also of the emotions, can be straightforwardly interrelated, even though the action that ensues may be haphazard and scattered among the members of the network. For there to be good 'mental' linkage, the natural network must exist 'physically': the persons who constitute it must come together *hic et nunc* at a point of space and time – as typically happens in the case of self-help groups, for example, which always meet in the same place, at a fixed time on a particular day, once a week, once a fortnight, or at some other regular interval (Silverman, 1980; Farris Kurtz, 1997).

3.2.1.3. Natural networks with mixed linkage

In everyday life, however, a natural coping network will more probably be only partly connected together, or partly disconnected, as it addresses its task. It will

TABLE 3.1
Summary of concepts

Natural coping network	Set of task-directed actions which existed before the networking practitioner's intervention. It is the 'natural task environment', i.e. the social setting in which the task first arose or in which spontaneous coping was organized.
Primary natural helping relationships	Everyday long-standing relationships which self-select when the task arises, and persist as helping relationships. They existed *before* the onset of the problem and continue to perform functions other than care. These relationships may also be *formal* in that they are established with welfare professionals already involved in the social network but concerned with problems other than the one considered.
Secondary natural helping relationships	Relationships formed after the onset of the problem. In a comprehensive welfare system, these relationships may be formal ones with professionals or voluntary workers concerned with the problem, or they may be informal ones with peers (in free mutual support relationships), or with others persons in the natural enviroment (i.e natural helpers, etc.).
Relational guidance	The relationship between the natural helping network and an expert who 'performs networking', i.e. the expert that (unlike the other professionals already involved as the deliverers of separate provisions) acts as the interlocutor for the network's overall coping action. This relationship not only adds a further node to the network but links it to the external statutory welfare domain, thereby annulling its naturalness (by turning it into a formal network).
Formal coping network	The set of natural relationships reorganized or activated under the relational guidance of an expert, i.e. following his/her deliberate networking action.

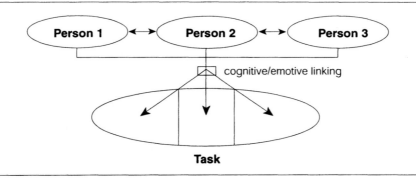

Fig. 3.3 Tightly-linked coping network.

lie roughly midway along the ideal continuum of tight/loose linkage that we have considered. When a helping network is not a mere analytical abstraction, it usually assumes a mixed form. It may contain isolated individual actions, as well as dual interactions, and interactions among interactions, which give rise to 'enclaves', or in other words, sub-networks (see Figure 3.4).

Let's return to the example discussed earlier.

When the father first noticed signs of his wife's mental disorder, he began to worry. He took some days off work so that he could stay at home and verify his impression that his wife was on the verge of a breakdown *(individual action 1)*. Then his youngest son, who had also noticed his mother's behaviour and was also worried *(individual action 2)*, asked him what he thought was wrong *(dyadic action 1)*. They talked about the problem with the other two children *(sub-network action 1)*. Their initial reaction was to try to hide everything by prevent-

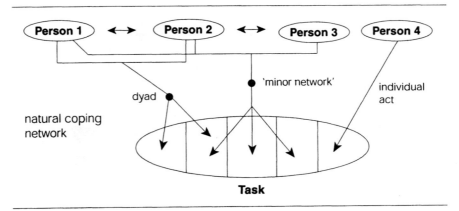

Fig. 3.4 Coping network with mixed linkage.

ing the woman from leaving the house. This provoked a major crisis. They therefore called in the family doctor, who decided with no further ado to have the woman admitted to the psychiatric ward of the local hospital *(individual action 3)* and telephoned his friend the registrar to make the necessary arrangements *(dyadic action 2)*.

3.2.2. *The natural network and its spontaneous tension*

A network's spontaneous movement, its almost reflexive adjustment to difficulties – whether the network internally restructures itself or whether it extends its compass – therefore consists of numerous individual 'movements', distinct 'segments' of the overall action. From time to time, these motions meet and give rise to interactions; then these dyadic interactions merge with others to produce 'sub' networks; and so on.

Each person does what s/he feels should be done: s/he acts under the dictate or the constraint of the stringent reality that we have called the 'task', and at the same time under the 'constraint' of his/her will. Each member of the network is a relatively independent force which applies pressure on the others and receives pressure from them in turn. Each member may freely influence the objective contingencies of the situation (the task), but each of them may be incited or constrained in their action by the others, and vice versa. In this way, each of them influences or impels the shared action and is in turn influenced by it.

A helping network always has supra-individual goals and dynamics which are *more* than the sum of its individual capacities for action. Every natural network has an intrinsic impetus towards collective, maybe unconscius, aims. The coping network has a 'personality'and it often runs on a collision course with the expert.

At the macro level, the history of social policies offers striking examples of clashes with expert systems fought and 'won' by natural networks. Consider the self-help movement (Gartner and Riessmann, 1984), and particularly the birth and growth of Alcoholics Anonymous (McCrady and Miller, 1993), which arose in conflict with the tenets of psychodynamic therapy. The proponents of the established theory started from a rigid definition of alcoholism as a 'secondary disorder', one merely symptomatic of deeper-lying personality disorders or of full-blown psychiatric pathologies. Ideas of this kind obviously did not contemplate action taken by the patient, who was assigned to a therapist so that the true causes of his/her condition could be treated, when the patient would continue to drink. Subsequent history has shown that the theory was flawed, but only because the patients rebelled and introduced alternative forms of therapy based on the idea that alcoholism or excessive drinking behavior is not a symptom but the disorder itself, which should be treated directly by the alcoholics themselves through their own action, however ingenuous, and mutual support, in order to achieve abstinence over time (Craig Clemments, 1997). Consequently, the fundamental curative principle of contemporary alcoholism therapy (mutual support) was not invented by the experts, but in defiance of them and their powerful convictions.

At the micro/meso level, the natural helping networks – whose independent capacities for action (for good or evil) are now being discussed – also comprise a variety of professional figures: doctors, psychologists, social workers, magistrates, and so on. In these cases, interweaving with the merely intuitive mindset of the members of the network directly or indirectly concerned with the problem – the informal agents – are other mindsets of a technical or administrative nature which may either combine with the former or clash with it. In the above example of the woman with psychiatric problems, when the family decided to call in the doctor, another logic, that of the health service, penetrated the previous mindset of social shame and demolished it with the decision to admit the woman to hospital. Once treatment began, the logics of the psychiatric service and then of the day hospital invaded the previous ones of the network (the family and the doctor) so that events slipped out of its control. When a family takes a problem into the formal sphere, it joins a larger game or a more complex network in which, as Reder and Lucey put it, 'there are comprehensive networks which develop independent dynamics within which the family may remain 'lost' '(Reder and Lucey, 1995, p. 13).

But we may equally say that if an expert intervenes in order to begin networking, s/he too may find him/herself somewhat lost.

3.3. What is relational guidance?

A natural network is a force in motion. If someone wants to assist it, they should have sufficient awareness of what it actually is: a force which is so powerful because it is dispersed among numerous and distinct volitions. Each of these individual wills is free to go its own way, and free to combine with others in the interplay of relationships so that it plays its part in the solution – or in the 'anti-solution' if its contribution is deleterious. A phenomenon of this kind has one distinctive feature: it can only be conditioned and perhaps improved, in its own movement.

'Guidance' can be defined as action taken to change the direction of a process already set on its path. It involves, that is to say, steering a dynamic which already exists. In social helping relationships, guidance, in contrast to standard forms of prescriptive intervention, should be viewed as the orientation of a phenomenon which is self-propelling although it is not always aware of the fact.

In social work, the relational guidance is the reciprocal influence between a network-in-motion and an expert who seeks to intercept and deflect that motion. To some extent, s/he too is caught up in the movement and is thus part of the network's inertial system. But s/he also remains partly external to it with his/her feet firmly planted on the ground. S/he is able from this steadier position to influence the network's inner relational dynamics and its axial shifts as it moves towards solution of the problem. Guidance is a process which shifts the direction of the network's intrinsic movement, so that it heads in directions other than those in which it would spontaneously go. Obviously, a certain amount of deviation takes place in any case, simply because of the added weight of the expert when s/he joins the network. But external guidance produces a more marked change of direction. The expert's anchoring in external reality – a non-material anchoring made up of two-way information flows – polarizes the network's motion like a magnet and alters its course (hopefully in a better direction).

Figure 3.5 shows that the network hinges on the relationship with the expert at time t0. It then moves forward and appears differently at time t1, and so on. The network 'triangulates' with the expert like a footballer: it passes the ball to the expert, dashes ahead, and then receives the ball back. The deviation produced by guidance is a vectoral function between the two entities that interact. The

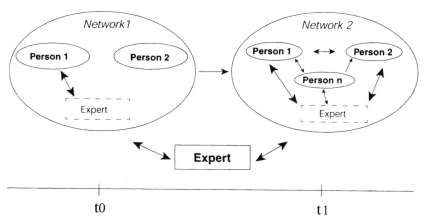

Fig. 3.5 Diagram of the network dynamic over time and its possible structural changes (the dotted line indicates the 'projection' of the expert inside the network as one of its members).

network and the expert may act in synergy, or they may diverge (Figure 3.6) until they become antithetical (Figure 3.7) in social control situations.

When providing guidance, the expert performs various functions which can be grouped under the heading of 'feedback' (Rubin and Campbell, 1998; Tornow and London, 1998). The expert resembles a satellite which receives signals from the network, unscrambles them and relays them back. On the basis of this input, the network may continue in the same direction or change course when it realizes where it is going.

Feedback is essential for any entity pursuing an unknown complex aim. Every end-directed system needs information as to whether it is moving appropriately towards that end. In a helping process, the expert provides the network with that information, while the network constantly supplies him/her with raw information (natural feedback) to be transformed into expert feedback.

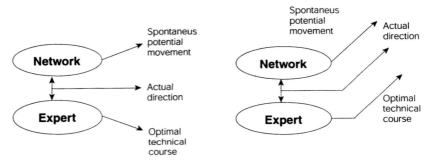

Fig. 3.6 Diagram of the direction taken by the network following expert intervention: the two paths (same direction) either diverge (on the left) or converge (on the right).

According to the behaviourist theory of human learning (Hilgard and Bower, 1975), feedback is a 'reinforcement' which alters a person's behaviour by modifying it, and thus directs the learning process. A's behaviour is followed by effect B, which may be a natural event or a reaction by another person. According to the type of reaction, A learns how to behave in the future, either altering his behavioural scheme or reinforcing it, in the sense of ensuring that it becomes constant.

The same applies to the 'behaviour' of a social network, granted the due differences. A network is neither as unitary nor as concrete as a real person. It therefore finds it difficult to obtain natural feedback.

The seat of consciousness of a natural network is not unitary but dispersed. Each member of a network may see the outcomes of their behaviour, but they are incapable of meta-observation: they are unable to see the superordinate behaviour of which their own behaviour is part. For this reason, a network may need someone who acts as a sort of rear-view mirror which reflects it back to itself, and who furnishes feedback to the network as a whole. The expert acts as a guide when s/he does not allow him/herself to be caught up by individual logic. S/he does not respond simply to someone or other in the network as if this person was his/her direct interlocutor, but instead behaves as if s/he was a simple member of the network. A digression is now necessary to clarify this point.

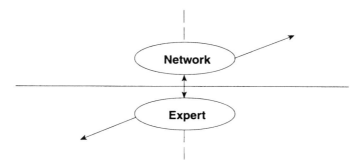

Fig. 3.7 Diagram of the vectors of direction if they move along opposite paths, i.e. when the intervention is not help, but control. The joint movement is cancelled out (in the case of equal forces) or it follows the direction of the prevailing force.

3.3.1. *Networking and on-line work: activities not to be confused*

We have seen that when an expert works with a natural network, s/he does so in two ways simultaneously: s/he joins the network – by becoming a new member – but s/he also remains partly extraneous to it by adopting a 'detached' or superordinate posture (see Figure 3.5). This a rather uncomfortable position, which would be impossible to maintain if the network – to which the expert both belongs and does not belong – were not an abstraction, an entity which the expert, or an even more external observer, has in his/her mind after selecting or creating it. If it were a physical reality, a container of some kind like a room or a garden or a box, the expert would have to decide whether to stay in it or get out of it. Interaction with a network – inasmuch as it is a non-physical entity defined by observation – permits the use of different rules.

In order to highlight the substantial difference between interaction-from-within and interaction-from-without – between 'being-in-relation' and 'relating to a relationship' – it will be helpful to give distinct labels to the two processes. I shall use the expression 'on-line work' to denote interactional activity as a member of a network, and 'networking' to denote the external activity of establishing global relationships with the scattered set of interrelated people located within the boundaries of the social network.

On-line work is the action undertaken by a member of a network, who not only belongs to the network – that is, plays his/her part in a shared task – but also actively seeks out interaction with others. S/he works in the spirit of the network, constantly seeking to interact with its members. This member can realize that what s/he is doing is only one part of the process (s/he is one node among many), and that others are working alongside him/her. As far as possible, s/he tries to facilitate the linkage between his/her action and that of the closest individual interlocutors in the network. S/he seeks to lubricate his/her own relationship, to smooth the interactions that pass through him/her as a network's node.

Every expert who engages in networking does on-line work. But the reverse does not hold. A practitioner engaged in on-line work does not necessarily stand in relation with the network *as a whole*. Although this point is obvious, it is often the source of confusion in practice. One frequently meets practitioners who belong to a coping network, who are maybe aware that they belong to it and are willing to interact, and for this reason alone persuade themselves that they are engaged in networking. In reality, they are not providing relational guidance but merely seeking to enhance the interactional exchanges in which they are directly involved. They move adroitly within the relational tangle that is the network to which they belong, diligently trying not to cause trouble, but rather facilitate its workings.

Natural helping networks often comprise practitioners who play the part prescribed by their professional role. They deliver the services that they should: a home assistant provides practical help, a psychologist provides support therapy, a psychiatrist drugs, a physiotherapist massage, and so on. As long as each of them confines him/herself to that role, and intends to do nothing more, we may rule out that they are engaged in networking. But we may also legitimately ask whether they are doing on-line work. In effect, they may very well not be, for belonging to a network, and efficaciously contributing to its overall task, does not necessarily mean working on-line internally to it: that is, being willing to interact, or facilitating interaction, with the other nodes in some way involved in successful fulfilment of the network's task. Someone may be objectively a member of the network, in that an external observer sees him/her addressing a portion of the overall task, but if s/he does not facilitate linkage with others in delivering his/her provision (albeit one necessary for the task at hand), s/he is therefore not working on line.

There is a propensity to self-referentiality among the actors in a network. Professional practitioners, especially, are closed in upon themselves and their work, rather than being open to relationships. Complex factors of an organizational, logistical and psychological nature may induce them to focus the range of their vision and action exclusively on what they are able to control directly (Payne, 2000). This closure may be due to laziness but also to feelings of superiority, or it may be due to professional rivalries: a psychiatrist may believe that his psychologist colleague is irrelevant to what he is doing; the psychologist may think the same about a social worker, and so on. This mentality is a breeding-ground for conflicts, overt or covert – where conflicts are investments of energy against interaction and cooperation (Edelmann, 1993). All this may cause the action as a whole to be skewed, sluggish or weak.

Although an individual expert may be truly satisfied with his/her own performance, the results of the action as the whole may be disappointing or indeed disastrous. By way of example: a psychiatrist interviews a patient and prescribes him drugs, but then takes no further action. In this case, he is part of the network but does not work on-line within it. If the psychiatrist is instead aware that the home assistant or a relative can check that the patient takes his drugs regularly, and therefore telephones or contacts this person to explain the purpose of certain therapies or to get information, then he is working relationally.

Professionals aware of the relativity of their action do not close themselves off from interaction. They therefore increase the likelihood that spontaneous yet efficacious dynamism will develop *vis-à-vis* the task. The same may happen if the persons involved (users, carers, volunteers) possess this sense of relativity, so that there are nodes in the natural network able to make it function more smoothly. It is not necessary for all the actors to be aware of their small role as internal micro lubricators: some of them may be so aware, perhaps a professional among them, but many others may not. What matters is that their behaviour should effectively facilitate short-range relational process through their action, and that this should improve overall co-ordination.

Let us suppose that one or several nodes expedite interactions, so that there is sufficient work on-line. Yet this not does not mean that the network's 'external' action is sufficent. This is obvious if we remember that coping theory tells us that the outcome of coping depends not only on the actor's capacity for action but also on the difficulty of the task. When faced by particularly demanding and complicated tasks, even an adequate network may fail to function properly. A natural network may develop dynamics which although healthy only partially reach the standard expected. It may fulfil its inherent potential but this may still not be enough. In this case, we may ask, is there nothing more that can be done?

We can always hope for a leap of network quality, and it is here that networking enters the scene as a relational strategy with full intentionality. The argument put forward here is that if a network is to improve its performance, whatever level it starts from, it must anchor itself to an external support. It can do this in two ways: either by linking up with a person who was not a network member until the networking started, for example a new professional practitioner who joins the network to perform that role, or by internally changing the role of some member. In the latter case, it must single out a special function performed by someone able partly to detach him/herself from the network and act as its observer/guide. If this someone is already a member of the network, s/he must be able to detach him/herself from his/her specific previous role, even though it may still continue, to assume the superordinate role of guide.

'Networking' as a relatively *deliberate* guiding action presupposes that the person engaged in it is at least minimally aware that s/he is dealing with a set of relationships and not with a person or a task. S/he must also be aware of certain general aims – above all that of ensuring that the network, as a set of scattered actions, *grows* with respect to a particular task. This point will become clearer if it is borne in mind that guidance is something more sophisticated than mere *co-ordination*.

Co-ordination is an endeavour to link together the set of individual actions taking place within the network as a whole. When a natural coping network is efficient, the co-ordination may be performed by only one of its members who is unaware of doing so (we know that this function can also be carried out in a *diffused* manner when several persons work on-line – that is to say, know how to adapt to each other). Frequently, it may be the user him/herself who performs this function, when s/he has good cognitive abilities – cases in point being disabled people – or a family carer. Impelled by the situation or by the requirements of the task, these persons find themselves at the *pivotal* point of the network and may therefore set about integrating and linking its various actions or functions. I say 'may set about integrating or linking them' because, as we know, a person who predominates in a network may do precisely the opposite – that is, centre everything on him/herself and thereby cause strains or perhaps even the break-up of the network.

In another chapter I have called this internal co-ordination 'informal co-ordination'. Networking as a relational guidance is something entirely different. It is the linking of overt behaviours (co-ordination) but also 'steering' and 'developing'. And it is deliberate. No networking takes place if an attempt is not made to catalyse end-directed social processes, and this attempt will always be unsuccessful in the absence of adequate distance and awareness. Distance and awareness are professional attributes, although they can be acquired by non-professionals as well.

TABLE 3.2
Summary of concepts

On-line work	Action by a single member of the coping network who seeks to link his/her contribution with that of some other people involved in the network. It is therefore an attempt, perhaps unconscious, by an individual component of the network to improve its action by relating it to that of another component (or a few others).
Acting in the network	Position of a person who plays a part, even in isolation, in a shared task. This is a member of the network who works on the task but does not do so relationally (not on-line).
Networking	Guidance (linking, steering and developing) of the various interrelated actions of the persons who constitute the coping network. This is partly external action which is deliberate (though not necessarily *professional)* and goes beyond simple co-ordination (functional linking).
Informal coordination	Minor networking activity performed within the network by one of its ordinary members without his/her being aware of performing the role nor of how to perform it (although s/he may do so efficaciously). The action is usually restricted to functional coordination.

3.3.2. The retroactive nature of relational guidance: feedback and its potential for reflexivity and change

Social intervention is 'guidance', and guidance is feedback. Put simply, this means that a social worker mirrors the action of others back to them. S/he is a 'reflective practitioner', to use Schön's expression, in that s/he acts on the network after observing the network itself, returning the material observed to it in redefined form (Schön, 1991). The network tells the expert what it wants him/her to do to it. In particular, the expert observes (a) what the network does and *reinforces* this if it is done 'well', (b) what the network *can* do and stimulates the network to do it.

A social worker always operates retroactively. S/he may work retroactively on an action already undertaken by others – and in this case truly acts *ex post facto* – or *ex ante* on a potentiality in order to *develop* it, and thus acts before the action real and proper takes place. I shall use the term 'stimulus' for this expert action intended to create conditions favourable for the network's activity before it begins. The judgement that a certain network can accomplish a certain thing obviously cannot be plucked from thin air. It must rest on indicators, even if tenuous, which the expert has decoded. For this reason, contrary to the super-ficial logic that deems it absurd, it is possible to classify a stimulus as a sophis-ticated form of feedback.

In order to understand the general idea of retroaction we may fruitfully draw on the oriental philosophy of Taoism. Deng Ming-Dao (1996) treats largely the same theme in the following illuminating passage:

> The strategists say: 'I dare not lead, but always follow' [...] We must make a careful distinction here: one should not be passive. One who merely waits is one who is too slow. Like a person who tries to sing while counting beats, if you wait for your cue to come, you have already missed it. You sing well only by knowing the beat and singing along with it. So if you apply the principle of 'behind' correctly, it means that wise persons are skilled at anticipating their opponents' movements and blending with these actions [...] If you understand and master all this, then you can fulfill another famous saying: ' I start out after my opponent, but arrive before he does'. (Deng Ming-Dao, 1996, p. 57)

This emphasis on feedback upholds the principle that an expert who must mobilize a social reality for helping purposes cannot act contrary to the wishes of this reality, or stimulate anything that it rejects. If clear signals are lacking, the operator must hold back and wait. Otherwise, should it be in any case preferable to do something and *stimulate*, s/he must be non-invasive. For example, s/he should act only as a 'probe' in the hope that the action elicited will improve the conditions of observation. The practitioner then latches on to this improvement, but not in the conviction that reality must be as s/he wants it to be. This point links back to the discussion in the previous chapter on the conditions which hamper repair work on the network's weaknesses. An expert who scans for weak-nesses and attacks them is not stimulating. Even less is s/he providing feedback: s/he is engaged in an project entirely of his/her making, and one not likely to bear fruit. If the seeds have already been sown, the gardener must water, hoe and nurture the garden; otherwise nothing will grow.

An expert who takes responsibility for providing a network with guidance becomes its *mentor* (Brooks and Sikes, 1997), a wise adviser who follows the network attentively but without being oppressive. This is how Elliot describes mentoring when discussing the reflective attitude of a practitioner:

> Rather than operating as an infallible source of relevant knowledge, the role of the reflective practitioner is to participate in a process of collaborative problem solving through which the relevance and usefulness of his/her

specialist knowledge can be determined and new knowledge acquired [...] From the perspective of the 'reflective practitioner' model, professional competence consists of the ability to act intelligently in situations which are sufficiently novel and unique to require what constitutes an appropriate response to be learned *in situ*. Competence cannot be defined simply in terms of ability to apply pre-ordained categories of specialist knowledge to product correct behavioural responses. Within this model of professionalism, stereotypical applications of knowledge are to be avoided and this implies that any attempt to pre-specify correct behavioural responses or 'performance indicators' is a constraint on intelligence practice [...] Learning to be a reflective practitioner is learning to reflect about one's experience of complex human situations holistically. (Elliot, 1991, pp. 312-314; quoted in Brooks and Sikes, 1997, p. 22)

The reinforcement of behaviourist theory is perhaps the best-known form of educational feedback, although given its intrinsic authoritarianism or artificiality, it is very different from the phenomenon being discussed here. It is worth dwelling for a moment on this procedure in order to highlight its difference from the more complex process of relational guidance. According to behaviourism, when an individual overt behaviour arises, an educator may consolidate it (by fostering learning) through the provision of some kind of reinforcement in one of its many different forms. However, there is a complication in even this apparently straightforward procedure. A behaviour undertaken for the purpose of reinforcement does not usually present itself *sic et simpliciter:* it must be identified (selected) among numerous competing alternatives. In a classic pattern of trial and error, the one good action (according to the observer) is necessarily mixed with numerous non-viable or irrelevant ones. Among the many behaviours that an individual or a set of individuals may undertake, there will undoubtedly be good ones. Yet, if there is no feedback – whether natural or artificial – to act as reinforcement, these actions may peter out.

Consider what happens in behaviourist rehabilitation training, for example when a therapist or a special teacher is trying to develop eye contact with an autistic child (Foxx, 1982). Let us imagine that, at a certain point, among the many actions that the child could perform, he allows his gaze to meet that of the teacher. This action by the child is the desirable one. However, it is intrinsically unlikely to develop further, because it is of no significance to the child (who is autistic precisely because he suffers from an empathy disorder). But the action is significant to the observer, who does not let the opportunity slip. He focuses on this particular action among the many irrelevant ones with which it is mixed, and gives it an exogenous meaning artificially constructed and transmitted by him in his quality as an expert. He thus fashions a meaning specifically for that child and 'attaches' it to his behaviour, so that it becomes meaningful for the child as well, and thus becomes an *action* in the classic Weberian sense. The teacher may, for example, smile or give the child a caress immediately after the eye contact has taken place. Or, since this display of interest is not likely to have much significance for the child, the teacher may give him a sweet, or something else presumably to his liking.

In social work, the reinforcement of actions important for the development of coping processes is never so straightforward as it is in the behaviour therapy of an individual. This is not only because a network is composite and therefore requires a clear overview, but also because there is a further complication, which should be emphasised. Unlike the special needs teacher, who from the outset has a clear idea of the action to be reinforced (which is not coincidentally called the 'target'), a social worker cannot have such an action *a priori* in mind. S/he does not observe the situation, waiting to *recognize* the appropriate behaviour as and when it emerges. On the contrary, the social worker observes with a mind cleared of all preconceptions, envisaging only a generic direction to move in, and therefore a broad category of actions that might work. There is no specific and pre-meditated goal to achieve or, therefore, to observe. S/he must move (and induce the network to move) towards an indeterminate end. As a consequence, the decision of what action to reinforce, and why, is considerably more demanding for a social worker.

Prudent feedback is an appropriate mixture of stimulus and reinforcement. One should not be put off by the behaviourist terminology, since the theory associated with it is of little relevance here: nothing is more alien to social work than the Pavlovian notion of stimulus or even the Skinnerian notion of reinforcement. I am not discussing something that triggers a reflex, but rather opportune pressure applied to set a network in motion, in accordance with the intrinsic relational dynamic. This involves, not reinforcement in the form of praise or moral reward, but the enhancement of or support for an action or set of actions deemed worthwhile from the external point of view of the expert, and from the emotional point of view of the interested parties (and undertaken by the latter).

These two operations of feedback and reinforcement act jointly as a *catalyst* for a dynamic which induces the network to move in the most appropriate directions – directions, that is, which do not counteract the impetus of the network and which have been deemed appropriate by an expert. This process is represented by Figure 3.8, where the two-directional arrow denoting the guidance-relationship has been split into one double-headed arrow which indicates pressure from behind (stimulus), and another which indicates backward action on things done (reinforcement) so that new ones may develop.

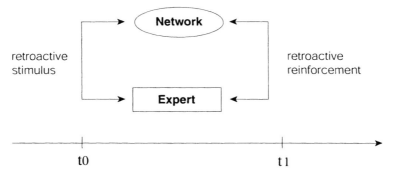

Fig. 3.8 Diagram of combined stimulus and reinforcement in the guidance process.

3.3.2.1. Possible simultaneity of stimulus and reinforcement: the case of verbal reformulation

The well-known reformulation technique provides a clear example of what is meant in practice by giving guidance to a complex action – rather than intervening in it.

Reformulation is conventionally considered to be an individual counselling technique, but we can equally well think of it as a networking one. In both cases the expert responds in the manner described by Carkhuff (1987): s/he waits for a discourse move by the interlocutor, restructures (i.e. reformulates) this move, and then transmits it back to the speaker.

Thus conceived, a reformulation is a reinforcement of what has been said and a stimulus for what is about to be said (see Figure 3.9).

Imagine a social worker engaged in a neighbourhood network session with a group of voluntary people interested in local social problems, for example the priest, the director of a voluntary association for the elderly, a group worker in a family carer self-help group for Alzheimer's disease (she is a retired nurse whose father is a long-term sufferer), a manager of the biggest juvenile association in the area, and perhaps others besides. After some free discussion, when the social worker feels the verbal intensity is flagging, and then all the people present fall silent, h/she can stimulate them as follows: 'When while ago Mary (the retired nurse) spoke, she seemed worried about the troubled situation of the most part of her groups' members, who are at risk to breakdown'.

With this reformulation, the expert guides the network in the sense that he *reinforces* (replicates) a specific aspect of the discussion so far, and in doing so *stimulates* closer examination of that aspect thereafter. He *selects* just one theme from all those that the network has developed thus far. This theme he then beams back like a differential mirror which reflects only one part of the image, the one deemed most significant, and obscures all the others. The part illuminated by the

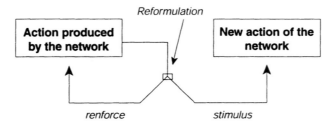

Fig. 3.9 Breakdown of reformulation into its dual functions of reinforcement and stimulus.

light of reformulation attracts attention and becomes important to all those present, triggering further input – remarks, questions, proposals, etc. – just as a good stimulus should. The course of the discussion is therefore shifted from its natural path, even though this deflection is already implicit in it.

3.3.3. *Different levels of guidance*

I would point out that reformulation, like every other form of guidance, does not operate only horizontally. In other words, it is not only used to steer the network on to paths on the same plane. Guidance also enables exploration upwards (or downwards) by shifting communication from one logical level to another. For instance, imagine that a person, Paola, makes the following declaration in an interview or a group discussion: 'My son's doing badly at school, and my husband can't be bothered. I'm tired and I can't take it any more'. Following Carkhuff (1987), this statement is stratified into at least three levels (Figure 3.10): a level 'of facts' *(content)*, a level of 'feelings connected with the facts' *(meaning)*, and a level of the 'feelings connected with self-perception' *(personalization)*.

The search for a solution – in this case to Paola's problem – may proceed in merely functional terms, in that it looks for some practical device to improve her situation. For this purpose, the expert will guide exploration of Paola's situation by reformulating the facts on a more superficial level. He may thus introduce different themes for discussion at that level. For example, if the expert reformulates by saying 'It seems to me that things are not going well for your family', he reinforces and stimulates Paola to talk about one or other of the family's various problems as she wishes. Or, if he says 'Your son's getting very bad marks', he reinforces and stimulates the discussion to focus on the son's problems at school (one of the specific facts that Paola complained about). Or, if he says 'Your husband doesn't give you any help', he reinforces and stimulates the discussion to centre on Paola's conjugal relationship (another of the specific facts mentioned). In each of these cases, Paola is prompted to discuss only the situation external to her.

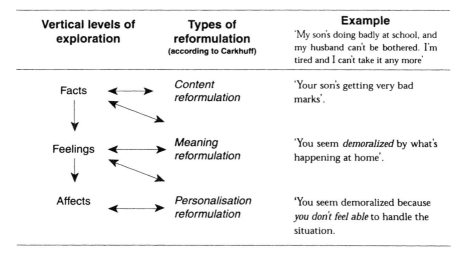

Vertical levels of exploration	Types of reformulation (according to Carkhuff)	Example 'My son's doing badly at school, and my husband can't be bothered. I'm tired and I can't take it any more'
Facts	Content reformulation	'Your son's getting very bad marks'.
Feelings	Meaning reformulation	'You seem *demoralized* by what's happening at home'.
Affects	Personalisation reformulation	'You seem demoralized because *you don't feel able* to handle the situation.

Fig. 3.10 Carkhuff's model of the relations among the different levels of communication (associated with different levels of exploration) and different guidance techniques

However, the expert might decide to probe below merely functional aspects and verbally explore underlying inner (psychological) dimensions as well. Let us assume that the expert decides that Paola's emotions regarding the problem should be brought into play. He might therefore reformulate as follows: 'You seem *demoralized* by what's happening at home'. In this way he verbalizes the emotion perhaps unconsciously expressed by Paola with regard to the facts set out above. He reinforces and stimulates exploration of the emotional meaning that the facts, though neutral in themselves, hold for Paola. If instead the expert says, 'You seem demoralized because *you don't feel able* to handle the situation', he steers the conversation towards an even deeper level: the self-affective one, or that of Carkhuff's 'personalization'. He wants to throw light on how Paola sees *herself* in relation to her task. The feeling of demoralization is connected not to contingent facts but to a key characteristic of the person concerned: Paola's low sense of self-efficacy (Bandura, 1997).

3.3.4. *Reciprocity in relational guidance*

Clarification is required of the reciprocity of guidance that I have just mentioned. I talked about stimulus or reinforcement as operations by the expert *towards* the network. Even if these expert operations must always be prompted by information and signals coming from the network itself, so that there is always a modicum of reciprocity, guidance seems by its nature to be a one-way process predicated on the expert. Of course, when the expert knows what the relational approach is, s/he will proceed with tact. Probably aware of Gibran's maxim – 'No man can teach you anything unless it already slumbers in your awakening consciousness' – s/he will take care to teach only things that the network is ready or willing to learn. But s/he nonetheless teaches; s/he may seek to steer the network where it wants to go, but s/he nonetheless steers it.

Guidance is unidirectional, therefore. Indeed, it is evidently so if we consider the high degree of intentionality that a sophisticated strategy must possess. But we should pay attention here. We know very well that in a helping process not only does the expert learn but the network also teaches: there must be an adequate amount of reciprocal learning. Can we stretch this principle to the extent of saying that the network *guides* the expert, not only in learning the *contents* of guidance but also the exercise of guidance itself?

On careful consideration, one sees that the network stimulates the expert to exercise guidance and reinforces him/her when s/he does it well. However, it performs this imperceptible function without knowing that it is doing so. This is rather like the famous story of Pavlov's dog, which he trained to salivate by giving it food when a bell rang. If the dog had been aware of what was actually happening, it could have just as legitimately said that it itself was training the experimenter: in effect, whenever the dog 'decided' to salivate, Pavlov gave it some food. The dog was the unconscious official recipient of the training, but nevertheless also the experimenter was trained by the dog.

A similar thing happens to an expert interacting with a network. A clear example is provided when an official expert (i.e. a practitioner with a diploma) is in actual fact the reverse: s/he is inexpert and still has many things to learn (because, for example, h/she is very young and h/she has just left college). If this practitioner is interacting with a mature, pre-existing network – for example, if s/he has been called in to act as the facilitator for a self-help group which has already been working well for a number of years – what may happen? If the novice practitioner is able somehow to express a relational attitude in the sense that s/he connects with his/he interlocutors and acts jointly with them, his/her appropriate guiding attitudes – which are likely to be rather haphazard at the beginning – will be immediately reinforced by the group, in the sense that the group will act in a way that the practitioner feels to be good. Inefficient attitudes, those contrary to the principles of relational guidance like directive or self-centred ones, will be 'punished' in so far as they have no effect or produce resistance. This is a powerful counter-feedback which orients the expert and helps him/her to learn.

We have seen in broad outline what the guidance relationship is: it consists of reciprocal stimulus and reinforcement between the expert and the coping network. An appropriate mix of stimulus and reinforcement moves the expert

TABLE 3.3
Summary of concepts

Reformulation	Guidance technique where the practitioner 'plays back' to the interlocutors (person or group) what they have previously expressed, reinforces it and stimulates further exploration of the statement (or of others correlated with it).
Levels of reformulation (according to Carkhuff, 1987)	The practitioner may choose at which level of communication to respond: that of facts, of meanings, or of the person him/herself.
Content	Playback at the level of the facts (external events) recounted by the interlocutor stimulates further exploration of the objective facts. Standard formula 'You're telling me that... [things are not going well in your family]'.
Meaning	Playback at the emotional level connected with the facts recounted. Stimulates the interlocutor to explore the subjective meaning of his/her statements. Standard formula: 'I see that you're [depressed, tired, demoralized] because... [things are not going well in your family]'.
Personalization	Playback which focuses on the affective level connected with the way the person sees him/herself (not necessarily in relation to the objective facts). Stimulates the interlocutor to explore his/her feelings towards him/herself, and the way that s/he sees him/herself (in general or with regard to the specific circumstance or problem). Standard formula. 'You feel (depressed, demoralized) because *you*... [e.g., are unable to handle complicated situations like that of your family]'.

and the network in a direction consonant with their interests, which in fact coincide because both sides are addressing the same task.

We must now ask what, metaphors aside, this *movement* actually is. What is the help produced by guidance – that is, by the fact that someone deliberately becomes a point of external leverage for the pre existing network's action?

We know that the expert triggers networking when the spontaneous dynamics of the network which s/he observes coping with its task are judged to be inadequate. Only if the network has lost its bearings are there justifiable grounds for linking it to an external 'satellite' personified by the expert which re-orients it. It obviously follows, therefore, that the relational guidance should somehow help the network to become 'adequate' in its future coping action. If the network is to acquire this adequacy, its movement (progress) must develop in two general directions:

(a) towards a better patterning of internal relationships, so that the network becomes 'more of a network', i.e. more extensive, better organized, more interactive, more aware, etc.;

(b) towards better joint end-directed action, so that the network follows the appropriate route in the search for the solution.

Point (a) has a structural prerequisite, namely that the network's engine and structure should be in good working order. Point (b) concerns the network in motion, when it is actually functioning. The guide must first increase the likelihood that the network is effectively a network in the true sense of the word. S/he must then help it handle its task in the best way possible. However, these operations need not necessarily proceed in the sequence in which they have been listed. In practice they often overlap.

3.4. A first operation of relational guidance: arranging/rearranging the inadequate helping network's structure

First of all, the network must become 'more of a network' when it already exists, or else it must bring itself into being if it does not. Becoming 'more' of a network means, firstly, that the natural coping should become more generalized, in the sense that the task is distributed among a larger number of people and, secondly, that these people should interact more closely, and also that the coping entity (the network) should grow more self-aware.

3.4.1. *Extending the network and the distribution of coping: the practice of linking*

When an expert looks at a task and asks who is coping with it, s/he often finds that the raw material of coping is lacking or in short supply: in other words, there are no copers (or there are too few of them). In another chapter, I have used the expression 'quanti-qualitative insufficiency' for this deficiency in the size of the network, although this is not to say that there is nobody at all concerned with the problem. We must not consider only the classic situations of marginalization, of objective poverty of social relations: for example when a client has no family or no friends. These are routine occurrences in social work. To understand this point it is necessary not to confuse a *social* network at large with a coping network. A helping network may be weak or extremely weak even though it is part of an extensive social network. A classic example of this situation is provided by the phenomenon of centralization, already discussed, when one or a few members of the social network manage to monopolize the task, or are forced to assume complete responsibility for it. Too many stand by and watch; too few act. Or there is the situation when numerous people tackle a problem and set to with a will, but an external observer nevertheless realizes that more people are needed. The helping network is qualitatively poor in the midst of abundance, something that may easily happen when the task is unusual or particularly complex, or requires too specific skills (Warren, 1981).

The guide in these cases must act as a mirror which shows the coping network its problem of structural inadequacy. The expert guides the network towards realization that it is inadequate, and the network guides the expert towards understanding of the right way to extend it. 'Who do you think can lend us a hand?'; 'Do you know anyone who can do this?'; 'Who could we invite to come to our next meeting?' are possible questions with which to confront the network with its inadequacy while simultaneously stimulating it to find a remedy for it.

It is typical of networking to seek to enable the people in a user's social circle not involved in his/her help to become so by entering the coping network (Whittaker and Gambarino, 1983). It may sometimes be necessary for the social worker in person to contact the person picked out by the network and explain what is expected of him/her. Or the expert may decide that it is better for the network itself (or one of its members) to make the contact, and this is often the most appropriate strategy. However, it is sometimes advisable that the person about to join the already-established coping network should know precisely what is wanted of him/her. S/he should also know that a formal project is in place, and that s/he is not merely being asked to do an occasional favour. If we take the case, for example, of a distressed adolescent who refuses to leave the house, the helping network may decide to ask a friend to telephone him once a day or drop in and see him. It must then be decided whether the request should simply be made by the adolescent's mother or sister, or whether the social worker should be involved as well, in order to give guarantees and to convey the idea of planned action. In the latter case it becomes clear to the friend that he is not simply entering a *natural* helping network; rather, that he is joining a more organized structure, able to give him help and support if necessary.

The social worker may also suggest to the members of the network that persons unknown to them – persons, that is, who do not belong to their social network – should be involved (Maguire, 1983). The network cannot think of anyone who might be usefully contacted, but the social worker has someone in mind. S/he may thus exploit his/her dual relationship with the person concerned and the network, creating a bridge which creates a relationship between two previously unconnected entities. This operation of creating connections or re-lational 'bridges' in order to enlarge the existing network – as schematized by Figure 3.11 – is perhaps the best known technique used in networking, to the extent that it is sometimes improperly regarded as identical with it.

In particular cases, enlargement of a network may start from scratch, in the sense that there is no pre-existing helping network. There is a task and an expert who sees it, but there is no unit of natural coping already in place. In reality, we know that an expert cannot perceive a task that no one else sees. In this case the task is not yet a *social* one. For this reason the expert must first verify his/her perception. S/he must check whether the task is recognized by *potentially* inter-ested persons when it is shown to them, and thus will generate a network there-after. As we have seen, tasks of this kind typically arise in collective situations comprising numerous people each with their own coping network, but where there is no overarching network that includes all of them. For example, every Alzheimer victim has a helping network of a certain size. Yet if a social worker considers all the Alzheimer sufferers in a particular neighbourhood and decides that the 'carers who now look after them – and those who will do so in the future – should have adequate support', it is clear that this is an abstract task which transcends the people concerned: it is not 'their' task (a social one). It requires the involvement of other actors, who perhaps do not exist. Each carer knows that it is his/her task to look after their patient, but they may be so immersed in this

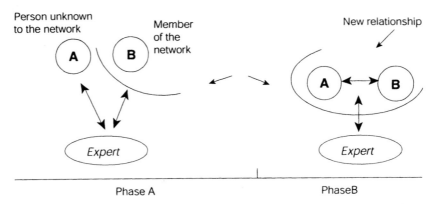

Phase A   PhaseB

Fig. 3.11 The dynamic of linking. On the left the initial situation, on the right the newly-created relation.

task that they do not perceive the need shared by all of them in the neighbour-hood. This more general task can be perceived by the social worker, and then by other persons viewing the situation from outside. And perhaps by one of the carers who has the energy and ability to abstract him- or herself from a particular stressful caring situation.

Let us assume that a community task such as the one just described goes entirely unperceived (Venkatesh, 1997). In this case the inadequacy of the network is total, given that experience sharing does not exist even in perception of the problem, and therefore the coping network does not exist. The expert must therefore act as a catalyst, working on the signals emitted by the individual and scattered potenti-alities already present. Without a social interlocutor, the expert in his/her capacity as a social worker does not exist. If s/he focuses on the task and attributes it to him/herself, believing that only s/he can handle it (for example in the usual fashion by delivering formal therapies or provisions of some kind), s/he undertakes action which is imposed on the social, not catalysed by the social.

It is easy to understand the need for a social worker to create a network *ex novo* when, for example, s/he intends to set up a self-help or mutual support group, like those for the kin of disabled people or AIDS sufferers, or abused women, or many other categories besides. But a social worker is not always fortunate enough to find a well-established self-help network already in place. Even less is s/he likely to find autonomous groups with an already fully-fledged structure. How-ever, should s/he do so, and if these groups are already working well on their own, the expert may consider whether it is a good idea, after politely asking permis-sion, to join the spontaneous system in order to contribute to it in some instances (Maguire, 1983). More often, the social worker instead finds him/herself ini-tially alone with his/her desire for an initiative of this kind to come about. The persons with the same problem – those whom the expert knows as his/her users, or presumes to exist in a given community – have no contact with each other, but each of them lives within the confines of their difficulty. The expert must therefore take the initiative by contacting a potential interested party, someone whom s/he presumes will see the usefulness of setting up a network, and then, when the nucleus has been created, enable it to expand through networking.

Except in the case of networks created *ex novo*, the enlargement of a network consequent on action by an expert guide has usually been preceded by a similar spontaneous expansion attempted by the network itself, with greater or lesser success. I have called the relations spontaneously activated by a network's action following the onset of a problem *secondary natural helping relations*. The new relations created by the deliberate start-up of networking by a practitioner should be therefore given another name, for example *secondary formal helping relations*.

Or at any rate they should somehow be kept distinct, because they are elements grafted on to the network which change its nature. After this restructuring by deliberate networking strategies the network is no longer entirely natural, but is organized or contrived or guided or formal, or what you will.

3.4.2. *Enhancing linkages and internal interactions: the network sessions*

Another function of relational guidance is to increase interaction within the actual coping network. Whether the latter is still a natural network or whether it has been enlarged by the practitioner does not matter: often, as we know, its functional inadequacy is due to a lack of interaction.

I have already pointed out that direct interactions are not necessary for a fully-fledged network to exist. A network may be such even though it is not 'humanly' interlinked; that is, even though there are no direct contacts among the people who make it up. There may be purely functional and indirect linkages, a set of independent actions which nevertheless can all be 'coupled' to the same task. Everyone does what they have to do, and then discovers that, although acting in isolation, they are all taken up with a task that ideally links them together. In this case we have the zero-density network defined above. If we find that this frag-mented configuration nonetheless works, we can only be grateful. But if the nec-essary linkage does not subsequently come about, this means that these individuals each acting on their own account must be brought together and co-ordinated. Decisions must be taken, courses of action must be decided, and so on.

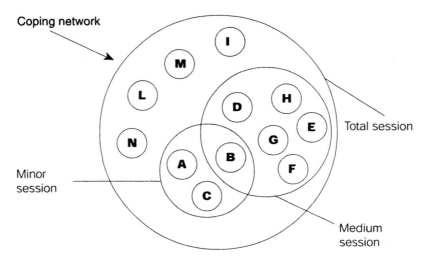

Fig. 3.12 Diffferent size of the network sessions.

The individuals in the network must meet, a process which can be facilitated by the expert guide. The parties can be gathered together in small groups at different times and places. Or if the social worker is lucky enough to happen upon a network small enough to fit into a single room, s/he may organize 'assemblies' at which all the members of the helping network are present. The classic examples are the meetings of self-help groups.

Garrison and Howe (1976) use the terms 'network sessions' or 'network meetings' for these gatherings, which may assume different forms and sizes (Figure 3.12). Network sessions, as Biegel and colleagues have shown, are essential tools for problem-solving (Biegel, Shore and Gordon, 1984). However, to reason in structural terms alone for the moment, they are also important for their ability to refashion the network, with effects that extend well beyond the room in which the session is held. Irrespective of the contents of the discussion that unfolds during the meeting, or of the decisions taken, the gathering of its members strengthens the network and catalyses relationships. All this is useful for focusing the latter on the task.

Periodic practitioner-led meetings to discuss the task may consolidate a helping network. This is important above all for a helping network with a high degree of formalization, or in other words, one structured to such an extent by the guide that it has little of its original naturalness left. An entity of this kind – one thinks, for example, of a self-help or mutual support group which has been functioning for some time, or of an open team (a small network of practitioners belonging to different services) – may have its interconnections strengthened by periodic network sessions, independently of its purely task-directed actions (Payne, 2000). For example, after a number of formal meetings to discuss the resettlement in the community of a young offender about to be paroled from prison, a social worker, the head of a resettlement community, and the prison educationist develop a certain familiarity and get to know each other, so that they coordinate their action or work together on other cases in the future.

On the promptings of this input, the helping network moves up the interconnectedness gradient illustrated in Figures 3.2, 3.3 and 3.4 at the beginning of this chapter. Therefore, if it is a loosely-coupled network, it will move to a medium level, if it has medium level of looseness it will become tighter, and so on.

3.4.3. Enhancing network reflexivity and the learning of self-guidance

A natural coping network has a fragmented psyche which, if it occurred in an individual, would be a severe pathology, but is the norm for a natural network. Relational guidance by the networker should piece these fragments together and provide them with a cohesive mental basis. If this happens – that is to say, if the network is able to 'think of itself thinking', if it grasps itself at least partially as a unit of consciousness *à la* Morin (1986) – then the network makes a leap of quality, as it does when it enlarges or creates internal linkages.

A specification is in order. Just as a coping network may exist without being aware of the fact, so there may be networking without there being awareness in the network that it is going on (there may not be this awareness in the network, but there must be in the networker!). Moreover, in principle there may be networking without this process producing greater awareness of it. However, reflexivity and self-awareness is *always* beneficial.

To clarify this point, we may return to the network with zero relational density illustrated in Figure 3.2, imagining a practitioner who decides to make it more efficient without using the instrument of direct networking: that is to say, without bringing the people concerned into direct contact by means of network sessions. Is this possible?

Let us imagine that an expert sees scattered individuals, all of them taken up with a task but only connected to that task, not to each other. The expert can coordinate these individuals by talking to each of them at different times and places. S/he bargains, discusses, reaches agreements so that each of them does what is opportune, but s/he never brings them together in groups of two or three, or more. They are co-ordinated but they are entirely unaware that they are.

Corrado, for example is a social worker in a Third Sector organisation. He has to promote a work integration programme for Antonio, a youth suffering from a slight learning disability who has completed one year of lower secondary school. Corrado has regular contacts with Antonio and his family. He has contacts with an official in the public agency that finances apprenticeships. He also has contacts with a local employer, a florist with his own nursery and greenhouses, who has declared his willingness to hire Antonio. Finally, he has contacts with the social worker in Antonio's village.

If everything goes well, Corrado's work will ensure that everybody does their part, performing largely what they have agreed to do *vis-à-vis* the task. It is unlikely that these separate actions will synchronize themselves spontaneously. But thanks to Corrado's work this may nevertheless happen. If it does, the sum of *x* individual interventions – constructed, though, bearing each of them in mind – produces a proper coping network, as if those involved have got together to create one. As if the synchronization was in their midst, so to speak, when it instead passes entirely through Corrado's head.

Is what Corrado has done 'networking'? Here we must be circumspect and sit on the fence: we must answer, 'Yes, but…'. It is certainly networking because the task is addressed piecemeal in unitary fashion. But there again, it is not, or not entirely. There are justifications for both answers, and the reason for the answer 'no' is that, although the network now does indeed work better as a result of Corrado's efforts, it has not increased in self-awareness. It is like a two-year-old child who can indubitably do many things but is unaware of doing them.

If guidance work seeks to foster connectedness by means of network sessions, for example, it may encourage the network to feel that it is a united or a finite entity. This does not often happen in the network's purely natural state, or when it has been linked together by the practitioner without knowing it. A coping network achieves self-awareness when it feels itself to be such, when it becomes the entity *per se (für sich)* of Marxian memory. It does so when each member of the network feels, albeit provisionally, that the task is shared, that the solution lies within the network, that the solution is constructed from the bottom up because there is no prefabricated part of it ready to put into place, that helping each other in full mutuality is crucial – in short, when the network has incorporated all the feelings and beliefs that constitute the relational approach discussed here. If the network is aware that it exists and that it is important despite its shortcomings – because it realizes that there is no other superior entity that can do better – this is full-blown empowerment, or something very similar.

A self-aware network – which grows in that awareness through the good offices of the practitioner and the good will of the members – has many more resources than a network that is not self-aware. This is especially so when a network defines itself with respect to long-term tasks, or when it is likely to be confronted by similar tasks in the future. In these cases, the network must not only be efficacious here and now in purely functional terms (those of mere management of the task); it must also become able (perhaps rearranged in some way) to perceive its own problems in the future, take responsibility for them, and deal with them in the most appropriate manner, perhaps without an expert.

If a network has to operate in the long term, it may be imbued with awareness of what it is and of how it should behave and a certain methodological sense of shared action arises. This awareness is initially possessed entirely by the expert and must in part be transferred to the network (I say 'in part' because it is obvious that a full sense of relational guidance is irremediably distant from the common mentality). In other words, it is important that the coping network should do relational guidance (networking) on itself and develop the capacity for meta-learning or learning to learn (Morin, 1986).

If a network is well-guided – that is, if it is provided with a model of how guidance is done – it will develop the ability to tell itself the things that initially the practitioner told it. It will learn to stimulate itself and to reinforce itself as it moves ahead to overcome the obstacles in its path. Consider, for example, what happens in a self-help group, although the same arguments apply to any adequately interconnected coping network. A random collection of people sharing a common task turns into a self-help group when these people become aware of themselves and of their power to act – that is, when they realize, each with his/her limitations and potential, that the helping process is their responsibility. At the beginning, the group may simply be a set of individuals in search of outside help, and this is usually the case of groups set up on the initiative of a professional groupworker. These people do not know that they form a network or that action is expected of them. The practitioner must remedy this 'ignorance' through guidance, by providing stimuli and reinforcement to enhance the network's awareness of its self-efficacy. However, if s/he intervenes directly, for example by explaining in minute detail what they are and how they should view themselves, s/he may cause dangerous confusion. Over-punctiliousness may communicate the opposite of what is intended: that the group's consciousness resides in the expert, and that s/he bestows it from above, so that the members presume that they will receive further attributes handed down from on high. Which is an excellent basis for further misunderstandings in the future.

We shall see in the next section exactly what guidance in problem-solving consists of. Here I merely point out that the practitioner must make the members of the self-help group (to remain with this example of helping network) realize that the problems that they are addressing – both the problem with a capital P that defines the group (alcoholism, for example, or single parenthood) and the specific sub-problems that arise during their discussions at meetings – all belong to the group as a whole. The practitioner will *stimulate* by saying such things as 'Has anybody got an idea of what to do?' or 'This is a problem: we should all think about it together', and then *reinforce* when the group comes up with an answer that s/he thinks is a good one.

A network of any kind increases in self-awareness when it gradually realizes that all problems pertain to it. The practitioner never solves problems on his/her own, or when s/he takes them outside the confines of that particular group of people (if anything s/he extends those confines). For example, an expert networker will send a member of the network to an outside therapist only in exceptional circumstances (Amodeo, 1995), perhaps for psychiatric therapy or counselling, but in no way will s/he take a decision of this kind with regard to coping problems. The group thus learns that it must get started and that it is capable of doing so. It learns that each of its members can do and say things on an equal footing with the others, so that the group becomes a coping network. Empowerment grows until, after a while, it is the group itself that takes responsibility for new problems as and when they arise.

Inevitably one of the group's members will say 'What can we do?' or 'Has anyone got any ideas', or similar, without the practitioner having to guide or compel them to do so. Again, after some discussion, solutions may be proposed, and the network (or some of its members) will perhaps know how to distinguish those that are feasible from those that are not, without the practitioner having to provide reinforcement. This, too, may gradually arise from the network's interior.

At this point we may ask what there is left for the practitioner to do. Should s/he take a step back, perhaps even withdraw? With the modicum of guidance methodology absorbed by the network from the expert, can it not now forge ahead on its own? If it were not for everything that I have said so far about the utility of the relationship between expert and the network, and if were not for the fact that the expert him/herself can learn from interaction with the network, it would be tempting to answer 'yes'. If it were not for these indications to the contrary, a strategy of gradual disengagement by the expert would seem advisable.

3.4.3.1. Performing 'double guidance': or guiding others who guide

A network can learn how to do guidance work on its own self. And if its inter-action with the expert is prolonged and clearly defined, this may well happen. In practice, obviously, this learning process will proceed piecemeal: some members of the network will learn earlier and better, others less so, and yet others not at all. One of them may indeed learn so well that s/he has the potential to become an outstanding natural helper – a 'practitioner' trained by the network itself. Numerous self-help/support groups can count on guides or experts of this type, who are 'lay' practitioners with little formal training (Skovolt, 1974). They should not be confused with the individuals that I earlier called 'pivot-figures', those able informally to achieve a certain amount of co-ordination. Here I am talking about individuals able to learn, and able to exercise, genuine relational guidance functions, or in other words, able to perceive the network as a whole and transmit feedback to it.

A professional expert might at this point imagine a guide operating at another level from the one that has been discussed hitherto. Once the expert is able to count on certain persons who know roughly what guidance is all about (members of self-help groups, voluntary workers, and the like), s/he may gradually steer them towards assuming responsibility for guidance. If s/he is involved in the network with them, s/he may take a step back and gradually let them take over the network. Or s/he could look for new helping networks in which to involve them, and for which they may become the 'guides'. Thereafter, however, the expert should not leave these natural helpers alone; s/he should instead supervise and help them in their work, thereby once again guiding them. This is second-rank guidance: it is, as Figure 3.13 shows, the guidance of a guide – or of several guides simultaneously.

Because they can count on the supervision of an expert, natural helpers – who are now themselves to some extent expert – are able to learn how to perform the guidance function better as they do it. As said, it is not necessary for the expert to single them out from the beginning. What is important is that natural helpers should know how to act adequately, that they should have some idea of what they must do and can do, and feel that they are being supported. In this way they can grow further and learn while they are being useful. The expert can foster second-level guidance by providing each lay practitioner with personalized support. However, a more relational manner of supplying this supervision is to join the people concerned together in a network, thus providing the basis for horizontal learning and support among lay helpers as peers.

When an expert is able to act in this way – when, that is to say, s/he is lucky or competent enough to be able to count on second-level collaborators who can sustain a network on their own – s/he greatly extends the range of his/her action. S/he is not someone who 'does the relational guidance him/herself' but a person who promotes and supports (guides) the guidance of others doubly within the spirit of empowerment.

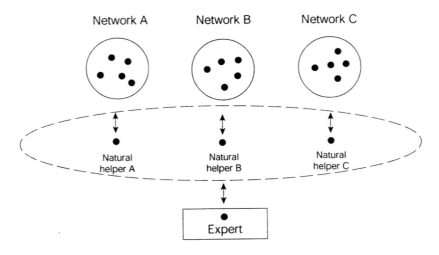

Fig. 3.13 Diagram of second-level guidance, where a professional practitioner guides the guidance provided by his/her 'lay' collaborators.

3.5. A second operation of relational guidance: joint problem-solving

We have seen that an inadequate network can improve structurally until it is able to act on its own. A fundamental requirement for efficacious action is that the network should be sufficiently extensive, with sufficient interactions and sufficient self-awareness. A settled network has a better chance of working and acting well, even if it has still not taken a step towards an 'external' goal.

A good driver should be able to fix an engine but also, obviously, able to drive a car. In networking, we may imagine guidance while the network gets settled, and then guidance real and proper, or orientation in dealing with the problem with respect to which the network defines itself, or the particular problem that it intends to solve.

3.5.1. *Tasks 'external' and 'internal' to coping network*

A coping network often requires concrete action directed towards a specific task. But this is not always the case. Sometimes an expert directs all his/her efforts – or a large part of them – at catalysing a network, without attending to any other task than that one – without, that is, anticipating what the network will do afterwards. Thus an expert may be concerned only to develop a network and make sure that it works, without having anything else in mind. An example:

> Adriana is a social worker for a small town council. She thinks that it would be worthwhile investing some of her time in encouraging the growth of a network of voluntary workers. She therefore contacts the people that she thinks may be interested and organizes meetings with them, so that they can get to know each other and look for other people to join the network. When this network establishes itself – when, for example, there are a dozen or so people who meet regularly – the social worker may be satisfied and thereafter work to ensure that the network holds together.

But what can this network do? It can set itself external objectives: for example, it could go in for political lobbying or organize community awareness campaigns on social issues or for advocacy (Barnes, 1996; Bateman, 2000) and so on. But it could do otherwise. It could serve only to provide emotional support or training for its members, who then act externally on their own account, drawing on the support or training provided by the network to improve their action as individual voluntary workers. They could collaborate with the social worker who has linked them together, assisting her in the various situations that she must deal with in her day-to-day work.

The same applies to self-help groups. These, too, are networks in which internal functions preponderate. For example, a self-help group for alcoholics can be seen as a relational context in which individuals – by means of periodic meetings, discussion, sharing, etc. – support each other and help themselves through mutual support. Obviously the group may occasionally set itself external goals or concern itself with outside problems. These problems may be those of the local community, or of the national community as a whole, so that the group organizes anti-alcohol campaigns, for example (Holmila, 1997); or they may arise from an emergency which affects one of the group's members. For example, typical tasks for the group might be trying between one session and the enxt to retrieve a member who has not been seen at recent meetings and may have relapsed, or helping a member who has lost his or her job or suffered bereavement. However, should it happen that no situations of this kind arise for a certain period, the group does not sit on its hands because it has nothing to do.

Another example of networks which may be only structural, and therefore do not pursue external goals, is provided by so-called 'policy-level networks' (Payne, 1993). Let us imagine, for example, that a city councillor for social services, or a local authority policy-maker, on his or her initiative or because s/he is obliged to do so by law, decides to improve co-ordination among the various public and third-sector organizations in the city. S/he therefore proposes the creation of a committee or panel, or something similar, where delegates from these organizations can meet. The purpose of a network of this kind may be static in that it serves only to foster co-ordination among the various agencies involved in local policies so that each can properly fulfil its mandate. It need not necessarily propose initiatives targeted on external, concrete problems, although this is always possible.

A network, therefore, does not always have to solve 'direct' problems; it may function purely for the value *per se* of relationality. That said, we may return to our central theme: what are the processes and mechanisms by which a well-established network can take action to solve concrete problems? And what form does expert guidance take when the network sets about doing so? These questions introduce the general topic of problem solving (Kahney, 1993) a procedure so well known that it has no need of detailed explanation here. Except for the fact that, unfortunately, it is usually described in individual terms which are misleading when applied to the networking approach. This requires us to make a further analytical effort, distinguishing between two versions of the method: on the one hand the classical procedure, which here is called 'linear problem solving', and the *relational* one, here called 'joint problem solving'.

3.5.2. *Linear problem solving and its limitations*

Solving a problem is like climbing a mountain. It begins with a single step followed by a multitude of others. It is usually the case that when a natural network is left to act on its own in complex situations, it will take haphazard steps, aimlessly groping its way through the task. The job of external guidance in this case is to reduce the level of randomness in the hit-or-miss process, increasing the likelihood that the network will actually get somewhere.

A common strategy among mountain climbers is to ignore the distant summit and divide the route leading up to it into stages. The goal thus becomes to reach the end of the current stage of the climb. No matter who the problem-solver may be (though caution is required on this point, as we shall see), s/he must move through stages or create the preconditions that lead towards the solution, or toward the definition of a lower-level problem.

The standard scheme of problem-solving comprises a linear sequence of steps. These are listed in Figure 3.14, with discussion of them postponed until the next section. If, as it is claimed, these steps exactly describe the sequence that necessarily leads to the solution, they must always be followed. When the problem is solved, this means that all the goals in the sequence have been achieved. Obviously, it does not mean that each goal has been defined and pursued intentionally, only that it has been accomplished.

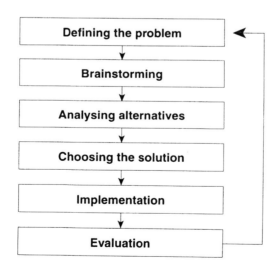

Fig. 3.14 Classical schemata of linear problem solving.

We can distinguish between the *process* of problem-solving (Perlman, 1957) and the *method* of problem-solving, defining the former as the *reality that progresses* towards a solution (i.e. a problem solved), and the latter as a procedure deliberately and rigorously applied in order to facilitate that process. When people get to grips with a problem, they may do so intuitively, immersing themselves in it and acting somewhat haphazardly. Or they may abstract themselves from the problem and address it in a meta-cognitive way (Winert and Kluwe, 1987) – that is, by thinking systematically about what they are doing, about the problem-solving process as such. The solver decides to spend as much time on each stage as necessary, so that s/he can be sure that at the end of it the conditions are in place for successful completion of the next stage.

In social work, the linear method of problem-solving is frequently recommended (Goldfarb et al., 1986), and it is indeed useful. But it should be revised to take account of the greater cognitive complexity of helping work when it is conceived as networking.

3.5.2.1. A first logical limitation: a solution generates further problems

The idea that solving a problem means finding a solution, which is then applied and then tested again, is a simplification that is unfortunately often contradicted by reality. Often, when various hypotheses have been formulated and weighed and a certain solution has been chosen as viable, as soon as the problem has been dealt with a new one arises, the solution of which generates a further problem, and so on. The chain continues until it is decided to call a halt because the situation has improved to a sufficient extent and it is thought that the solution is adequate, or for other reasons. A once-and-for-all solution is usually 'hoped for' by applying standardized procedures. However, as we know, these are solutions which are such 'by definition' – that is, regardless of whether or not they actually are solutions (they are only purported solutions). But when action must be individualized so that it fits only one specific contingent situation, every solution fragments into numerous sub-solutions each of which requires a specific problem-solving process.

This consideration adds to everything said in the previous chapter about the indeterminacy of action in social work and its tendency to open up into a wide range of possibilities. Social workers know where they start from but they do not know where they will end up. And this uncertainty does not only stem from the fact that there may be several potential solutions to be addressed. Even when the choice eventually falls on a specific solution, the process does not always finish there: it may resume, and once again slide into the unpredictable.

Like a set of Chinese boxes, extracting one solution often means that further problems come into focus, in accordance with Popper's idea. These further problems may arise after *application* of the solution – that is, at the end of the problem-solving sequence, during the evaluation phase. Or these further problems may appear and be addressed on purely cognitive grounds, before tangible action is taken. In the former case, it is the transformation of reality produced by the action that brings out new problems, ones which were previously hidden or unforeseen. In the latter case, it is the mental insight of a purely imagined solution which, again at the cognitive level, points up new problems and therefore new solutions – these too hidden at the beginning of the problem-solving process.

In both cases, the emergence of a solution gradually comes about through the problem-solver's interaction with the products of his/her action or his/her thought, which retroact on him/her to create further matters to resolve. Once again, it is evident that simple linear action (one problem, one solution, one application, etc.) does not correspond to the multifaceted nature of social reality.

In practice, the problems deriving from a solution spring not from thought or action separately, but more often from both spheres together. It is obviously impossible to stretch the cognitive phase *ad infinitum* while seeking to itemize and resolve all possible problems beforehand with limitless mental effort. Such an endeavour would obstruct action and prevent it from yielding the information that clarifies how the problem-solving process should proceed. Sooner or later action must be taken, although it is still not entirely clear what form it should take. But it is equally evident that immediate action, once a solution has been thought of, is often not possible.

An example may help:

> Imagine a social worker who has identified a problem, for example a case of sexual abuse. The victim is an eight-year-old girl (Michela) and the abuser is her stepfather (Alfonso). Let us also imagine that the social worker, perhaps jointly with colleagues or other interested parties, comes up with a solution after carefully weighing the alternatives. This solution is to 'organize a protection network' around the little girl at risk. Consequently, the social worker decides to ask the other members of the family to help.

The social worker may adopt the strategy suggested by Smith (1995). In this case, therefore, progress from the problem to the solution requires the system of relations to be reorganized so that persons able to supervise and dissuade are interposed between the child and the abuser. This is easy to say but how can a solution of this kind be applied *in practice?* For it is evidently more an aspiration, an 'aim' than it is a 'goal'. Nor can it be implemented without mediations, as explained in the previous chapter. It is simply the envisioning of an *aim* of the type 'It would be good if the situation could become such and such'. But then the problem immediately arises of what to do next. In practice, the next stage may be the solving of a myriad of sub-problems, all of which can be converted into concrete goals of the type: 'Who are the people best able to give protection?', 'How can they be involved?', 'How can they be helped to perform their role properly?', and so on. Sub-problems like these must be systematically addressed and solved so that the premises are in place for application of the solution originally devised. Once action is under way, it may produce new problems or new opportunities which were not imagined at the beginning, given that the information necessary has only subsequently been produced by the action.

3.5.2.2. A second logical limitation: 'the' solver does not exist

Another distinctive feature of problem-solving in a reticular framework, as opposed to a linear one, is that one of its cornerstones disappears: the 'solver' does not exist in a social coping network. Whoever invented the problem-solving procedure (assuming there ever was such a person) devised it with the intention of 'doing a favour' for its user, namely the *solver*. The method tells the solver that when s/he is confronted by a problem of any sort, s/he should do 'such and such' – first define the problem, then examine the options, and so on. This is methodological advice intended to make the solver more efficient. And every possibility is envisaged of him or her except 'non-existence'.

We well know that this pillar of common-sense disappears in networking situations. If we ask ourselves who constitutes *the* solver (in the singular) in social welfare problem-solving, we must answer that such a figure (unlike what happens in the technical disciplines) cannot exist. The solver is dispersed or scattered among the various elements that make up the network. We also know that a person who sweeps away the problem before him or her cannot be a 'networker': a person who applies relational guidance in networking practice must endeavour to *catalyse* the problem-solving process rather than simply implement the solution. If it is true that there is no individual solver in social care or welfare, even less can one be an expert who claims to be a networker. Guiding a network means providing stimulus and reinforcement so that the problem-solving (i.e. the progress through the stages specified by the method) takes place within the helping network rather than within the mind, however methodical, of the individual solver, who, as we know, is an integral part of a social network. I shall apply the term 'joint' or 'relational' to this type of problem-solving in order to emphasise that it is always action with a broad spectrum of subjectivity.

3.5.3. *Joint problem solving in network action: operational features*

What is guidance in problem-solving processes when the solver is an entire network? The expert must first of all carefully observe what is going on. S/he must immediately determine whether the network has already started to move through the various stages of the problem-solving procedure. If it has, then s/he need do no more than reinforce the process. If it has not, if it has skipped one of the stages – which may easily happen if the natural network is inadequate – the expert must induce it to revert to that stage and complete it so that it can then move smoothly through the next one. When this reorientation (the stimulation) is successful – which is apparent when the network responds positively to the expert's inducement – this will reinforce the ensuing action, and thereafter throughout the entire process.

Every stage of problem-solving is a broad abstract aim to be achieved and filled with *ad hoc* content. Responsibility for ensuring that each stage is completed, and that all of them are linked together, attaches to the expert. Filling each of them with content that fits the contingent situation is the joint responsibility of the network and the expert. I shall now briefly discuss all the steps in relational problem-solving, highlighting the main differences with respect to the standard model of directive problem-solving (Fig 3.14).

3.5.3.1. Defining the problem

The way in which the problem is perceived is the most delicate operation in the entire process because it is the most basic one. It is for this reason that this book devotes an entire chapter to the topic, pointing out that a problem does not exist unless it is shared – that is to say, unless it is perceived by a network. If a problem is perceived only by the expert, it is a technical problem that should be solved by him or her. It is not a social problem. However, a distinction is in order. It is one thing to *feel* a problem – that is, be aware that something is wrong, or sense a difficulty of some kind – and another to *define* it in the most appropriate manner for it to be addressed operationally. Although a problem may be clearly perceived by a practitioner's social milieu, and not just by him or her alone, this does not entail that it has been methodologically formulated in the best way possible, so that it relates to the social entity that perceives it rather than being estranged from it.

A network may feel a problem but define it in such a way that it is deflected elsewhere. The network may view the problem as someone else's problem rather than its own. It thus commits a major preliminary error, which the expert guide must try to prevent. I have discussed at length the error of defining a social problem as the problem of an individual or his/her pathologies rather than as the deficiency of a coping network. To provide some concrete examples, the problem is not 'Luigi the alcoholic who cannot stop drinking' but 'all of us close to Luigi who do not know what to do with him'. The problem is not 'Alfonso the stepfather who sexually abuses Michela', nor is it 'Michela traumatized by Alfonso's abuse', but 'we who are close to Michela but do not know how to protect her or how to help her overcome the trauma' (or 'we who are close to Alfonso and do not know how to prevent him from abusing Michela or how to get him to control himself'). The problem is not 'Cristian the young drug addict in prison for drug-dealing and petty theft' but 'we who are close to Cristian and do not know what to do when he comes out of prison in six months' time', and so on.

As we know, the problem should be framed as *action* by a network. 'Action' here does not relate to internal variables like feelings, moods, emotional distress, and so on but primarily to more comprehensive potential operations as yet unperformed. And then not to actions by one person, or a few persons in the network, but action as far as possible undertaken by everyone concerned.

When a problem is improperly defined as someone's problem, the network may think that it is the person afflicted by the problem that should change. In practice, two things may happen. Either the network sends the person away to be changed, for example by a clinical therapist, or the network decides that it itself must change the person. It will think 'Who can change Joe Bloggs?' or 'How can 'I' the network *alter* Joe Bloggs?'. But it should instead think: 'How can I the network – including Joe Bloggs – alter myself so that conditions improve for Joe Bloggs and for all of us?'.

This brings us to the core of the ecological perspective in social work (Germain and Gitterman, 1996). The unit of meaning that should be changed is the context of action surrounding a person, not some state internal to him or her – or rather, not his/her inner state *directly*, given that the person is part of the context which changes, so that s/he too will be changed in the end but without being the explicit target of the intervention.

Acknowledging the existence of a particular impasse in the human ecology – which means recognizing its inadequacy – is the obligatory first step for a helping network. If it appears that the network has not taken this step, then the social worker must try to steer it back on course. S/he must ask questions which prompt the network to focus on the action that it has failed to take, questions of the type 'What is the problem that we must tackle together?' or 'What could we have done that we haven't?'. In practice, it is less important that the coping network should exactly and lucidly define the problem as its own problem; it is more important that the opposite situation should not arise: namely a decision by the network that the problem 'belongs to someone else', which may easily happen. The task of the expert in this phase is to manage the situation so that this disorientation does not occur.

3.5.3.2. Brainstorming

The second step in problem-solving is the fostering of indeterminacy, by which I mean the removal of compulsory solutions (courses of action taken for granted) and the opening up of the field to imagination/realization of the unthinkable. In the case of a serious and long-standing problem, it is probable that the persons concerned will have already tried solutions that have failed, given that the problem still persists. Although these solutions have proved unsatisfactory, those who have used them are still attached to them, finding them cognitively difficult to relinquish. Why does a problem exist according to the persons caught up by it? Because the solutions envisaged by those persons, and which they have probably implemented thus far, do not work. And yet they can envisage only those solutions. They tell themselves, 'There is a problem because *those* solutions, which are *the* solutions to the problem, for some reason, in these circumstances, do not work.' Paradoxically, they stubbornly cling to their behaviour. If they can think of any solution it is the one that has already failed, and they discount any other.

The purpose of brainstorming is to counteract the compulsion to iterate what has already proved unsuccessful. It starts when the problem to solve has been defined and those concerned begin thinking about *potential* solutions, not about the *de facto* solution or the best one. Brainstorming is the creative generation of possible 'in theory' solutions, ones that are feasible in principle (Rikards, 1974; Avolio and Kahai, 1998). We know that every problem can be subjected to a large number of hypothetical transformations, from the most sensible to the most original or impracticable. Bringing these possibilities out into the open so that the mind's eye can focus on them clearly is the purpose of brainstorming.

Brainstorming is a mental activity of free association whereby a product of the brain (an idea) elicits a new idea which then generates further ones. A 'storm' of thought throws up diverse innovative, even bizarre, solutions which would be unthinkable with the mind at rest.

Brainstorming works best when it is performed by a group or a network, i.e. in an inter-mental face-to-face context. Although it is today possible to brainstorm electronically (Roy, Gauvin and Limayern, 1996), here I shall concentrate on non-virtual contacts among people during network encounters or meetings. Whatever the setting, the product of one participant's mind stimulates another's mind, which stimulates another, and so on, until the chain of association may return to the first mind. One person says something ('To solve the problem, we could do x') and this idea x triggers an association of ideas in another person, who says 'We could also do y', when idea y would have never come to mind had it not been elicited by x.

The quantity of ideas brought out by collective brainstorming is an emergent *product* of interpersonal relationships, a genuinely joint action. When acting individually, a person only partially elicits his/her own mental products, so that the creative stimulus of surprise is limited (Goldfarb et al., 1986). Contact with diverse points of view produces something which is more than the simple sum of its parts (Kramer et al., 1997), and obviously also more than what emerges from one part alone (Valacich, Dennis and Connolly, 1994).

An expert who guides a network problem-solving process must pay particularly close attention to brainstorming, no matter how s/he may conceive it: indeed, s/he may not call it by that name or may not laboriously formalize it. The expert must make sure that the network produces a sizeable number of possible alternatives, without initially worrying whether they are sensible or practicable. S/he must also make sure that these alternatives are sufficiently diverse. If there is differentiation, this means that the options have been produced by the network in the true sense of the word. It means that the largest possible number of people have been involved, that they have had their say regardless of constraints of role or status. For example, if a social worker who must manage home help for an elderly man discharged from hospital to convalesce, organizes a meeting among the doctor, the district nurse, one of the man's granddaughters, and a voluntary worker, for there effectively to be a network it is indispensable that everyone present must feel that they are equals (disregarding the specific aspects of the work of the professionals involved). From the coping point of view – that is, from the point of view of what needs to be done to help the old man – an idea suggested by the granddaughter is just as good as one suggested by the nurse, and an idea suggested by the nurse is just as good as one suggested by the doctor, and vice versa. The hierarchy principle tends to disappear, in a social network that functions as such.

The expert stimulates a *plurality* of views and reinforces them when they are expressed. S/he acts as a mirror to the network, prompting it through questions like: 'We've still only a few ideas of what to do, are there any other suggestions?', or 'X has said such and such, does that bring anything else to mind?', and so on. If one or a few persons monopolize the discussion, the expert may encourage the others to speak, so that it is the network that operates, not some particular individual. If someone is prevented from speaking by shyness or by fear of what the others might think, or by some other destructive group's forces (Nitsun, 1996), the presence of the facilitator may be of help: not just because s/he is constantly non-judgmental in attitude but also because s/he will forestall any negative criticism in the group. In his/he role as facilitator, the expert may be assisted by transmitting the specific technical knowledge to the group that the purpose of brainstorming is the creative production of ideas – even bizarre or irrelevant or foolish ones – and that criticism is reserved for the next stage in the problem-solving process.

3.5.3.3. Analysing and criticism of possible alternatives

Brainstorming creates a list of possible options, a mental list or a real one written on a piece of paper, if it is decided that it would be useful to structure the procedure to such an extent that its various stages are written down (Goldfarb et al., 1986). In the next phase, that of criticism or intermediate evaluation, each alternative is examined and its pros and cons are discussed. The various hypotheses are criticised, sometimes harshly, in order to determine their theoretical soundness on paper before they are implemented.

This stage tests the practitioner's ability to *interact* with the network in the full sense of the word. The expert probably has his or her own opinion about every point on the list ('This is feasible and this is not'), and so too does the network. It is here that the different views – the expert and the experiential – may clash, and it is therefore here that the expert must be more careful, providing guidance rather than intervening. S/he must constantly work both sides of an intrinsic ambivalence. On the one hand, s/he must elicit and respect the opinions of the network. But at the same time, and at this stage more than any other, the expert must express his/her views to the network, since s/he possesses the vital asset of expert judgement which it would be unwise not to use.

The expert is also an effective member of the network, not just a detached supervisor. S/he therefore has the right as well as the duty to contribute cognitive input. Yet the higher his/her status as expert – the more effectively different s/he is from the other members of the network – the more likely it is that difficulties will arise. The riddle is a technical one, perhaps the main technicality in networking: how can the expert make his/her opinions mingle with those of the others without suppressing or distorting them. Obviously, the safest way to proceed is to stick to the role of guide: without directly expressing opinions, therefore, but stimulating the network to explore the problem more deeply when the expert realizes that crucial aspects have been ignored. For this purpose s/he may employ hints or stimulus-questions of the type: 'If by doing this, such-and-such happens, what can we do?'. By reflecting back his/her doubts rather than his/her certainties, the expert avoids repressing or distorting opinions by the authority of his/her role – which might otherwise happen if s/he passed peremptory judgement on the issues under discussion. If, for example, during a network meeting between the relatives of an elderly man and a voluntary worker, the expert says that the action suggested is too demanding – for example, the man's granddaughter cannot call in every morning to make sure that he has got up – this opinion may become a self-fulfilling prophecy only because it has been asserted authoritatively. Obviously, if s/he deems it appropriate, the expert may express his or her opinion, but this should be done in awareness of these effects.

3.5.3.4. Choosing a solution and coping with related problems

Point-by-point analysis of possible alternatives flanks the mere list of solutions produced by brainstorming with a double column of pros and cons. Thus each possible solution is matched by judgements on its feasibility and possible doubts. The logical next step is the devising of an operational conclusion, which means choosing the solution deemed most practicable.

Choices must be based on criteria which, even if they are not explicit, must nevertheless be present. From the point of view of the members of the network, the general criterion is obviously that the pros must outweigh the cons: the solution selected must be the one that exhibits the best ratio between benefits and costs. From the point of the view of the expert external to the network, the criteria must also be methodological in nature, like those singled out by Goldfarb and colleagues: firstly, the criterion of avoiding solutions that remove the problem from the network – that is, solutions which require all-encompassing outside intervention; secondly, the criterion of giving priority to solutions that require cooperation among the members of the network (Goldfarb et al., 1986).

It may happen that although some solutions proposed during the brainstorming session have the advantage of a good costs/benefits ratio, they cut out the network even though they have been devised internally to it. For example, the members of the network may think it a good solution to 'find a place for the old man in a nursing home' or 'have a mentally ill relative admitted to a long-term care facility' or 'consult a psychologist' or 'get the police to arrest the drug pusher' or 'ask the town council to do something about people who are HIV-positive', and so on. Each of these solutions highlights the prevalence in the network of exogenous expectations, in the sense that the network expects the problem to be dealt with by an external agency. This attitude is passive; or rather, the network is active in its mental production of the solution but then asks for the solution to be implemented outside its boundaries. The solutions suggested may even be acceptable, but only provided they are not exclusive, and thus leave space for action by the network. If the proposal to consult a psychologist means that the latter is supposed to solve the problem, then it is a bad proposal. If it instead means that the network wants to have a psychologist as one of its members because his or her presence will improve its performance, then the situation is entirely different. The same applies to the request by the network for the town council to do something. If the intention is to involve the local authority in the network's activities, then the proposal is acceptable. And so on.

Other solutions suggested during brainstorming may confine action to the network – that is, they assign action exclusively to the network's members. Solutions of this kind, however, may differ in terms of the amount of cooperation (interaction) that their implementation requires. For example, if it is decided that the needs of a learning disabled child can be best met if his mother 'quits her job and stays at home', this solution does indeed restrict the action to the network (assuming that the mother has taken part in devising the solution), but it concentrates such action on only one of its members. As we know, centralization of this kind is hazardous. It is therefore up to the expert, while assessing solutions and choosing among them, to guide the coping network towards decisions that fulfil the criterion of the greatest amount of cooperation possible in those particular circumstances.

The criteria that should guide the choice of a solution in this phase of the problem-solving process facilitates those involved in their selection. By urging the network to respect these criteria, the expert performs a methodological function which increases the likelihood that efficacious choices will be made. Yet there is another function that the expert must perform during this phase, a function which concerns how (rather than what) to choose, and which we may call meta-methodological. The expert is responsible not only for ensuring that the network chooses solutions which involve it as much as possible in their subsequent implementation, but also for ensuring that the decision has been taken by the network as such. How has it been decided that this solution is better than the others? Has the decision been truly 'relational' in the sense that it comprises the opinions and feelings of the greatest number? Have the majority of the network's members been able to express their points of view?

Often, decisions which solicit action by a network have not been taken by the network but by one of its most influential members, or even by the expert. Some of the people present – perhaps even the majority of them – have had the solution imposed upon them. In this case it is not the network that chooses; the network is only the container in which the choice is made (by someone). The expert-as-guide must make sure that this, the most delicate phase of the problem-solving process does not drift towards an individualistic configuration. If this happens, inappropriate messages will be transmitted: that the network has limited intelligence, in the sense that its capacity to understand is not shared, but concentrated in one particular person; that the majority of its members are mere executors unable to think for themselves. The expert must prevent the choice from becoming a hasty decision taken by one member of the network with which the others merely comply. To do this s/he must try to ensure that, potentially, all the persons concerned are aware that they are taking a decision, that they can and must speak their minds, and so on. The expert must skilfully counteract domineering personalities, which may be those of colleagues with prestigious roles, and encourage/support weak or intimidated personalities.

It does not necessarily follow that if everyone in the network has their say, conflicts will arise to complicate the entire process. Often, an immediate sense of common purpose is created, even if everyone expresses their opinions, given that what should be done is obvious. All the intelligences involved, no matter how numerous, may converge, either spontaneously or through reasoning and discussion. This may happen but it may not. If unanimity is not forthcoming, the expert can at least obviously steer the network towards the most relational method of decision-making: the democratic method of putting the matter to the vote.

Once the decision has been taken, the expert must encourage the network to remain at the reflective stage as long as necessary, dissuading it from rushing headlong into action. As we have seen, when a complex solution has been selected, the related problem of how to implement it – of what strategies, devices or techniques to employ – may arise. The expert refers to the network any sub-problems correlated with the solution, so that the network addresses them and solves them.

3.5.3.5. Applying the solution, dealing with related problems and evaluation

Having reached this stage of the process, the network has a clear idea of what action should be taken – what I have called the solution – and also a set of more specific goals, which are the small-scale solutions to problems correlated with the main one. Each goal requires action by some member of the network, or by several of them together, so that it becomes clear, or relatively clear, who must do what, how, when, and if possible why.

Let us return to the example of Michela, the eight-year-old girl suffering abuse, and Alfonso her abusing stepfather. If the solution, as we have seen, is to reorganize the family network so that there is always someone able to police and dissuade between Michela and Alfonso, those involved should by now also know how this strategy will be implemented.

It may be agreed, for example, that before the mother goes out of the house and leaves Michela on her own, she will always call in an aunt or a neighbour or anyone else who has declared their willingness to help; that Michela must avoid her stepfather when he approaches her; that the mothers of her schoolmates will take turns to bring Michela home after school when her mother is unable to do so herself; that someone will try to persuade Alfonso to talk to a psychiatrist, who has already agreed to treat him at fortnightly counselling sessions; that Michela should go on summer camp with a voluntary association for twenty days and then attend a day centre (this latter proposal was made by the expert, who in this case was the community social worker).

During the implementation stage, the expert must ensure that the shared action is adequately defined, and that there is sufficient co-ordination and planning (sufficient, note, nothing more). The moment has now come to put what the network has decided into practice. In addition to the cognitive work of all the previous stages, there is now the operational work of concrete action focused on the unsatisfactory reality of the problem. The network has devoted cognitive effort to mapping out a feasible scenario of action. It must now get to work. Each person concerned will do or not do, do well or do badly, what they previously decided in their capacity as members of the network. According to the type of task and the type of network, action by individual members may vary greatly: it may be simple and brief, or it may be something more complex and permanent requiring concentration, application and ingenuity.

The expert in his/her capacity as a member of the network will also have something specific to do, if this has been agreed. Otherwise s/he will concentrate on the more demanding tasks of observing and guiding – or, put otherwise, monitoring the action as a whole and providing feedback. While the actions agreed are being implemented, problems associated with them may emerge concerning some person or persons in particular. The expert must determine whether the network as a whole is aware of these problems – and not just the person(s) concerned – and that it is doing something about them. If the network is indeed doing something, then the expert need only help the process along. If it is not, s/he must direct the network's attention to the problems so that it recognizes them and takes action to deal with them.

Besides monitoring in the form of watching for possible difficulties in the implementing of individual actions, there is a deeper-lying monitoring which consists in overseeing the route or direction followed by the action as a whole. Is the network proceeding towards the outcome desired? Is the situation evolving as expected? If not, is there reason to worry and tell those concerned? Or would it be better to wait, in the hope that things will work out by themselves? We may call this process 'evaluation', by which is meant not only the final review of how things have gone but also continuous appraisal while they are unfolding. How things have gone may in many cases be self-evident. It is more difficult to construe the signals of their satisfactory progress during the initial and intermediate phases, when these signals may be still weak and ambiguous.

3.5.4. *A word of caution on the problem-solving procedure*

The most striking aspect of the problem-solving procedure is its extreme methodicalness. There is nothing wrong with this, given that problem-solving is a method. But methodicalness may get out of hand and lapse into over-fussiness. The reader should therefore not take what has been said too literally. I would emphasise once again that not necessarily, and not in every intervention, must the expert and the network meticulously move through each canonical stage of the problem-solving procedure described. Sometimes, the outcomes typical of each stage arise spontaneously, or almost. The process flows smoothly along and no deliberate effort is required to define the problem, for example, or to evaluate the alternatives. What it is sensible or opportune to do is obvious, or becomes evident with little effort, so that it is not necessary to apply the relevant procedure, nor for the expert to guide the network towards that procedure. It is obvious, however, that while the expert

TABLE 3.4

**Comparison between traditional problem-solving
and relational problem-solving**

	Simple linear method	*Joint (network) method*	*Key questions*
Defining the problem	The expert states the problem clearly in operational terms.	The expert steers the network towards perceiving and formulating the problem as a coping problem (for the network itself).	What should we tackle together?
Brainstorming	The expert calls to mind any idea (however bizarre) that might constitute a 'solution'.	The expert prompts the network to come up with any idea (however bizarre) that might theoretically constitute a 'solution'.	What potential actions could we take to solve the problem?
Analysing and criticism of the possible solutions	The expert weighs the pros and cons of every solution imagined.	The expert guides the network as it weighs the pros and cons of the various solutions imagined.	What advantages/ disadvantages can we see deriving from this or that action?

Choosing the solution	The expert makes up his/her mind and chooses the solution.	The expert guides the network as it decides which solution is the most suitable (if necessary by means of the democratic method of putting it to the vote).	So which of these various solutions is the best for us?
Anticipating possible new problems	The expert considers what possible future problems s/he may encounter when applying the solution and solves them.	The expert guides the network towards identification of possible problems or other decisions to be dealt with before implementing the solution.	Is there any other problem that we should deal with?
Implementing the solutuion	The expert does what s/he has decided to do.	The expert guides the network as it implements the solution that it has agreed.	Is what each of us must do clear? Are we all doing or able to do what we have decided?
Perceiving further problems	The expert deals with any further problems that may have arisen.	The expert guides the network as it deals with difficulties resulting from implementation of the solution.	What unexpected situations have arisen that we must now deal with?
Evaluation	The expert conducts final assessment in order to verify that the problem (the situation) has been resolved.	The expert guides the network as it assesses the congruity of the new situation with the old one.	Have we achieved what we wanted?

is guiding the network towards the solution, s/he should check that the essential logical steps of problem-solving have been fulfilled. This monitoring should always be performed; but then, if it is not necessary to spend effort to ensure that every step is covered so much the better.

3.6. Formalization of relational guidance

Let us summarize. A social worker gets together with a set of people confronted by a task about which they are aware to a greater or lesser extent. The action that springs from the interweaving of these various entities and their reciprocal influence is true *social* work, that is, the social that works. If this work and the consequent modification of reality is directed towards a goal – in other words, if on one side or the other (but broadly speaking mainly on the expert one) there is some degree of intentionality and purposiveness – we may speak of professional guidance.

A further key aspect to consider is the variation in this degree of intentionality and therefore in the extent to which the guidance functions are formalized. Not all guided networks are equal in this respect; indeed, they may differ greatly. To clarify matters, we may imagine a continuum which stretches from interventions with the minimum amount of structured guidance, at one end, to ones with a maximum amount at the other (see Figure 3.15). According to whether social networking action lies at one extreme or the other, it assumes very different features.

By 'degree of structuring in guidance' is meant a mix of features; a state of affairs midway between (a) the extent to which the guider (expert) is aware of what s/he is doing; (b) the extent to which the network realizes that it is being guided and accepts it; (c) the extent to which the guidance function is externally conditioned, and in particular the extent to which it is imposed by the networker's professional role in the agency for which s/he works.

3.6.1. *Networking with a low level of initial obligation: networks for community development*

Located at the extreme left of the continuum is a broad category of social interventions which share a feature in common: they are indeterminate to the maximum degree, both as regards their causes (the reasons why they have been implemented) and their goals (the activities which will be implemented). Whether we observe them when they are already in progress, or when they have been completed, or when they are only hypothesised and have yet to come into being, the processes triggered by these interventions are free from external conditioning. That is to say, they are free to develop according to the internal circumstances of the situation that has produced them – although it would be more appropriate to say that they *should* be free to develop as they wish lest they rapidly peter out.

These social initiatives, however important and worthwhile, may not exist. They are optional events: if they exist, then so much the better; if they do not,

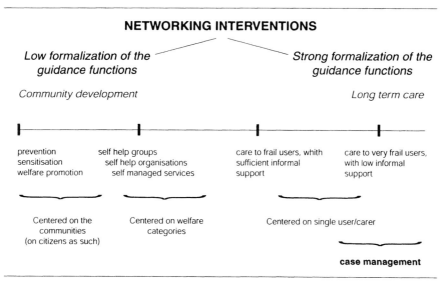

Fig. 3.15 Typology of network interventions according to their degree of structuring.

then (literally) nobody is going to die. They are a bonus, or even in certain cases a luxury, for a given area or local community. Nobody can demand them, because if they were the object of *specific* demands (imposed by law for example) they would be unlikely to come about.

Concrete examples of initiatives of this kind are community schemes intended to change (or influence) citizens. They may also merge pre-politically with community action, thereby generating the collective processes of consciousness raising or socio-political emancipation described by Alinski (1971). More precisely, these initiatives should be related to the community development, the enhancement of community spirit or of solidarity among citizens (Chaskin et al., 1997). They include sensitization or prevention campaigns, advocacy projects, and so on. Lying further to the right along the continuum are schemes targeted on specific categories of users. In this case the aim of the community action – of many persons in a network, or in a network of networks – is to foster the growth of self-managed social services or policy-making programmes, mainly in the form of self advocacy and mutual support (Barnes, 1996).

If we inquire as to the source of these initiatives, we find that they are bottom-up processes: they are not the result of authoritative input set out in laws or plans or projects by policy-makers and then implemented (this is obvious, otherwise it would be statutory not community action, and therefore would not be networking). These initiatives are kept going – at least in their initial stages – mainly through the efforts of voluntary action (even if they are promoted by professionals). Nobody forces (nor could they) these people to contribute their time and energy. They do what they do freely and willingly for the most disparate of reasons: a sense of civic duty, gratification (sometimes of a questionable nature), pride, self-interest, and so on. Many of them are not paid, nor do they expect to be. They are not answerable to anyone for the success or otherwise of the undertaking.

Relatively unstructured networks like these do not usually deliver statutory services. Their action – in keeping with their voluntary nature – proceeds largely unrestricted by the narrow confines of role.

As for relational guidance functions – these too can emerge spontaneously. That it is the expert (or lay person) who pulls the strings may be something that is not decided but comes about by itself. Sometimes a certain amount of bargaining may be necessary among the members of the network, but more frequently guidance arises as natural leadership. It may sometimes be performed unknowingly, in which case one talks not of network intervention but of a simple social process because intentionality is lacking. Sometimes guidance may be scattered among several subjects so that it is actually non-existent.

Let us look at an example.

> Augusto is the director of a third-sector agency contracted by the local authority to provide assistance to non-European immigrants in the form of accommodation and walk-in help. For some time Augusto has been thinking of launching (on his own initiative) a campaign in a neighbourhood of the city to make the local population more welcoming, or at least less hostile, to the immigrants living in the agency's hostels located in the area.

This task is neither written nor imposed by the contract with the city council. Of course, if the co-operative succeeded in its project, the result would take pride of place in its annual statement. If it did not, nothing would happen. Nobody expects a campaign of this kind to be mounted, so that it would be a bonus if it actually happened.

> The workers in Augusto's non-profit organisation are stretched to the limit by their day-to-day jobs. And the director thinks it a bad idea to burden them further with the project and force them to neglect their work. He has therefore shelved the idea for the time being, also because the resources for the project would have to be found outside the agency. One day he bumps into a former friend from university, now a teacher and the vice-headmaster

of a lower secondary school. During their conversation, Augusto discovers that the friend had a lively interest in social issues and every year sets study projects for his pupils on emerging problems. Last year, for example, he organized a project on drug addiction; the year before on violence in the family. This year the topic is immigration. Augusto immediately sees an opportunity to involve his friend's school in his sensitization campaign. He imagines involving the pupils first, followed by their parents (with some sort of show put on by the immigrants), and then other people in the neighbour-hood (other students/parents from other schools). He asks his teacher friend if they can do something together, and if they can meet in a few days time to discuss the project.

At this point, we shall shift to the temporal dimension to project us into the future. How will Augusto's friend's respond? If he says 'no', for example because he has too many things to do, then the matter will go no further. But if he says 'yes', that he would be happy to involve his school in the project, then the ground has been prepared for the process to begin (nothing else, but this will do for the time being). If this happens, Augusto immediately asks two repre-sentatives of the largest foreign communities in the city to take part in the project. He thus sets a networking process in train although he cannot predict its eventual outcome.

What will happen in, say, three months' time? Will something similar to what Augusto imagines come about, or something different, or nothing at all? Will Augusto be the guide for the initiative, or will it be his teacher colleague, or someone else? Will the scheme achieve its purpose? All these questions depend on answers which for the moment are not forthcoming, but this does not matter.

3.6.2. *Networking with a high level of obligation: long-term care networks*

Located towards the other end of the continuum are network projects which still possess the flexibility and indeterminacy of the ones discussed above, but differ from them in that these features are more and more conditioned by the objective or the final outcome as one moves towards the extreme. Although these forms of networking may articulate themselves and define themselves in different ways, they must obligatorily perform certain functions and achieve their purpose. If they do not, then the networking method can legitimately be jettisoned and the work done by other means, for example by having users admitted to residential facilities.

These are interventions that concern themselves with the most intractable of care situations. Unlike the ones discussed above, they are aimed at achieving, not

222 / RELATIONAL SOCIAL WORK

desirable communitarian (collective) states, but *necessary* personal ones (necessary, that is, for the survival of the minimum of dignity of the persons concerned).

Long-term care, even irreversible care in the sense that there is no hope of its ever becoming unnecessary, is the kind of intervention that falls in this category (Kerson and Kerson, 1985). The users are non-self-sufficient elderly people, the severely disabled, mentally ill people, or people with severe learning disabilities (Malin, 1995) The needs of these users are absolute because they determine survival itself. And satisfaction of those needs should also be all-important for those responsible for them. In the absence of a family or an informal network, the local authority, directly or via independent providers, must take responsibility (Freedman, 1993).

The network approach postulates that care for these persons should be provided in their own environment, preferably in their homes, without subjecting them to the 'blanket' security offered by residential institutions. However, this raises the problem of the responsibility and of the degree of *acceptable* security (which need not be *total*) which networking must nevertheless guarantee. Numerous agents, and numerous fragments of care, set to work and interweave with the largest possible degree of freedom but subject to a constraint that must, in principle, be absolute. This constraint is that the fragments must pull together to form a unitary and meaningful whole. Maximum freedom in procedures must combine with its opposite: the absolute obligation to achieve results. Nobody with institutional responsibility (social workers, administrators, policy makers, etc.) can take this matter lightly: the network must function properly and guarantee the provision of care.

If an elderly man is bed-ridden and therefore needs someone to look after him twenty-four hours a day, the network may do what it wants (indeed, it *must* be free to do what it wants) but only provided the man receives the minimum quality standard of care. A freedom which does not achieve that precise result is pointless, even though conceptually it is so important that, as we have seen, it is the defining property of the networking approach. If the elderly man is neglected by the coping network to such an extent that he suffers, or even dies, from his point of view and also objectively no theory can convince us that residential care would not be much better.

Obviously, in a network responsible for long-term care, the action may not be voluntary in nature. So much the better if a network comprises people who give care because they want to, and are happy to do so, or if these people can be found outside the natural network. If this is not the case, then it will be necessary to foster responsibility and motivation in the customary manner, reimbursing the carers for their expenses or partly paying them for their services. Or it may be necessary to call in public practitioners who act out of official duty and the binding responsibilities of their role.

3.6.2.1. Case management

A caring network, however fragmented, must function properly. We know that it can function on its own if the informal predominates. It may function with the unobtrusive and occasional guidance of an expert if this suffices. If not, if the network is inadequate or is stuck, when it is instead *necessary* that it should function, then someone, usually a professional, must assume specific *responsibility for guidance* on behalf of the local authority that employs him/her (or for which s/he works on a contractual or freelance basis). In the ideal-typical situations at the extreme of the continuum, when fate decrees that the severe personal conditions of the user combine with the fragility of the helping network, the expert who tackles the situation and sets about networking must officially assume the guiding role. S/he must be formally appointed as guide, and be accepted as such by the partners in the network. The more navigation is insidious, the more guidance entails the assumption of a binding accountability which cannot be shared with the other members of the network (at least initially). An expert who guides a network in this constrained and formal manner can be called the 'case manager'.

Without going into the methodological details of the well-known case management procedure (Weil et al., 1985; Davies and Challis, 1986; Challis and Davies, 1986; Rose, 1992; Orme and Glastonbury, 1993; Quinn, 1993; Payne, 1995; Siegal and Rapp, 1995) it is evident that a number of general problems arise at this point. These problems are most apparent in the case of highly professionalized coping networks: that is, when a case manager must work together with colleagues from a mix of different agencies and also assess their performance. When the guiding expert is working in largely informal circumstances and therefore interacting with non-professionals, s/he may find it easier to gain acceptance as the guide because it is obvious to everyone that s/he is the expert.

3.6.2.2. The problem of inter-professional collaboration: networking and teamwork

If other professionals are part of the network as the deliverers of specialized services – and if there are many of them, as likely if the situation is serious – matters grow more complex. On what basis does an expert act as guide, given that the other members of the network are experts as well? Who among all of them should be the guide? In some cases the answer will come automatically without discussion being necessary. In others it will be necessary to reach an agreement so that the distinction between the guide and all the others is made clear.

Furthermore, when the guide has been chosen and recognized, will there be collaboration? Each professional member of a care network must *recognize* the higher-rank responsibility of the colleague acting as the guide and feel the *obligation* – in the technical sense of *deontology* – to join in with the network and act collaboratively. These professionals should not find it too difficult to accept these conditions, given that the colleague who acts as guide must obviously be acquainted with the principles of guidance (otherwise s/he would be self-contradictory): s/he will know about the feedback principle and will therefore also be aware that direction by fiat must be avoided because this is perhaps the main cause of conflict. Therefore, given the combination of (a) the fact that the guide will take care not to bruise the sensibilities of his/her colleagues and not to trespass on their autonomy (but, if all goes well, enhance it) with (b) the fact that these colleagues cannot give free rein to their personal concerns or place overriding importance on their autonomy, then probably, thanks to the synergy between the two circumstances, things will go as they should. The network should function properly even though it is burdened by the weight of its tasks, as well

TABLE 3.5
Summary of concepts

Networks with minimum obligations	*Networks with maximum obligations*
• The network's action is free and largely undetermined.	• The network's action has a low (but never nil) level of indeterminacy.
• The aim is mainly to promote the growth in the community of new initiatives, services and attitudes (community development).	• The aim is mainly to provide long-term care for users suffering from severe or extremely severe disabilities.
• Initiatives are optional and depend on the availability of natural resources in the local community (it may happen that no results are achieved).	• Initiatives are the statutory duty of the public welfare system and depend on formal resources (objectives must necessarily be achieved).
• Action is largely voluntary.	• There is little (but never nil) voluntary action.
• Initiative and key decisions are bottom-up.	• Initiative may be top-down (duty-bound).
• The role of network-guiding expert is not formalized. It usually arises spontaneously within the network (often in the form of natural leadership).	• The role of the network-guiding expert must be formalized (perhaps as case manager). It may sometimes be assigned by virtue of professional role or it must be agreed by the members of the network.
• The network furnishes little or no specialized care. Actions are minimally defined according to role (whence the importance of the activation function).	• The network may provide a great deal of specialized care. Many of its actions are role-prescribed (whence the importance of the co-ordination function).

as by the potential confusion caused by the interweaving of so many professional roles.

But this is the situation that is hoped for, the one that ought to be the case. Matters may turn out otherwise. A correct relational attitude by the individual professionals so that their cooperation combines with a solid ethical sense of propriety may not come about, or it may not be enough. A long-term care network cannot base itself solely on a commitment to cooperate by each professional because otherwise the damage caused would be too severe (Fried and Cook, 1996).

At this point it is necessary to highlight the (obvious) difference between networking and teamwork. A multi-professional team consists of practitioners with different skills and roles who work for the same large agency or for different agencies in the locality (West, 1994). They are usually co-ordinated by a service manager who is empowered to require each of them to comply with the strategic and functional purposes that s/he has in mind. In networking everything is less structured, and therefore often more complicated; it is looser than a simple 'care package' or 'open teamwork' (Payne, 2000). The professionals who come together in a coping network not only belong to different services but are matched by their 'natural' counterparts: the family, the community, and so on. All these components stand on an equal footing in principle (and also in practice, if the network functions properly). The hierarchical principle that drives a team does not apply in networking, where the emphasis is instead on collaboration among different workers in different organizations and among different types of people at the local level.

When scattered professionals are all involved in the same case, it is likely that each of them will have a single 'vertical' preoccupation: to deliver the specific provision for which they have been given responsibility by their employer. Each of them is duty-bound to provide his/her services but not duty-bound to collaborate with other members of the network. If a practitioner does not feel responsible for interprofessional cooperation, what can be done? The presence of a guide who knows what to do usually increases the likelihood of cooperation, but not always. When the interlocutors are the guide's colleagues – experts like him/her or even more so – and do not see the need for cooperation or reject it, what can be done?

The relational discretion of the practitioners – that is, their freedom to decide whether or not to cooperate or to work on line – should be codified in some way. But if this disciplining of professional interaction becomes too restrictive, if the practitioners involved lose their will to interact because they find it meaningful, or alternatively if protocol and 'defensive' compliance with procedures prevails, the elementary conditions for networking break down.

3.7. Summary

The guidance-relation is the crucial link between a natural helping network and an expert who knows how to deploy one. By means of this linkage – and the subsequent provision of guidance by the expert – the natural network is helped to *restructure* itself. In other words, it is helped to alter its structure so that it can address its task better, steer itself towards solution of the problem, and undertake meaningful and adequately end-directed action (problem-solving). The expert for his/her part is assisted by the network in performance of his/her institutional role, which is to solve or reduce the problems of his/her users or the community in which s/he works.

Guidance by the expert is a deliberate undertaking which requires a good deal of expertise. In particular, the expert must know the *retroaction rule*: that is, the principle whereby a social worker acts mainly through feedback and not through prescriptions. Feedback may involve weak or latent information transmitted by the network to the expert so that it acts as a *stimulus* for activities that the network has not yet begun. Or it may involve more explicit information on actions already undertaken by the network so that the feedback assumes the more canonical guise of *reinforcement* for decisions or actions deemed appropriate to the *goals* pursued.

By means of guidance, the expert may support indefinite processes where the network's freedom of action is maximum, or more controlled processes where the obligation of providing a *secure* care structure is binding (for example, when care is provided for severely handicapped or house-bound people). In these cases, an expert who wants to exploit the potential of networking in terms of flexibility, creativity, extra resources, common-sense, and so on, must assume formal responsibility for the efficacy/efficiency of the network as a whole by taking on the role of case manager.

A case manager must engage wholly in networking and interact with all his/her interlocutors. S/he must not be a mere system organizer. Of course, it may happen that circumstances force the case manager to intervene prescriptively (not reactively) when urgent decisions are necessary. However, a professional's sense of reality should outweigh his/her observance of methodological procedure; or better, the latter should be at the service of the former. If the expert decides that the networking approach should be abandoned to ensure minimum standards of security – when it becomes clear that an unstructured approach may in certain circumstances not offer sufficient guarantees – then it should indeed be discarded. But this should take place in the awareness that this is not social work and that it is therefore necessary to proceed with circumspection.

CHAPTER 4

Case studies

Networking best practices described
from the experts' view

4.1. Introduction

The purpose of this, the last part of the book is to illustrate the concepts discussed thus far from a different perspective: that of the social worker who puts them into practice. It addresses the following questions. What is meant by saying, not in abstract but in concrete terms, that a social problem is an event that emerges from relations or the absence of relations? What is meant by saying that it is unproductive for a social worker to treat a problem as the business of one person, or even several persons, but always taken individually? What is meant by saying that the solution is not distinct from the problem but is simply a different future arrangement of it? What is meant by saying that processes of this kind must be 'guided'? These and other questions, however abstruse, are so evidently bound up with the tangible reality of social work that it is possible to adduce numerous examples to clarify them. Here I shall provide only some such examples, taken somewhat at random, in order to illustrate and supplement the abstract notions discussed hitherto.

One of the main aims of this part of the book is to draw a dividing line between clinical treatment and social work. It endeavours in particular to differentiate between two areas where confusion seems inevitable in that both adopt the same underlying orientation, namely the relational approach. I said earlier that the relational orientation assumes systemic features in the clinical field, while in the social one such features become increasingly 'reticular', which is to be relational in the true sense of the word. In this part of the book I shall strive to make this crucial distinction clear.

The systemic approach concerns itself with understanding and modifying dysfunctional individual states (symptoms) caused by closed and fixed relations. These states are imagined to be located within the person who manifests them (they belong either to the emotional-affective or cognitive-behavioural domain, or more often to both). Relations enter the picture because they create the problem, but ultimately the problem is always (conceived as) an individual symptom. Intervention therefore consists not in coping – i.e. in undertaking a particular task – but in an attempt to modify relations *as such*. The intervention is narrowly restricted to reversing relations from what they have become, so that it ultimately seeks to reverse their individual effect. Technical action operates backwards: it attempts to restore a previous, more favourable situation, rather like bending a twisted piece of metal back into its original shape. When an expert uses the systemic approach, s/he already knows what the various people concerned should do (more or less).

The networking approach instead comes into play when shared action on a task is envisaged. For various reasons, this action has not yet been taken. Whence derives the problem and – although it is not known how it may arise – the solution. I shall not dwell on the individual inner states of the persons who take part in this process, nor on the rigidified configuration of their relationships called a 'system'.

The next three sections enter the social sphere and therefore the true domain of networking. Examples will be provided of three forms of relational guidance in settings where social work takes place: education, long term care and community development. The socio-educational example (the case of Marco, the classroom clown) will provide a bridge between the systemic and networking approaches, in the sense that the joint action undertaken by the coping network that sought to solve this particular problem was intended to deal creatively with a superordinate systemic dysfunction which apparently created individual dysfunction in Marco.

4.2. Marco and his behaviour problems in the classroom: a socio-educational example

> Marco is a fifteen-year-old boy who has lived for the past year in a third-sector residential community home for minors. He was moved to this unit because of severe problems in his family: his drug-addicted father has served repeated prison sentences for small-scale drug dealing and recently tested positively for HIV. Three years ago his mother moved in with another man, a habitual offender without a steady job. She too has had problems with drugs, as well as being involved in prostitution, which she may not have entirely left behind.

She now works in various casual jobs. Four years ago Marco was placed in the care of his maternal grandmother. However, partly because of health problems, she was unable to look after him properly, and he lived on the streets until a social worker was able to find him a place in the community unit.

Three months ago Marco began attending lower secondary school (after repeating two years at elementary school). Giovanni, the social worker responsible for coordinating the agency, has talked to Marco's teachers on several occasions. Today he has received a telephone call from the headmaster, who wants to talk to him.

Giovanni ponders Marco's case on his way to the school. Despite his poor academic performance, Marco is a gifted child, a factor that perhaps makes his situation even more difficult. Compared with his classmates, Marco has had much more experience of life, with overwhelming problems of which he must nevertheless make sense. His personality has been marked accordingly. Whether the damage is irremediable or whether there is still some hope for Marco is impossible to say.

Some of Giovanni's colleagues are angry that it took so long to refer Marco to the residential unit, but nothing can be done about that now. Marco's relationships, his educational failings, his role models are now a matter of fact. Nothing that has happened to him can been undone; and even if it could be, the undertaking would serve little purpose. The forces of Marco's past have shaped him into what he is today. Moreover, his difficulty is not focal but affects his entire personality; a personality in part already formed and in part still in the process of formation. There is no telling what the outcome will be.

Giovanni thinks to himself: until Marco was thirteen years old he was left alone amid his hardly salubrious family relationships. When it became clear that the malfunctioning of these relationships had produced a dysfunctional child, it was decided to remove him from his family and place him in a 'therapeutic' environment where he was entrusted to the tender mercies of us specialized social workers and educationists. And yet, because we have studied and earned our professional qualifications, everyone thinks that we can do more than we are actually capable of. People think: 'Now they'll deal with it'. The headmaster, too, is going to say: 'Please do something, we don't know what do. We can't cope with Marco'.

Even though this is what everyone expects – Giovanni reflects – we social workers cannot take on everything that others delegate to us. It would be wrong to consider us technicians specialized in personality repair. If that were the case, what sort of social workers would we be? For fully thirteen years a set of natural relationships have worked day and night to turn Marco into what he is. How many years of our artificial relationships will it take to change him?

My psychologist friends working as specialists in the Social Services Departments are called upon to deal with highly specific matters: a phobia, a particular type of behaviour, an idea, and so on. When I talk to them, they tell me that they are often unable to alter even these circumscribed problems by means of therapy. They have to work obliquely on natural relationships. So what can we social workers do, who have to deal with the entire personality, and with the impact of that entire personality on relationships? We have to tackle problems head-on. Specialists worry about how particular structures of relations create a particular human symptom, and therefore about how these structures can be reversed or steered in a different direction. We cannot work so subtly. The relationships of our kids are not dysfunctional in only one of their components: indeed, they often give the impression of being utterly inadequate.

From our point of view, Giovanni muses, we educators can consider ourselves (if we wish) to be the *linchpins* of the most difficult re-education projects. For this reason these projects should involve *external* society; if they do not, we will be crushed under the weight. Or in order to protect ourselves, we shall have to rid ourselves of them as soon as possible. The rehabilitation of a young person is a *common good*, not just because it helps those concerned but also because it is beneficial to society as a whole. The point is, though, that this good can only be achieved by *joint* endeavour. Only through the shared effort of some external *community* can it be obtained. Marco should begin to relive his life by being stimulated to re-orient himself by a new and hopefully healthy environment – or at least one healthier than the one he is in now.

Nobody knows *a priori* what incentives or what forms of help will work with Marco. Nor does anybody know how to offer them without Marco spurning them. But we do know that the help must be *multiple*, in order to counteract the manifold harmful influences that have damaged the boy. Reasoning *ecologically*, the closer the involvement of healthy settings, the more it is likely that virtuous processes – ones unthinkable at the moment – will be gradually set in train. In concrete terms, the more the school, the parish, sports clubs and cultural associations, local families, and so on, can be involved, the better things will be. Our organisation should be at the centre of this interweaving set of positive influences. We social workers will still have a great deal to do. As well as our primary task (monitoring children, educating them, etc.), we must stimulate, link together, support and supervise other actors that could be involved. What we will do is only *part* of what will be done overall.

There are risks in this 'networking' strategy, of course, thinks Giovanni. The main one is that placing Marco in healthy but not particularly robust settings may achieve the opposite of what is expected. It may happen that these settings will be disrupted or impaired, and therefore fail to exercise a beneficial influence on Marco. The boy's personality and relational power – a power deriving from his anomie, from his belief that he is not subject to rules – may prevail over the less forceful personalities in the natural environment in which he has been introduced.

'What do you think has happened in Class 1b where Marco is now?' Giovanni asks himself. 'Precisely this: Marco has sparked off a *social* problem, an ecological upset in the entire school as well as outside it. It is certainly this that the headmaster (I'm about to enter his office) wants to talk to me about.'

The headmaster's first words to Giovanni are as expected. 'Things can't go on like this. Since the beginning of the school year, Marco has gone from bad to worse. He constantly misbehaves in class. Especially with the Italian teacher, a young woman, maybe, but able to cope even though she's a novice.'

> The Italian teacher is also in the office. She tells Giovanni that she has reached the end of her tether. She has tried every form of punishment she knows (detention, warnings, black marks in the class register) but to no avail. Now she proposes that Marco should be suspended from school. She has never wanted things to come to this but now it is unavoidable. Marco must be kept away from school for a while. Perhaps this will make him understand.

Giovanni says that he appreciates the problem. He fully understands the situation in the classroom because crises sometimes erupt in the residential unit that he runs, and the only solution is to send those responsible away for a while. However, he asks the headmaster and the teacher to give him some time to assess the situation. With a boy like Marco, a drastic solution like suspension from school might have the opposite effect to the one desired. Giovanni makes a proposal: if the headmaster agrees, he will work with the teacher, and perhaps the other teachers of Class 1b, to see if together they can come up with a solution if one exists. His experience with severe behaviour problems may be of help. The headmaster decides to convene a meeting of all interested teachers for the following afternoon.

4.2.1. Creation of the intersubjective base for understanding the relational core of the problem, and of the early coping network

Giovanni is talking to the Italian teacher and the mathematics teacher (for some reason the others have not come to the meeting). The Italian teacher immediately starts to talk, giving vent to her anger and frustration.

She says that she has to shout from the moment she enters the class to the moment she leaves it. It's a constant battle. She tries to explain something, to call the children's attention to a point, and when it seems that the class is concentrating, Marco comes out with one of his wisecracks or starts acting the fool. The children laugh and the chaos resumes. Once again she has to shout at the children and threaten them with punishment, finally managing to restore order. She starts teaching again, perhaps turns her back to write something on the blackboard and all hell breaks loose once again.

Giovanni asks the teacher for her views on the problem. Her answer is as expected. In her opinion it is an individual problem: Marco and his constant fooling around are the cause of the difficulties in her class. It is he that is entirely to blame. His misbehaviour seems deliberate, it seems as if he enjoys what he does. Indeed, it seems as if he plans his actions and that creating chaos is his *objective*.

The solution proposed by the teacher is suspension. She expects nothing miraculous, but at least it is important to send out a signal, to halt the spiralling disintegration of the class. Probably, she says, the problem can only be effectively solved by getting at its roots: not punishment, therefore, but treatment. Perhaps some neurological or personality disorder is responsible for Marco's behaviour. She is not certain, but this might very well be the case: a personality disorder. Unfortunately, she does not know of a therapist able to take on a case as difficult as Marco. She knows from her colleagues that there have been problems in the past when specialists from the social services department have been called in. If there were a psychologist who could 'withdraw' Marco from the class for a term and then send him back 'restored', willing to cooperate and with his personality problems solved, that of course would be wonderful. But if this treatment is not possible, then the only answer is suspension.

While the teacher is talking, and then explaining the same things in different words, Giovanni reflects. It is obvious that the teacher is reasoning with common sense. But although her arguments are plausible, they are operationally unfeasible. The solution that springs from her view of the situation (take Marco to an eminent psychiatrist who will cure him) is not viable; it is merely a pious hope. The teacher is reasoning in individual terms, both as regards her explanation of the problem (the problem is Marco and his deviant behaviour) and its solution (the solution is intervention by an expert).

This is cause/effect linear logic: Marco causes the problem, the specialist changes Marco, the problem is solved. That Marco causes the problem is what appears on the surface, but beneath there lies a much more complex reality. In the first place, we have seen that Marco has been affected by a complicated web of past events triggered by his relationships; events which have acted on his

ACTION UNIT   **TASK**

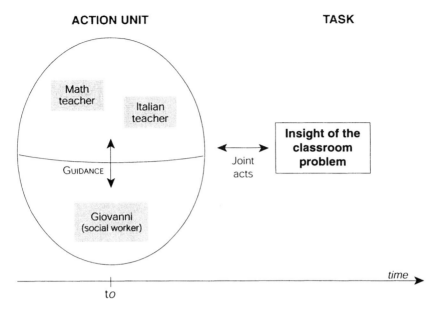

Fig. 4.1 The coping network at the beginning of the networking process (To).

personality and made him what he is. But apart from this consideration, which is of little interest to the teacher, it must be said that Marco's character is not the origin of the problem, in the sense of being the cause of an effect.

Marco is part of the problem, but he is one element in it among several. The chaos in the classroom is a *social* dysfunction because it involves all Marco's relationships, not just those circumscribed by the space/time of the class. This dysfunction concerns (a) the distress of the teacher *jointly with* (b) the distress of the many parents whose children are failing to learn *jointly with* (c) the distress of some children in the class who want to work and are unhappy about the disruption *jointly with* (d) the distress of the headmaster, who is accountable for the quality of the service provided by the school *jointly with* (e) the distress of the tutors who work with the children in the apartment unit, and so on. Perhaps, at bottom Marco too suffers to some extent. Although he appears to enjoy playing the fool, perhaps he feels unconsciously that he has no restraints, that he lives in a world in which there are no adults to understand and take care of him. He enjoys demonstrating his power to upset the teacher, but underneath he may feel alone, ignored by people with the strength and ability to give him security. If Marco is the cause of a problem, he is also one to himself.

From a different point of view, a class which fails to function properly, which is unable to assimilate Marco for all his personal difficulties, is a *social* problem for another reason. It testifies to a failure by society as a whole to *rescue* Marco as he drifts into deviance. Marco is being lost; he is sliding down a slippery slope. We educators, Giovanni thinks, have caught him at the last moment, but now other agencies and significant individuals must play their part. That the school feels that it is unable to cope, that it does not know how to act and asks to be relieved of the task, is a *social* dysfunction in two senses. Firstly in the generic sense that it is bad for society that this should happen, secondly in the specific sense that the problem stems from society itself. Compulsory school is a fundamental instrument of socialization (or in Marco's case of re-socialization), and the fact that a social agency of such importance is failing is the real problem to be addressed. Is it not Marco's fault that the institutions of society are unable to handle him.

But let us return to the class and to the turmoil apparently (that is, as far as can be seen) caused by Marco's misbehaviour. The teacher of mathematics now speaks, and he says something important. Yes, Marco misbehaves during his lessons as well, but not as badly as he does with the other teacher. It varies from day to day, but Marco is usually involved in the lessons and is responsive. Giovanni now asks the two teachers to look at what happens in the class from a different angle. He points out that the interpretation that Marco is to blame for everything that happens has led to solutions (warnings, punishments, etc.) which have not worked. It would therefore be helpful to look at the problem from a different perspective.

The social worker takes a sheet of paper and draws a diagram of what happens in the class (Fig. 4.2). He shows it to the Italian teacher and she agrees that this is the way that events unfold.

4.2.2. *Sharing the systemic nature of the Marco's individual problem*

The diagram depicts a set of relations. These relations constantly repeat themselves and grow increasingly stable. One may therefore say that they constitute a typical example of a *relational system*. The three components of this system (the teacher, Marco and the audience) weave together interactions which eventually condense into two main types of relation: a confrontation relation *(symmetrical)* between Marco and the teacher, and an acceptance relation *(complementary)* between Marco and the audience. Giovanni helps the headmaster and the two teachers to analyse these relations one by one.

The symmetrical relation between Marco and the teacher. Giovanni states a premise: looking at a relation means looking, not at the individual behaviours

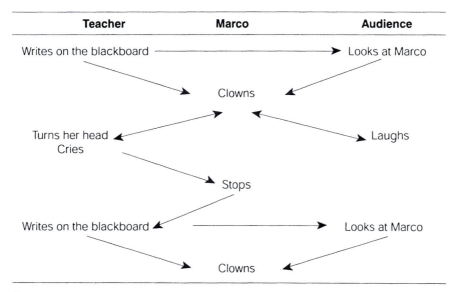

| Teacher | Marco | Audience |

Fig. 4.2 The relations in Marco's class plotted as a relational system.

of the two interacting persons but at how they interrelate with each other, at the interplay between them. If we look at individual behaviours it seems that one *causes* the other. For example, the fact that (a) the teacher turns to write on the blackboard seems (b) to trigger Marco's misbehaviour, and this in turns seems (c) to cause the teacher's angry reaction, and so on.

If instead we look at the relation structure, Giovanni asks, what do we see? The mathematics teacher, after a moment's bewilderment (he has never thought of behaviour in this way), remarks that the two persons seem to be attracted by their mutual *opposition*. This is what 'symmetrical relation' means, Giovanni points out, but what does this mean in more intuitive terms? The Italian teacher (on whom the discussion is focused and consequently feels somewhat flustered) replies that the two people are battling for *power*, and on an equal footing.

> In class, the teacher seems to say 'You must do what I tell you because you're subordinate to me', and Marco seems to reply, 'In reality I'm in the one in charge here. I decide whether we're going work or whether we're going to mess about'.

Marco and the teacher withdraw *status* and *affect* from one other, forcing the other into aggressive behaviour. The teacher seems to say: 'I don't respect you as a pupil, I don't accept you', and Marco seemingly retorts: 'I don't respect you and accept you as a teacher. I'm not interested in your lessons if you're unable to control me'. When a seesaw exchange like this begins, it never ends. Each party seeks to finish the contest in the uppermost position, but in this case the upper and lower positions cannot be accomplished once and for all. The contest continues as if driven by an inner dynamic.

Giovanni draws attention to the fact that so far it is not the relation between the teacher and Marco that has been analysed, but the relation between the teacher and Marco's disorder. In other words, they have only discussed what happens between the teacher and Marco in concomitance with every aspect of Marco's disruptive behaviour. But, Giovanni points out, relatively few of these open conflicts occur during a typical schoolday. What happens the rest of the time, when Marco (even he must catch his breath!) keeps quiet and behaves himself? Is there a relationship with Marco *independently* of his disorder? On reflection, the teacher is forced to admit that there is not. She is unable to see Marco in detachment from his disorder. When she meets him in the corridor or when he is behaving in class, she finds it difficult to treat him like any other pupil. Whenever she sees Marco, or even thinks about him, she grows irritated, not only by his behaviour but also by him as a person.

The complementary relation between Marco and the class. If Marco's classmates are viewed as constituting an 'individual', a relation structure very different from that with the teacher becomes apparent. After a moment's thought, Giovanni tries to explain. Whereas Marco and the teacher interrelate by opposing each other, Marco and the class interrelate by attracting each other. What Marco does is accepted by the class; and vice versa what the class does (laughs, approves, supports, etc.) suits Marco just fine. The class 'completes' Marco's behaviour, bringing it to full realization (in the language of behaviourism one would say that the class *reinforces* Marco's behaviour). Viewed in relational terms, Marco's tomfoolery and the laughter of his classmates constitute a unit. It is difficult to determine what causes what: whether the clowning causes the laughter or whether the laughter causes the clowning. The process is circular.

The mathematics teacher points out that Marco assumes the role of leader in the class; a role that would not exist if the followers did not complement it. Marco's classmates spur Marco into acting towards the teacher in a way that they could not (would not) contemplate. They prefer to keep their heads down. They want to enjoy the results of Marco's actions (entertainment, a break in boring routine, a vicarious challenge against authority, etc.) without suffering the consequences (loss of the teacher's esteem, punishment, etc.). They are able to conceal themselves behind the individualistic illusion. It seems that it is only Marco who challenges the teacher, only he is branded a deviant; he who has nothing to lose: neither the esteem of his parents, who are non-existent, nor of the teachers, who have never bothered about him. But in reality Marco and his audience constitute a unit.

The audience's behaviour forms a seamless whole with Marco's. By hiding behind Marco, his classmates also interact with the teacher. For that matter, if they were not present, the relationship between Marco and the teacher would not be fully understandable. The teacher's irate reaction is also provoked by the laughter of the class. If the class kept quiet, and showed more interest in her explanations than in Marco's clowning, would the teacher get so angry? Instead, the class's amused reaction to Marco's behaviour is also due to her reaction. If she did not react angrily and lose her temper when provoked by Marco, would his antics be so comical?

Giovanni says that he is satisfied with the way things are going. In order to gain further understanding of what is happening in the class, and from a different perspective, he proposes that they should concentrate on Marco (after all, he is the reason for the meeting) and perform an *empathy exercise*. Giovanni explains what this is: imagining yourself in the place of the person observed in order to see reality through his/her eyes: empathy, as native Americans say, is 'walking in the moccasins of the other'.

What does Marco actually feel, given the relation structure that surrounds him? The mathematics teacher speaks first. He says:

> If I were Marco I'd feel rejected by authority, by the teacher who represents the institutions in the classroom, and I'd instead feel attracted by the defeat-ist mentality of the audience. I'd feel rejected, attacked by an impotent authority, and it would be precisely this that gives me satisfaction. I could fight and show how strong I am. And in doing so, my role as leader of the class would be reinforced. I could boost my credibility as a delinquent. Whenever authority attacks me, tries to change me, I refuse to change and I come out the winner. The distance between me and authority increases and this consolidates my image as a delinquent, as someone able to challenge authority successfully. Whenever I get a black mark, whenever I'm sent to the headmaster, that's a campaign medal for me. In the eyes of my classmates (and also my mates in the neighbourhood when they hear what I've done) I gain more status if I get three black marks in a day instead of just one.

The Italian teacher listens to this analysis and gains some insight: now her problem seems (somewhat) more meaningful; now things are beginning to make sense. A deviance-fostering 'ecology' has been created in the classroom, a *relational system* which sucks everyone into it. The more she piles on the punishment, the more Marco becomes skilled in challenging her and getting away with it, to the noisy applause of the 'spectators'. It seems paradoxical, but the teacher has been acting as a sparring partner, as an expert coach who has refined Marco's anti-social skills. Quite contrary to her intentions, obviously. But Marco and the audience for their part have also acted as a sparring partner for the teacher, creating a dangerous situation in which her aggressive behaviour towards them has been exacerbated. Marco and the audience perform this role perfectly: they would, she says, try the patience of a saint. This realization consoles her some-what but she knows that it is no justification for her behaviour.

Her relationship with the class cannot be enacted like a normal relationship of everyday life: it is a professional relationship with specific obligations. If Marco implicitly communicates messages like 'You're worth nothing as a teacher, what you teach doesn't interest me', a professional cannot descend to the same level and reply 'You're a fool if you don't appreciate what I do, and I'll force you to respect me'. This reaction may be understandable on the human level, but it is a disaster on the professional one. The teacher realizes that she has fallen into a trap: she has been ensnared, so to speak, by the system of relations in her classroom.

4.2.3. Enlarging the pre-exixting coping network

Giovanni sums up the discussion so far. He points out that observation has shown that the disorder in the classroom is caused by everybody, and that respon-sibility for it must be apportioned among all those concerned, even though Marco's behaviour is its most evident manifestation. If the disorder (a) resides in numerous people (also outside the class), and (b) derives from direct and indirect interactions among these people, it is evident that it is a *social* disorder, one which is purely relational. It is also evident that change – improvement or resolution of the situation – can be introduced from various quarters. Change has numerous points of access to the system, although they are not yet known. And this is an important conclusion. The admission that it is not only Marco that must change, even though he is the toughest part of the conundrum, is an encouraging start.

Before moving to discussion of possible solutions, Giovanni says that there is still an important issue to resolve: what should be done about Marco's suspen-sion? The two teachers look at each other, and it is clear from the expressions on their faces that they have reached the same conclusion. After everything that has been said thus far, the Italian teacher says, it is obvious that suspension is not a good idea. It would simply be an exacerbation of the remedies tried so far (the shouting, the black marks in the class register, and so on), and these have already proved inadequate. If the wrong strategy is being used, implementing it even more stringently does not turn it into the right one (Watzlawick, 1988). If you try to unscrew a bolt in the wrong direction, the more force you use, the worse the situation becomes: not only do you waste your energy but you screw the bolt tighter. In the classroom, the more you insist on the wrong methods, the more you tighten the system and the more difficult it becomes to loosen it.

Giovanni now emphasises an idea that he thinks is important. In his view, the conclusions reached thus far cannot be generalized. Suspension in itself is neither a good thing nor a bad thing. He would not want the teachers to think that suspension is never a good idea. To be sure, less use should be made of it, because it is a drastic and unpleasant medicine to be used only as a last resort. But this is not to say that it is not sometimes necessary. Suspension will very probably have no effect on Marco, because we already know how he has reacted to it in the past, but it may be 'beneficial' for other children.

The mathematics teacher looks puzzled, so Giovanni elaborates on his explanation. A suspension can be effective only on one condition: that it removes status from the person concerned. When a headmaster orders 'For five days you must stay away from school', the child should feel diminished in his/her status and value. S/he should feel (and regret) that the punishment has reduced the esteem in which s/he is held by the headmaster and his/her parents – the esteem, that is, accorded him/her as a 'good student'. Suspension therefore presupposes that the recipient subscribes to the values system of the person who imposes it. But this is not the case of Marco. Things have deteriorated to such an extent, it seems, that he is utterly indifferent to the esteem of his teachers. And if esteem is entirely lacking, it cannot be taken away. By contrast, he is extremely concerned about the esteem that he finds on the other side of the 'divide', among his classmates. Indeed, a deviant may be defined as someone who in his/her mind and reference (sub)culture converts official disesteem into esteem.

The effectiveness of a suspension depends on the *relation* with the recipient, and with Marco it may prove to be a high-risk strategy (McManus, 1995). 'What can be done, then?', asks the Italian teacher. Giovanni replies that coming up with an answer to her question will require another meeting, and perhaps more than one.

* * *

Giovanni asks the teachers to think about who else could be involved. The more people present at the next meeting the better, because a wide range of ideas will be needed. He also asks the Italian teacher to write a summary of the conclusions reached at today's meeting to assist those who may come to the next one.

On his way home, Giovanni has good reason to feel satisfied. Things have gone much better than he expected. He has had the good fortune to find two teachers willing to cooperate. Especially the Italian teacher – the one more emotionally involved in the problem – who listened to what he had to say without raising too many objections. After starting with the unshakeable belief that the fault lay entirely with Marco, and that it was only Marco that had to change, she immediately grasped the 'ecological' idea that the problem instead consisted of everyone concerned. Helped by her colleague, she accepted that her own aggressive behaviour was not unrelated to the problem. She had already realized on her own that punishment was failing to work. During the discussion she was ready to go further and accept that it was precisely the punishment that was the problem and that new solutions were needed.

Giovanni is too well acquainted with the world of the school not to recognize his good fortune at finding a flexible and motivated teacher, one ready to question her own behaviour. He could just as easily have found a tired, demotivated teacher, constantly on the defensive, or so angry that s/he would accept only solutions 'against' Marco which increased his punishment or his isolation. That this has not happened – although Marco has done everything possible to bring it about in these first months of school – can be seen as a sign that the fates are with him. Finally, there is a relationship that is beginning to go well for Marco.

Giovanni is also satisfied with the way that he has worked, and with the method that he has used.

> Three days ago he was on his way to the headmaster's office to hear him say, in substance, that the school has done everything possible. Changing Marco is not the business of the school but of the tutors responsible for him, or of some specialist. Let them take over. The school can only instruct children who want to learn, it cannot re-educate delinquents.

And yet, Giovanni reflects, he has been able to counter this argument – which is not without its logic – by virtue of the headmaster's open-mindedness and informality. He has been able to connect the school with his centre and to create a cooperative relation between them which, although not yet formalized, has the authoritative backing of the headmaster. He has been guided by the 'minimalist' idea that just as the centre on its own cannot handle Marco, with his complex past, neither can the school. Instead, now that they have begun to interact, both institutions may become more effective. Each of them may support and stimulate the other in a constant process of reciprocal reinforcement.

The first concrete result of this relation is that now, as Giovanni makes his way home and his mind begins to turn to his many other problems, two teachers have undertaken to *act* for Marco's good for a week, which will also be for their own good and for that of the community. They will try to persuade other colleagues, the headmaster, some parents, and others concerned, to come to the next meeting. And another thing: the teacher who wanted Marco to be suspended is now prepared to explain to her colleagues why this punishment could be counterproductive. Even though the process has not yet begun, and only its preconditions have been put in place, an encouraging step forward has been made. And in any case, thinks Giovanni, what is networking if not the constant development of preconditions?

Wednesday, 21 January, 15:30. The second network session convened to improve action on Marco's class has just begun. The two teachers have persuaded the headmaster to come (he is present at the meeting, in fact, but has already announced that he cannot stay until its conclusion because of other commitments), as well as two other colleagues who teach Class 1b (the English teacher and the gymnastics teacher), the two parents' representatives on the class council, and the educationalist from the school for children with learning difficulties. After introductions and a brief speech by the headmaster, the Italian teacher illustrates the discussion and conclusions of the previous meeting.

Giovanni already knows the main points of the teacher's summary because they worked on it together two days ago. While she is talking, therefore, he watches the reactions of those present. He realizes that the two teachers have done an excellent job of networking. There are more people present than he expected: except for the children, everyone involved with Marco's problem has come to the meeting, and all of them can help produce change.

> This, he thinks to himself, is a good example of a coping network: the most disparate persons come together voluntarily (without compulsion) to address a shared task, each of them free to think and act, the only condition being that they do so in connection with the others. This is not a hierarchical organization (it includes the headmaster, but he has equal status with the others) in that the objective set by the group for itself cannot be imposed by fiat.

The Italian teacher is explaining what this objective is. When she makes it clear that it is not to change Marco but to create a better 'ecology' for him, many of those present react with bewilderment. The teacher tries to explain what she means: everyone concerned must create the conditions in the school so that Marco (and anyone else) feels fulfilled. A climate must be created and activities devised which involve even the most difficult children and induce them to cooperate rather than resist (McCombs and Pope, 1994). The teacher uses rather general language but she nevertheless makes herself understood. Question: what conditions would make it more probable that Marco will enhance his self-image and shed that of being a *deviant?* How can his self-esteem be made to grow together and in harmony with that of all the other members of the class, rather than being shaped by default? The teacher uses an overhead projector to show the diagram drawn at the previous meeting. She explains that Marco finds self-fulfilment in his struggle with authority, but he finds nothing to give him equal gratification in what is normally expected of a child in a school classroom.

The OHP transparency arouses curiosity, and many of those present ask to speak. The mathematics teacher, too, comments on the previous meeting, while others seek to clarify their ideas. In short, the idea that the disorder, and the responsibility for it, is shared rather than being (only) individual is gradually gaining ground. Giovanni knows that the meeting should have a more advanced and practical purpose: deciding how to change the climate surrounding Marco's disorder, and also deciding on the responsibilities and actions of those involved (as well as others who could be approached) to achieve such an indefinite and demanding outcome. But for the time being it is obvious that those present still need time to define and re-define the task presented to them on the OHP transparency.

As discussion grows animated, Giovanni withdraws from it to reflect on method. Networking, he thinks, is a mediated intervention. The real action is undertaken by the persons involved (i.e. the network). He, as the conscious operator, assists and guides, giving the process free rein to develop. His role is to provide bland guidance: he must supervise, monitor and ensure that things go as they should.

> So far everything has gone smoothly, thinks Giovanni, my direct interven-
> tion has not been needed. Should the network break down, however, I shall
> have to move out of the background and make my presence more visible and
> tangible. But so far there has been no need for this. Everything is going
> surprisingly well. And these are all people who are cooperating willingly.
> They are simply happy to get involved.

From now on, however, things are going to get more difficult. So far the network has functioned only to the extent of achieving a shared and more precise awareness of the nature of the problem. We have tried to grasp the systemic nature of the situation in Class 1b. But unlike professional methods, where the expert (usually) keeps this awareness to him/herself, Giovanni says to himself, I have tried to spread it around. At the previous meeting I played a direct role in sparking this shared awareness: I almost acted like a teacher does, explaining the ideas that are now spreading through the group and consolidating themselves. The network is assimilating them and redistributing them.

4.2.4. *The beginning of brainstorming and the search for possible solutions*

When the discussion finishes, a new phase will begin in which there is no pre-established aim. Everyone will share the same *task* (improving the ecology of the school) but they will not know how to achieve it. There is not, in fact, *one* goal to pursue nor *one* path to follow. The aim is so broad and so indistinct that it can be reached from various directions, or, if things so badly, from no direction at all. My function as a social worker, and therefore as an outsider to school, Giovanni thinks, is not to point out a distinct route but to help the group of people involved to proceed amid indeterminacy, or in other words, to help all of them

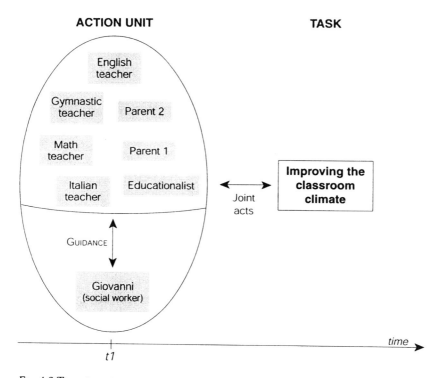

Fig. 4.3 *The enlarged coping network at the time 1.*

together to understand which route is probably the best one. They will proceed armed only with a compass, not with a detailed map of the terrain.

> This is the most difficult part for me, Giovanni says to himself: I must stop myself from imposing what I think should be the way ahead. Very soon they are going to turn to me and ask what they should do, seeing that they consider me to be an expert on delinquents. If I try to apply my expertise, it will overwhelm their ideas and we shall soon lose our way. My expertise should be placed at their service, and their intelligence should be at the service of my expertise, so that what emerges is not what is best but what is most practicable in this situation.

A social practitioner performs a twofold role, Giovanni reflects. On the one hand, he is one among many *in* the coping network and he must agree with the others what part he is going to play. On the other, he must simultaneously act *upon* the network, providing it with emotional and methodological support. He will have to make sure that the network functions, which means that he will have to ensure that all those present at the meeting – both from within the school and without – contribute their ideas and voluntarily assume the roles assigned to them and then perform them as well as they can. All of them are able to propose courses of action, which should be coordinated and oriented. This coordination may even arise on its own with some sort of spontaneous synchronization. If this does not happen, as the person who knows what is happening, I shall have to 'lubricate' harmony among the network's parts.

The discussion begins to flag. The phase of gaining awareness of the problem has now finished. Giovanni waits for a while to hear whether anyone will start off a new round of discussion by asking the classic question 'That's all very well, but what should we actually do?' Nobody answers the question, however, and Giovanni therefore redirects the discussion. He returns briefly to what the Italian teacher said at the beginning of the meeting and tells the group:

> Our task here is to come up with ideas on how to answer the following question: What can we do to improve Marco's situation at school and of everyone else involved with his problem? This can be broken down into four sub-questions:
> (a) What action can the teachers take (regardless of the irritation or awkwardness that they might feel while doing so) to involve Marco and his audience in what they are doing?
> (b) What action can the parents take (regardless of the fear of disorder and over-hasty solutions) to support Marco and the school in their endeavour? What can they do with their children, Marco's classmates?

(c) What action can be taken by the tutors at my Centre to support the parents and the teachers in their task?

(d) What action can be taken by the headmaster so that the entire organization of the school facilitates and supports these various activities?

A parent now speaks. He says with regard to point (d) that he finds it strange that a professional organization like a school does not have established procedures for dealing with behavior problems. How is it possible that the teachers are left to cope with difficult children entirely on their own? Why do the teachers have to make things up as they go along and expose themselves personally in this way, battling with Marco and destroying any possibility of establishing an effective educational *relationship* with him?

The English teacher says that it would be a good idea to devise a 'school policy'. This could be done by codifying a set of values and rules shared by the teachers, the pupils, all the rest of the school staff, and the families. A sort of charter, he says, an official set of regulations to be posted on the noticeboard in every classroom. These rules should be drawn up with the direct involvement of the children. Once a year each class would hold an assembly to discuss and approve the items on the charter. The teacher says that a system of this kind is described in a book that he is reading (Sharp and Smith, 1994), and that it seems feasible in their school. The important thing is that the charter should not be imposed from above. It should not suddenly appear on the noticeboard. Instead, as said, it should be the outcome of joint discussion. The parent who spoke previously asks why this cannot be done? The headmaster, who thus far has not spoken, now says that he has no objection. He will call a meeting as soon as possible to decide how to proceed. In the meantime, he asks the English teacher to write a short report on what he thinks should be done.

A second parent speaks. With regard to point (d), he says, it needs pointing out that many children are bored during lessons. With all due respect to the teachers, if a child is constantly disruptive, this means that the lessons are not sufficiently 'entertaining'. Not that the school should be an amusement arcade, but it should at least be stimulating. At least, that is what he thinks as a non-expert. Everyone agrees with him: the quality of the teaching influences the quality of school behaviour. The educationalist points out that, in her view, there are two problems to consider: on the one hand, the quality and the appeal of the teaching; on the other, the ability of certain children to understand the topics explained to them. The more difficult children, the ones with learning problems or those who lack motivation, would find it difficult to follow even the most brilliant of lessons. It is therefore necessary, she believes, to proceed on two fronts simultaneously: help the teachers improve their teaching skills, and help the intellectually weaker children by giving them support and individualized lessons.

Giovanni points out that *helping* (the teachers or the children) does not always mean *giving* help. It can also mean encouraging relational (mutual) help. He asks the educationalist if she is aware of significant examples of good teaching in this school, or in the other schools for which she responsible. Are there other teachers experimenting with innovative methods that they should know about? Would these teachers be willing to feed their experiences into the network, sharing them with interested colleagues? The educationalist replies that she does know of teachers of this kind. The headmaster asks, 'Then would you be willing to coordinate a teacher learning and support group (Thomas, 1992), a sort of mutual help group open to anyone who wants to join it? The most experienced or most skilled teachers could share their knowledge and techniques with the younger ones. The younger ones could stimulate the more experienced teachers to rethink harmful habits and established routines, and so on'. The educationalist says 'yes'. (The headmaster now announces that he has another appointment, apologises, and leaves the meeting).

The Italian teacher points out that she has often thought about changing her teaching style, not least because of her difficulties in controlling her classes. But she has never gone further than this declaration of good intent. If a support group started up, she would be happy to join it. She also has some ideas on minor innovations that she would like to discuss with colleagues, in particular on how to encourage pupils to help each other to learn.

This is a technique called 'tutoring', which she has read about in a book on networking in schools (Topping, 1988). It would be a good way to assist children with learning difficulties, or to help those who have fallen behind with the syllabus. Marco is a case in point. Small self-coaching groups could be set up, perhaps in friendly competition with each other (competing for prizes, for example). Care should be taken to ensure that each group is a mixture of more gifted and less gifted children, and that they take turns as group leader, writing up the minutes of the meetings, reporting to the class, and so on. The teacher explains that she has never tried to put these ideas into practice, because she is not certain that she could handle what seems a very complicated technique. However, if she could discuss it with a group of colleagues and hear their suggestions, she would certainly be willing to try it out.

A parent intervenes to say that if this tutoring project gets under way with official backing, the parents would be likely to support it. Some parents could make their homes available for meetings, giving the children a hand if need be.

The parents' representatives undertake to convene an assembly to talk to the parents about the project, and to see how many of them would join if it got under way. At the parents' meeting – suggests the Italian teacher – the behaviour of Marco's 'audience' should also be on the agenda. The parents could discuss and agree on what to say to their children to persuade them not to encourage Marco's misbehaviour unwittingly. A parent says that his daughter has told him that some of the children in the class are tired of the disagreeable atmosphere in the class and are beginning to realize that things cannot go on like this. Perhaps the parents could encourage these children to take action on their classmates. The precise form of such action could be discussed and decided later.

Giovanni now informs the meeting – with reference to point (c) – what he undertakes to do: he will tell his colleagues, the other tutors working at the residential unit, what has been decided at the meeting. The gymnastics teacher says that, in his view, that it is important that the Centre should continue to work with the school. In particular, the new regulations should also be somehow applied by the Centre externally to the school. Giovanni acknowledges that this is an important point. It would be helpful if the rules, the pledges, and punishable forms of behaviour were the same in both institutions. The initiatives taken at the school would therefore be managed through an even more extensive network. For example, if, as is unfortunately probable, punishments will have to be meted out at school, they could also be applied outside it, at the Centre, where they would be likely to have more effect (for example, a ban on going out to eat a pizza might be more painful than a ticking-off from the headmaster).

The Italian teacher again speaks, but this time to complain. What has been decided is all very well in the long term. Even if the decisions taken are implemented, they will still take time to have any concrete effect. In the meantime, tomorrow she has to go back into class and confront Marco and his audience. While waiting for the network to produce results, she will have to continue her solitary battle in the front line. A colleague, the English teacher, points out that there is a difference, however. Whereas before she entered the classroom feeling that she had no control over events, now she knows that these events are about to be tackled collaboratively. Tomorrow, however little it may seem, she will enter the class a different person, more confident and therefore less aggressive. And she will also be aware that she is being 'virtually' supported by the entire network of persons with whom she has now shared the problem. This will already reduce the tension.

Giovanni intervenes to stress that this more relaxed mood may enable the teacher to see Marco as a person (in difficulties) and not as her persecutor. It might help her to establish a genuine *helping relationship* with him, not just a disciplinary one. The teacher should try to ignore Marco's irritating behaviour as much as possible and involve him in classroom activities *as if* he were not annoying her. For example, she could call him to the blackboard more frequently, give him little chores to do, praise him if he deserves it, have the occasional nice word for him: in short, treat him just like the others. These devices too, Giovanni admits, will probably only have results in the long run, but the teacher should be immediately ready (emotionally) to use them.

The English teacher says that as far as he can recall there is a specific technique which may have immediate effects. A colleague talked to him about it some years ago and said that... it's difficult to explain, but in any case, the basis of the technique is to keep disruptive behaviour under control by authorizing it at very specific moments. The educationalist says that this is a technique widely used in psychotherapy and called 'paradoxical prescription of the symptom'. Instead of mobilizing enormous mental energies to impede Marco's tomfoolery, the teacher could authorize it, or even prescribe it. She could say at the beginning of the lesson:

> Today we're going to talk about something rather boring. What can we do about it? I suggest that every quarter of an hour we devote two minutes (only two, mind) to relaxation. If anyone wants to, they can fool around during those two minutes. Even Marco, who's our specialist. It'll help us to concentrate for the rest of the time.

In this way disruptive behaviour is socially *redefined* and brought under the teacher's control. If, as we saw from the diagram, the mainspring of Marco's behaviour is *opposition* to the teacher and that he gets most pleasure from the fact that such behaviour is forbidden, when it is instead prescribed the dynamic breaks down. It is one thing to play the fool in defiance of authority; it is quite another to play the fool in obedience to authority.

Giovanni stresses that this technique could prove useful. But caution is necessary. In his opinion, it should only be used after all the other remedies decided at the meeting have been started. If it is implemented on its own, when a network has not yet been established to link with Marco mentally, it may prove a merely systemic and somewhat dangerous manoeuvre.

Giovanni asks: if a technique is chosen at random, and if it is intended only to curb or even eliminate unwanted behaviour, what risks does it create? The mathematics teacher tries to answer: logically, if all goes well, it may happen that because the boy is authorized to play the fool, he may stop misbehaving because he dislikes doing it to order. But, Giovanni asks, does this mean that the problem has been solved?

Let's suppose that Marco stops playing the fool. But if this sort of behaviour ceases, it may be replaced by something different. And this is the point, because Marco may substitute fooling around with some other more disruptive or destructive types of behaviour. If a dentist extracts a crooked tooth, can he assume that the new one will grow straight?

The mathematics teacher completes Giovanni's argument. If Marco stops playing the fool, he may start assaulting his classmates or committing acts of vandalism, which is behaviour that the teacher cannot obviously prescribe.

A technique is useful if it achieves an effect, but the solution of social problems is not an effect or a chain of programmed effects. A technique must be implemented in a *context* of favourable conditions. When Marco is surrounded by a supportive network of relations (Jackson and Veeneman Panyan, 2002), when he feels that he can fulfil himself in class by means other than misbehaviour, then the time is ripe to remove his pleasure gained from playing the fool. Only when he is ready will a technique to help him to shed his dysfunctional behaviour be entirely appropriate.

The educationalist says that she agrees. In her view, the note of caution sounded by Giovanni also makes sense philosophically: education cannot be conceived 'in negative' as merely the removal of behaviour. A parent makes the more down-to-earth point that it is a pity that Marco, with all the misfortunes that have beset him, will see one of his few opportunities for self-fulfilment taken away by a team of teachers and specialists. Marco should be given a chance to go *beyond* his tomfoolery, to leave it behind because he has found better alternatives, not to have it merely suppressed.

Giovanni winds up the meeting by reiterating that they have decided to take joint action to find better alternatives for Marco and for all the children in the school. He briefly summarizes the tasks assumed by all those present and suggests that they should meet twice in a month to evaluate how things are going and to coordinate the activities. Then, everyone goes home. It is left to the reader to imagine what happens subsequently.

4.3. Elena, suffering from Alzheimer's disease, alone in a country which is not her own

An example of long-term care

Twenty years ago, Elena, sixty years old and recently retired, a widow and without children, took a sudden decision. Born in Germany but resident since childhood in the United States, she decided to move to Italy and live there permanently with her extremely elderly mother, whom she would bring with her. After a short holiday spent in the country village from which the parents of one of her American friends had emigrated, she was convinced: it was there she would spend her old age. With her savings and her pension, and also thanks to a favourable exchange rate, she had a small villa built which was ready almost a year later, just before the death of her mother. Left alone, and with the smattering of Italian that she had picked up by virtue of her sociable nature, she found it easy to join in the life of the village. She took part in parish activities, made friends, gave lessons in English, looked after the small children of a neighbouring family, and made frequent journeys to every part of Europe.

Giuliana is the social worker in the largest mountain district of the province. She is responsible for elderly people in several villages with a total population of around fifteen thousand people. This morning she is busy as usual: two hours on call, then two home visits to make before midday, when she has a meeting with her service director. Yesterday she received a phone call from Angela D. about the problems of a neighbour of hers. She is due to arrive now, at a quarter past eight. Giuliana has given her an appointment because she asked for one. The woman enters, sits down, and tells the story of her neighbour. It is Elena.

To cut a long story short, she says, after twenty years in the village Elena is just like one of us. When Elena arrived from Colorado, Angela was young and had just married. She came from a nearby village. Both she and Elena were therefore newcomers and they became close friends. Her children, for instance, have always called Elena 'auntie'. Angela describes some recent events: for instance when, on the advice of a lawyer, Elena decided to sell her house to someone in the village but retained her right of occupancy (having no heirs, she wanted the money immediately to spend on her trips abroad, on her frequent donations to a missionary with whom she corresponded, etc.). She has always been self-sufficient; indeed more than self-sufficient because she has always helped others. But in recent months she has changed. She has started talking to herself, she repeats the same things over and over again. Sometimes she loses her temper, which she never did before. She has now taken to roaming the village in the evenings. One cold night she was found wandering after midnight without an overcoat. At her age this might be expected: she was eighty-one years old last month. She is in excellent health, but her mind is beginning to give way.

Recently Elena has let herself go even more. It may be dangerous to leave her alone in her condition. So, Angela says, she has decided to contact the local social services: her husband has been saying she should do so for some time. She doesn't know if she's done the right thing, whether it's her responsibility, but in the end she's decided to come...

4.3.1. *Identifying the coping network and gross assessment*

Giuliana has heard about Elena the American woman and her work in the community. Her colleagues in the home help service have mentioned her from time to time because she has sometimes helped them by doing small services: administering medicine, providing some companionship for the bed-ridden, and so on. Now it is Elena that needs help.

Giuliana points out to Angela that, judging from what she says, Elena's problems have already been evident for some months. Presumably, therefore, some sort of action has already been taken. She says:

> From what you've told me, your neighbour has been unwell for some time. Who's been looking after her? Who in the village has been keeping an eye on her, or helping her? Apart from yourself, obviously.

Angela mentions various names. It seems that there has already been a certain amount of mobilization to help Elena. The social worker starts to work with some degree of method. She wants to know who her potential partners are, the people that she can count on when organizing care for Elena, apart from Angela (who strikes her as sensible and reliable). Two years ago she attended a training course on networking, and there was one notion that she understood very well because it matched her own experience. She has been working for ten years and is well aware that when a problem arises, especially if it develops gradually as in Elena's case, a network soon forms to deal with it (a 'natural coping network'). This network, no matter how inadequate it may be (otherwise why should she, the social worker, have to intervene?), immediately sets to work, driven by the logic of the situation and calling on everyone concerned to do what is needed (if they want to, that is). In this case, who belongs to the network?

Elena's neighbour lists the people who have helped thus far. Obviously, given the relationship with Elena, they have been mainly herself and the members of her family. Herself most of all, but also her husband and her two children. To tell the truth, they are beginning to resent the situation, she says. They complain that there are special rest homes for elderly people like Elena. However, so far they have not refused to help if there is something that needs doing. Her husband has taken care of the small maintenance jobs that need doing around Elena's house, which she always used to do herself but has recently neglected. For instance, every evening he goes to check that Elena's chickens have been shut up for the night and fed. Eventually they will have to be got rid of; and the vegetable garden, which hasn't been sown this year, will have to be dug up. Her husband gives Elena a hand with cutting the grass and pruning the fruit trees – as he has always done for that matter. She, Angela, has taken care of Elena's food. Previously, she made sure that Elena was preparing meals and feeding herself properly. But for some weeks, since Elena's condition began to deteriorate, she has done the cooking herself. Sometimes she takes food to Elena's house, sometimes she has her round to eat with her own family. Elena's cleaning is done for payment by Ida, a woman from the village who goes into her house every morning.

As she has already told Giuliana – Angela continues – a few weeks ago Elena left her house late at night and wandered the streets without a coat. She risked at least a bout of pneumonia. An old friend of Elena's called Grazia, who lives in a nearby village and is also widowed and childless, has just spent the weekend with her, to keep her company and also to keep an eye on her. Grazia knows how to take care of Elena, with whom she shares a deep religious faith. They have often gone on trips together in the past, visiting sanctuaries and centres of worship. When Grazia talks about their travels together and reminisces about places and events, except in moments of exceptional confusion Elena is able to remember and to communicate. She was relatively calm in the company of her friend last weekend. At times, indeed, she seemed her old self, and she passed the two nights peacefully. But now the problem is what to do next. Grazia cannot spend her entire time at Elena's house. She could at least spend the nights there – they've already discussed it – only she doesn't have a car and can't drive. She would have to take a short cut through the fields, a twenty-minute walk which would be impossible every day.

Giuliana asks whether the doctor is aware of the situation? Yes, Dr. Manconi obviously knows everything, Grazia replies. He says that his diagnosis is Alzheimer's disease (or something similar). He says that it is progressive, that unfortunately it will only get worse, and that the social services should take an interest as soon as possible. Indeed, when talking to her husband Dr. Manconi told him that he would phone the social worker. But Angela saw him yesterday and he said that he hadn't had time to make the call. He promised to do so, but it seems to Angela that the matter is more urgent than the doctor apparently believes. That is why she has made the appointment with Giuliana and that is why she is here talking to her now.

Oh, but she was forgetting: there's the schoolteacher Mario. As the parish trustee he has helped Elena ever since she arrived in the village and needed someone knowledgeable to help her with the paperwork to apply for Italian citizenship, even though (Angela has never understood why) she never completed her application. Mario has also helped her with money matters and has the counter-signature to her bank account in case of emergencies. All the shopping that Angela has recently done for Elena she has agreed with Mario: he will drop by at the end of the month to pay her. It was Mario who had the idea of selling the house so that Elena could use the money while she was still alive. It was he who dealt with the lawyer, found a purchaser for the house, and so on. Elena understood very little about legal matters – she says that she didn't even understand very much when she was in the United States, and there the bureaucracy is much simpler – but she trusts Mario and the parish priest.

Some time ago, Mario contacted a friend of his who works as an official in the local authority in order to ascertain Elena's welfare entitlements, seeing that she is a foreigner. For example, does she qualify for a place in a rest home? No, was the answer, because her pension is not large enough and the municipal council cannot help because she is a foreigner. She has no relatives in the United States. Only a niece, who seemed rather strange on the two occasions when she came to visit Elena, and since then there has been no further contact apart from the odd Christmas card. Ask the niece for money? Difficult. It would be a problem just to find her...

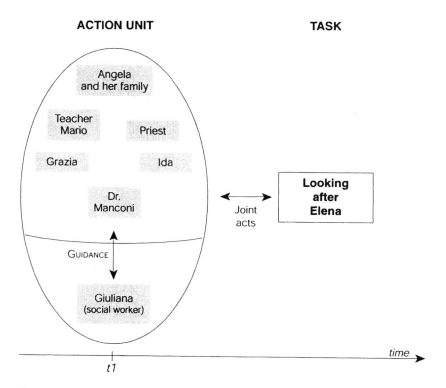

Fig. 4.4 The chart used by the social worker to visualize Elena's initial help network.

The social worker has been listening for all this while, occasionally taking notes. It seems to me, she says, that you neighbours have already organized yourselves well. If I understand rightly – she looks at her notepad on which she has jotted down some names – besides your family, five people have helped Elena since her problems began: Grazia, Ida, the schoolteacher Mario, the parish priest, and Dr. Manconi. Is that right? Angela says yes, but of course there are lots of other people who know Elena and feel affection for her, who every so often drop in to see her or stop her in the street for a chat. But the people who have done something concrete to help her in recent months are those that Giuliana has mentioned. Angela reaches into a drawer and pulls out a diagram of circles, or what to Angela look like circles. Giuliana shows it to her and Angela realizes that she was right: the diagram consists of concentric circles divided into sectors, in which, Giuliana now explains, she will insert the names just mentioned according to their closeness to Elena (whose name she writes in the centre circle), putting Angela precisely 'here' (see Figure 4.4).

Giuliana again checks the diagram and says that it is very important for her to meet these people and hear what they have to say. Together they can decide what to do. For the time being, she has gained an idea of the situation. She thanks Angela for her information, and also for what she is doing for Elena, together with all the others. Would she be so kind, she asks her, as to tell those people that the social worker has been informed and would like to meet them as soon as possible? She will phone Doctor Manconi, but would Angela tell the others that the social worker would like to talk to all of them tomorrow, after she has visited Elena to see at first hand what sort of state she is in. Before saying goodbye, Giuliana asks Angela for her telephone number: this evening she will ring to tell her exactly when she can be there for the meeting tomorrow. It will probably be at the end of the day, around six o'clock. She'll have to put off an appointment but she should be able to make it. In any case, she will know for certain this evening. Goodbye for now, and see you tomorrow.

When Angela has left, Giuliana thinks about what may happen. She has looked after numerous elderly people – it's her job after all – but this is a special case. Is it true that Elena is not entitled to a place in a rest home? If it is (she will have to find out, perhaps her boss will be able to tell her when she sees him at midday), then one escape route that has so often rescued social workers from complicated and unmanageable situations (or manageable ones which require more time than available) has been shut off. Here, a care system truly centred on home help will have to be organized. This is a classic situation of community care, with the rest home option unavailable and with a total absence of family members as carers.

It will have to be the community that looks after Elena, thinks Giuliana. And it seems in any case that the community has already been working well. So far Elena has been adequately taken care of. Given the basis that already exists, it looks as if things may go smoothly. The essential thing is that the entire burden should not fall on the shoulders of just one or a few people – Angela or Grazia. If it does, the situation will soon deteriorate. Its is essential to set up a real caring network.

At half past four the next afternoon, Giuliana calls on Angela as agreed so that she can take her to Elena's house for the home visit. Elena has been relatively calm all day, Angela says, almost always alone except for the two hours in the morning when Ida was doing the cleaning, and at lunchtime when Angela was with her. After lunch Angela put her to bed. She rested until an hour ago, when she got up by herself and was seen in the garden by Angela's husband. She was talking to herself but did not give cause for concern. On their way to Elena's house, the social worker asks if Angela has been able to contact the other people concerned. They are all coming at 5:30, Angela replies, apart from the schoolteacher Mario, who is busy all afternoon with a meeting of the municipal council. He says, however, that he will ask Angela about what has been decided, and the next time, if he has more notice of the meeting, he will certainly be present. Giuliana tells Angela that she has talked to the doctor, who has confirmed his diagnosis of cerebral arteriosclerosis complicated by diabetes and says that it is very important that Elena should take her drugs regularly. He asks if it is possible to ensure that she does so.

Elena is a little old lady with a sprightly manner and a sharp gaze, although her attention sometimes tends to wander. She answers Giuliana's simpler questions appropriately. Several times she asks Angela who the other woman is. On each occasion it is explained to her that she is the social worker sent by the local authority services to see if she needs anything. But shortly afterwards Elena asks again.

After talking for while, Giuliana takes a form out of her bag and begins to complete it. Either asking Angela or on the basis of her own observations, she marks a series of crosses on the form and adds some notes, explaining to Angela that it is a self-sufficiency test used to establish exactly what Elena can and cannot do on her own. When the form has been completed, a score is calculated which roughly indicates the level of Elena's care needs. She says that this is only a broad appraisal intended to give an idea of whether more detailed assessment by a team of specialists will have to be made at a later date.

For the time being she asks what Elena is able to do in the home: if she is able to put herself to bed and get up (yes); if she can get dressed and undressed (yes);

if she is able to cook (yes, but you have to watch her); if she can keep herself clean (she can wash her hands and face but she often forgets; she can't take a bath by herself any more); if she can make phone calls (yes, even too many: she'll telephone at any time of the day and always ask the same thing); if she can walk, get up the stairs, etc. (here it is obvious that she has no problems); if she can see and hear the television (no problems here either). Then Giuliana asks what Elena can do outside the house: if she can get out to do the shopping (yes, but she forgets what she has to buy); if she is able to take the bus (yes, but we have to make sure that she doesn't); if she calls on friends (yes, when she goes out during the day she drops in on neighbours, but you can't tell if she does so deliberately or if she's just wandered in); if she goes to church (yes, until a short time ago she went to mass every morning, but now she sometimes forgets) or to the cemetery (yes, every so often she visits her mother's grave: the cemetery is close to her house). The social worker then asks about 'significant others' (as the form calls them), but this was talked about yesterday, so it is only necessary to write the names and addresses of the people who will be at the meeting. We'll do everything there, Giuliana says.

By now it is 5:30. Angela has made an appointment with Ida and Grazia at her house. They'll be waiting there. Should she go and get them or should they both go to Angela's house? Giuliana smiles and says that she'll do whatever Angela decides. After all, it is her house: what does she think would be best? Angela shrugs... Well, perhaps, seeing that Elena is calm – she has just finished watering the flowers, she's rearranged the pots on the balcony, and now she is sitting at the table with a newspaper in front of her – perhaps it's better to go to Angela's house, because she is not really sure that Elena is unable to understand, and she might be alarmed by a meeting here, she might hear things that would make her anxious. All right, says Giuliana, we'll go to your house.

Angela lives just fifty metres away. The two gardens adjoin each other. When Angela and the social worker arrive, Ida and Grazia are already waiting. They talk to Angela's husband, who has just got home from work and is working in the garden. Giuliana introduces herself: 'I'm the social worker,' she says, 'together with a colleague I'm responsible for all the old people in this area'.

Angela ushers them into the living room while her husband makes the coffee and brings some mineral water. While the others take their places and talk, Giuliana takes her notes and charts out of the folder and reflects on what is happening. She reminds herself that this hastily-arranged meeting, with this handful of people – and not even all of them because Mario the schoolteacher and Dr. Manconi are absent, as well as the priest (by the way, did they forget to invite him?) – this meeting is in fact extremely important because it will be the basis of everything that happens from now on (Not for nothing meetings of this kind have a technical name: 'network sessions' but 'meetings' will do just as well). What should happen here, then, that is so important?

> If everything goes well – thinks Giuliana – this little get-together should create the 'spirit' of the network, the awareness shared by all of us that we've come together to do something, and that there is no-one beyond or above us that can do it better. And it should also create – again, obviously if all goes well and I haven't adopted the wrong approach or style, as I've unfortunately sometimes done in the past, or if nobody objects – a genuine relationship between myself as a representative of the public institutions and with a specific role, and these people who have decided to take action because that's the way they are and because they want to.

Giuliana continues to reflect. The local authority has responsibility for the universal and impersonal fate of the elderly people that fall within its jurisdiction. Through me, here, in this informal sitting-room now permeated by the aroma of coffee (which Ernesto, Angela's husband, is now serving), this public authority is now in contact with a group of people who have taken the fate of one of their neighbours directly to heart. It has always been strange to feel herself embodying in her actions – a person so reserved and blithe like herself – situations which seemingly belong to another world when she reads about them in books: 'the encounter between the institutions and civil society', 'the interweaving of the formal and the informal', 'the synergy between expert competences and experiential competences', and so on. All these principles, what are they now? They are her, Giuliana, sitting on a chintz sofa, surrounded by people who perhaps do not really know why they are here but know everything else. She knows old people in general; they know Elena in particular. Now they are waiting for her, the social worker who has assembled them, to explain the reasons why.

4.3.2. Construction of the inter-subjective action base: defining the problem as a task for the network

Giuliana begins as she always does by greeting those present and thanking them for coming. She says that yesterday Angela told her about the situation. That she, Giuliana, has already spoken to the doctor and has met Elena just shortly before. As they have probably already realized, there is no hope that Elena's condition will improve. She is irremediably ill. She will always need help.

She has asked them to come here today because Angela has told her about what they have done to help Elena since she started to lose her self-sufficiency and to be a cause for concern. She has a good idea of what everyone has done, and she knows that there are other persons who cannot be present today, like Mario the schoolteacher and Dr. Manconi. Yesterday with the help of Angela she completed the chart which she is now showing them. It contains the people who are dear to Elena and who she would certainly want to see here if she were able to compile the chart itself. Is it accurate? asks Giuliana. Is everyone on it who should be, or has somebody been left out?

Ida points out that Angela's two children are missing. They are on the chart but why are they not here? Has Angela, their mother, forgotten to invite them? Angela says that it hadn't cross her mind, that perhaps she took it for granted that these were adult matters; although, to tell the truth, Pietro, her eldest son, is already an adult (he's nineteen years old). He's upstairs studying, she can call him (her other son Luca, who's thirteen, has gone to football training and will not be home until 6:30).

After a while Angela comes downstairs to say that Pietro won't be coming. It's not that he isn't interested but he's studying, he's got to prepare for a test at school. The social worker is now speaking. More precisely she is stating the 'problem' to the network. Elena needs twenty-four-hour care. So far, those present have been able to take look after her, mainly because Elena does not yet need constant supervision. But it is obvious, she tells them, that from now on your efforts will have to be supplemented and supported. You cannot continue as before. Indeed, that is precisely why Angela came to me yesterday to ask for help.

> So, seeing that Elena is at risk if she is left alone, although everything done so far has been fine, from now on it's going to get more difficult. What can we do to solve the problem? It's a tough situation and we must think carefully. Let's see if those of us here are enough, including the absentees, who have said they're prepared to help. Or if we'll have to find someone else to give us a hand. Whatever the case may be, it is not likely that one person will be able to do everything. If one of us were Elena's daughter or husband or daughter, perhaps that would be enough (I say 'perhaps' because care-giving is hard even for people looking after their loved ones), but Elena doesn't have any close relatives, so each of us can only do a small part of the work. So we must all work together. That's why we are here, to see how we can put a lot of little pieces together.

After a moment's silence, Ernesto says that if they could get Elena admitted to a rest home, that might be the solution, because if you have no relatives, as the social worker has just said, a rest home is the only option. He knows that there is a difficulty with the fees, he's talked about it with the mayor, and also Mario the schoolteacher has investigated the matter, but there must be a solution. With all the money that gets wasted, the council must realize...

Her husband's vehemence somewhat embarrasses Angela, she doesn't want to make a bad impression on the social worker. She intervenes to defend the council, saying that as far as she can see it is a question of law. It is not that the council does not want to help; it is simply unable to. Ida objects: she says that the council always does exactly what it wants, that you can get round the law. Ernesto agrees with her, he reminds them of various by-laws passed by the local authority. Soon everyone is talking about the council. Giuliana interrupts:

> Ernesto, by saying that the only solution is a rest home what you're really saying is that we're no longer able to cope. Your proposal is different from mine. I said that, since so far everything has gone well, together we can work out ways to do things even better, with less effort and less worry for all of us. I said that we could try to do it ourselves. Do you think that's possible?

Angela intervenes to say that if she has understood properly, the rest home is not an option for the moment. So it is pointless to discuss the matter now, because they cannot do anything about it. The only alternative is to do as the social worker says. 'Of course it's difficult, all of us have our own things to do. We can't be constantly looking after a sick person.'

Grazia asks to speak. She says that she will try to talk 'in Elena's stead'. Elena is not present at the meeting, she says, because she no longer understands. But only six months ago she understood – and how! – and if she could have attended the meeting she would have said things that she, Grazia, will say in her stead.

> Elena would probably tell us to do everything to get her into a rest home. She has never wanted to be any trouble, to be a burden on others. It's the last thing that she would have wanted. We all know her, and if she were here she'd say: don't bother about me. Of course, if she knew that she didn't have enough money to pay for the rest home, she'd be embarrassed... and perhaps humiliated. Perhaps she would say that the best solution would be for her to die as quickly as possible. But in any case what would be her main concern? Not to be a burden on us...
> If Elena were here and said these things to us, how would we answer? I at least would say that she is one of us, that she has always been liked and accepted, that she has always tried to help others.

The other day, says Grazia, she spoke to the priest, who was worried about Elena's state and remembered the good works that she had done in the village. Of course, as a Christian, she, Grazia, would have a problem with her conscience even if Elena was a bad person, if she were selfish and unsociable, if she had never done anything for the community. But we are all indebted to her. Personally, she has always been a great comfort and help to me. So, Grazia continues, what the social worker proposes – that we should each do a 'little piece' for Elena – is fine by me. Elena will never realize what Grazia has done for her and will therefore never thank her, but never mind.

Ernesto asks to speak because he wants to make something clear. He wasn't saying earlier that he didn't want to do anything. He'll certainly try to help Elena, as he always has done. He mentioned the rest home because he thinks that the council should pull its weight. Why should the council get away with doing nothing?

Angela says that she doesn't want to keep contradicting her husband, but it seems to her that the council *is* doing something, even if it can't give Elena a place in a rest home. Already the fact that the social worker is here with us now, and is trying to help Elena, is a great comfort. Since she met the social worker yesterday and talked to her about the problem, she feels that a weight has been lifted from her shoulders. The situation seems less intractable than when she and her family seemed to be carrying almost all the responsibility.

Ida agrees as well. She says that Elena is not so difficult to look after. She knows because she does all her housework every morning. The real problem is supervising Elena, keeping an eye on her. But for the rest she's reasonably self-sufficient. She spends a lot of time peacefully on her own. Until her condition really deteriorates, the problem will be the nights, because the days won't be difficult to organize. Also because the social worker is involved now, and then there are other people who could help.

Giuliana says that she wants to take up a number of points that have been raised so far. She agrees with Grazia that the community is in some way 'indebted' to Elena. This will make it easier to find other people willing to lend a hand. Among the people that Elena has helped, or among their family members, there may be someone willing to assist, if asked, and certainly among Elena's fellow parishioners and the voluntary workers in the community. It is too early to say who these other carers might be, however. We must think about this together: my role here is to help you establish links with the external community so that you're not left alone.

She also agrees with Ernesto. He is right to point out that the council, too, should take responsibility. Her role as social worker will also involve acting as a go-between between the group and the local authority, her employer, to ensure that Elena's care does not depend wholly on the good will of her neighbours. There are many ways in which the local authority can make itself useful, with its district nurses, care assistants, day centre, meals on wheels, and emergency helpline. It is still too early to decide exactly what to do, but what is certain is that they will not be alone. And Ernesto is also right in what he says about the rest home. She knows that there are difficulties (she talked to her manager yesterday) and that for the time being they're stuck. But she's going to find out more and take legal advice as well. If Elena becomes unmanageable in her own home (but for the moment she agrees with Ida that home care is feasible), then it's just as well to know whether or not there is a last resort available.

The social worker proposes that the meeting should finish at this point. Much has already been done, but deciding how to organize things properly will take the whole of another meeting, which should obviously be held as soon as possible. She is available at the same time tomorrow, half past five, if they agree. Mario the schoolteacher will obviously have to be invited, as well as the parish priest if he can come. She will report to the doctor if it is impossible for him to be present. Can Angela get in touch with them? For a little while Angela, Grazia and Ida will have to continue on their own, looking after Elena as they have done so far, but at the next meeting we'll decide how the work can be shared better. But she was forgetting, says Giuliana, can she have everyone's telephone number? And she'll leave her visiting card so that they can contact her if anything comes up before tomorrow evening.

4.3.3. *Care planning: brainstorming and the joint definition of caring tasks*

After she has said goodbye and left the meeting, and as she is driving home, Giuliana tries to put her thoughts in order. She has managed to guide the network, she has acted as the mirror in which the network can see itself and gain self-awareness. She has done, she thinks, what the books say an expert social worker should (although you can never really understand the books, they make everything so complicated). She feels that she has been efficient, but what does that actually mean? On other occasions she has been even more efficient, but she was working with people who resisted her, and the network never got started. Here she has luckily found a group she can rely on. What has happened, in fact, is that her professional reliability has been matched by the reliability of these people. From this encounter a reliable coping network has emerged, one stronger than the natural helping network that was already in place. If she had to make an assessment now, she would say that they can go ahead with due caution; that the goal of ensuring security and human warmth for Elena can be pursued with a good chance of success...

Then, she thinks, there's this business of empowerment. It is natural that ordinary people should find it difficult to understand that they can 'do it themselves'. With all the professionals and the specializations and the rest homes available, a person is right to say: 'The most that I can do is demand that the social services do their job properly. And if they do not, I shall complain bitterly and loudly'. So why should this person think that it is his or her responsibility? Just as no-one would think that they should bake bread every night because there's the baker to do it for them, so they think that the rest home should take care of Elena. 'Why should I do it?', they say. Or on the other hand, 'why should it be 'granted' to me to do it? With all those who live on our taxes, who earn their salaries by delivering services, it's logical that they should take responsibility'. When someone thinks like this, they close themselves off mentally without realizing it, because it is natural thing to do.

I like Ernesto, Giuliana thinks: he's typical of the reasonable person trapped in this kind of mentality. A generous person who, without realizing it, thinks and speaks as if he were not. But he's right in a way, given that the institutional resources exist and can and should be used. Only when social workers use them, they do so in a way that tends to confuse people like Ernesto, who are unable to grasp that social services should be used to *support* them, not to substitute for them. And they are even more confused if the social workers are mixed up as well: if they don't have a clear idea of what they are doing and use services to substitute for what people are able to do.

Giuliana personally thinks that her ideas are clear on the matter. But all the same, how can she expect Ernesto to understand these things immediately? Perhaps he will learn with time, if the group continues to act and learn together.

The next day, again at 5:30, the network has gathered at Angela's home. All of them are there, apart from Ida, who has had to go into town on urgent business. If she can manage it, she has said, she'll come along later. Nor has the priest been able to come, but he'll get in touch with the social worker (he's obtained her telephone number from Angela). However, Mario the school-teacher is present, and also Pietro, Angela's eldest son. Giuliana introduces the newcomers and then briefly describes the purpose of the meeting.

> As we decided yesterday, the purpose of this meeting is to organize ourselves so that we can ensure constant supervision for Elena. The time will soon come when she can't be left alone, when someone will always have to be with her. We've got to solve the problem in such a way that the task is as easy as possible and nobody is penalized. What I mean is, each of us can make a reasonable contribution without being required to make sacrifices. We've all got lost of other things to do...

Grazia asks to speak. She says that she has been thinking since yesterday, and seeing that she lives alone she has a suggestion to make. She could spend the nights with Elena, who trusts her, and if necessary she could spend Sundays with her as well. Elena is used to having her around, and this could be the best solution.

Angela says that they've already talked about this possibility, except that Grazia is underestimating the transport problem. Although Grazia says that she can manage, it's too far to come every day on foot. It might be a pleasant stroll in summer, but in winter it's impossible.

But the problem can be divided into two, the social worker says. There's surveillance of Elena by day and surveillance of her at night. With her proposal, Grazia may have solved the problem of the nights, but according to Angela the solution is not viable.

Angela has told us, continues Giuliana, that there's a problem of transport. Can Grazia accept responsibility for looking after Elena at night and also for arranging her own transport? Isn't she going to leave anything for the others to do? This seems to be Angela's message, the social work says. But joking apart, if Grazia takes on this major commitment of staying with Elena every night, can't we do something to help Grazia?

First of all we've got to sort out the problem of Grazia's transport every day to Elena's house. Ernesto now speaks to say that, of course, he can lend a hand, but only to drive Grazia to Elena's in the late afternoons. He can't take Grazia home in the mornings because he has to go to work. Someone else will have to be found.

Ernesto has offered to go and collect Grazia every day, the social worker says. What do you think? Mario the schoolteacher (who so far has been silent) now speaks. In his view, if he has understood what the social worker is trying to do, then the commitment made by Ernesto (who's a generous sort, he knows him well) strikes him as excessive. Tying yourself down like that every day is a big commitment, even if it only requires a quarter of an hour every day. And then there's the problem of the petrol. It won't cost all that much, but why should someone trying to help also be out of pocket? His suggestion that Ernesto's petrol money should be taken out of Elena's pension, which he Mario, administers. Ernesto could be paid an agreed amount every week. It won't be very much but it would be only fair, Mario says, seeing Ernesto gesture as if to say that he won't hear of any such payment.

Mario the schoolteacher – the social worker recapitulates – is concerned that Ernesto should not do everything on his own, that he shouldn't be the person who always goes and collects Grazia. What do you think?

Grazia speaks up to say that she feels rather awkward. It's true that she's getting on a bit, that she may have a touch of phlebitis, but she's hardly an invalid. Thanks for the offer of help, she says. Being able to count on transport every so often will certainly be useful, but a bit of exercise will only do me good.

Angela says 'yes'. In fact, she thinks that the problem of getting Grazia to Elena's house can be solved as Grazia proposes. She can go on foot. It was the prospect of *always* having to go on foot that worried her. If there's a minimum of organization to give Grazia help when she needs it, that should be sufficient. 'I didn't want to say that she can't walk... Ernesto can also count on Pietro's help. He's only just got his licence but he's a good driver. So if one day Ernesto can't go and get Grazia, then there's always Pietro (who nods, seemingly content with his role). Otherwise I can go,' says Angela.

'But,' Angela continues, 'there's still the problem of the mornings. Who is going to take Grazia home? Neither Ernesto nor Pietro nor I, Angela, can commit ourselves on a regular basis (I could sometimes take Grazia home, but I have to get the family ready, take Luca to school and do the housework).' Giuliana says that Angela has put her finger on the problem: who will accept the task of taking Grazia home in the morning?

Realizing that nobody is going to speak, Giuliana adds that it does not necessarily have be someone in the room. There might be someone else that they can think of. She asks: do you know anyone who could take on this commitment? Mario says that it would have to be a pensioner, someone who has the mornings free. For the moment no one comes to mind, but he will have a word with the priest. If it proves impossible to find somebody, Giuliana says, I'll ask a voluntary association for transport of the disabled on contract to the local authority if they can take her. However, we shouldn't expect too much, first because they are always overloaded with work, and second because the problem is transporting, not an invalid (Grazia smiles) but a *carer*. She's already talked to the head of the cooperative about problems of this kind, but he told her that the contract with the authority is extremely inflexible on this point. The service is provided for patients, not for carers. Giuliana says that she lost her temper (not with the voluntary association but with whoever had made the rules so inflexible). She had also asked her service manager to take the matter up with the regional administration. Perhaps he'll be able do something but they shouldn't raise their hopes. If this solution is not available, Mario the schoolteacher says, at least for a while, until they come up with something better, perhaps they could call a taxi. He realizes that money shouldn't be wasted, but when it's necessary to spend money, then it should be spent. There's no point in keeping Elena's money in the bank if Elena has problems that it could solve. Mario understands that Giuliana agrees with him because she nods her head. She has seen so many old people rely entirely on inadequate public welfare while their pensions and attendance allowances pile up in the bank or at the post office because they think they should save, because you never know...

But, says Giuliana, there's another question that has to be settled. If Grazia is going to spend the nights with Elena, there's problem of finding someone to substitute for her should she – because she's tired or ill or simply wants a break – needs some respite. Angela says that she could take Grazia's place if necessary, if it's only for a few nights. Otherwise they could ask Ida, perhaps give her a bit of money, seeing that it's her work (Mario nods). Or they could ask her friend, Anna, whom Grazia also knows (she too nods). She belongs to the pastoral counselling centre and has been doing voluntary work for years.

We may now interrupt the account, assuming that the meeting at Angela's house continues. The reader can presumably imagine the outcome of the meeting, and of the ones that follow. The intervention seems to have been set up well (thanks to Giuliana's good work) and it is not difficult to predict that Giuliana will now set about consolidating what has been decided so far, summarizing and reminding each of those present of their commitments. She may also introduce the other important question of day care, stimulating the group to come up with solutions to this problem, as well as to the other secondary ones that arise. She listens to everyone's opinion, she pushes for the most reasonable and feasible proposals, she seeks to ensure that the most generous members of the network do not subsequently find themselves in difficulties, and so on.

Specific mention, however, should be made of one proposal mooted by the social worker. It is perhaps one that the reader would not predict, given that Giuliana herself cannot say why it sprang to mind at the end of the meeting. On realizing that the agreements reached by the various persons present would not be simple to manage, and that with all her numerous other cases to attend to and amid so many distractions she would find overall coordination extremely difficult, she made the following suggestion. Why not ask Angela – who had always been at the centre of the network and who has proved herself so sensible and sensitive – to be the informal manager of the network, to act herself as the networker, given that in part she is already doing so. Not exactly in those terms, of course. While she was formulating the question, Giuliana realized that it would to be too technical for those present. Consequently, she simply asked if she could rely on Angela to keep her informed on how things are going, and especially if she could contact her immediately whenever a problem arose. Giuliana then asked all those at the meeting if they would refer any problems or questions to Angela, who would then pass them on to her. She suggested holding a meeting once a week – she was always available on late Friday afternoon – at which she would be present, while for the rest of the time, in the case of unexpected problems or changes of plan, it would be Angela who decided what to do, after discussing the matter with the others.

4.4. Father Damiano and development of an anti-alcoholism self-help community movement in Trentino (Italy)

Father Damiano had been chaplain in a local hospital for four years, in a small town in Trentino, a beautiful province in the north of Italy. One day on finishing morning mass in the hospital, he went upstairs to the psychiatric department, where he had an appointment with the consultant, Dr. Enzo D. He was in a hurry because his doctor friend – a friendship forged by many battles fought together – was rarely to be found in the department. He only dropped in for an hour or two in the mornings before spending the rest of the day at the community.

With his blend of spirituality and social commitment, Damiano was adept at observing and noting. Since his arrival in the area, he and his brethren had managed to convince the Franciscan order that their monastery should be opened to the outside world and turned into a reception centre for socially excluded people. The non-European immigrants then beginning to arrive in Italy were also to be welcomed. Damiano set to work, pulling strings and working behind the scenes, and the reception centre opened. His role as chaplain was too restrictive for his ebullient personality. He threw himself into his work and, if need be, he could also get angry.

But on that particular day Damiano had no wish to lose his temper with the chief psychiatric consultant. After all he was his friend. Except that Enzo was always too caught up with his work. He had taken the Italian law of 1978 which closed the mental hospitals very seriously indeed (which was why he was Damiano's friend). But, Damiano thought to himself, when someone refuses to understand there is nothing you can do. As a good Franciscan he would stick at nothing, he decided, he was going to get angry. He was going to tell Enzo why he had come, and he was going to ask him some questions. 'How many times have I talked to you about alcoholics?' 'How many times have I told you that it is not true that nothing can be done to help them, that it is only an excuse to say that it's their fault or that there's nothing to be done for them?'

Enzo has heard these questions over and over again. Father Damiano has a big heart and great perseverance, he thinks. He could move mountains with his grit and persistence, but what does he know about therapeutic techniques? How many times have I told him that psychotherapy for alcoholism is a waste of time, that it makes no difference? Where is the sense in organizing a service for alcoholics at the hospital when so much effort is being made to demedicalize their treatment?

Father Damiano knows very well how many nurses Enzo has in his department (exactly six). And how many doctors (two). This handful of people must run the SPDC (the hospital's small psychiatric department), the residential apartment units just opened in the community, and the planned day centre. Indeed, today he has a meeting to discuss funding with the chief administrator of the local health unit. Just imagine him allowing his two psychiatrists to take it easy in the comfort of the hospital, making technical diagnoses when even a child knows what alcoholism is all about. And then the real problem – and Damiano should know this too – is that nobody knows what to do when the diagnosis has been made. Of course, psychiatrists are masters of mystification; they can spin out a therapy for years without anyone realizing. Is that what Father Damiano wants? Has he never read *Medical Nemesis* by Ivan Illich? Is he concerned for the good of alcoholics or for the good of psychiatrists?

The defect of psychiatrists, even the more intelligent ones, Father Damiano thinks to himself, is that they never listen. To be sure, as a man of the church, he knows more about the Bible and the Gospel than he knows about therapies. But it's not so difficult to understand something about psychiatry as well. He would never consider talking to a traditional psychiatrist. They only dole out drugs or dawdle over psychoanalysis for years. Or they 'decondition' relapsing alcoholics by attaching electrodes to their heels and jolting them with shocks, in the old behaviourist manner. Well, he doesn't think that does any good. There's no time to waste. He hasn't come here to persuade his friend Enzo to revert to being a classical formal psychiatrist. It's fine with him if he continues to be the militant 'anti-psychiatrist' that he's always been... He's not trying to convert him (has he ever?) but he knows that only his psychiatrist friend, so unconventional and so committed to his work, can do something. But first he must put aside his natural conceit as a chief consultant. He must abandon the certainty that he knows everything about psychiatry, even where and when it fails to work. When psychiatry fails to work, where it can go no further, then a friar has something to say.

Father Damiano begins to tell Enzo about his experiences at the hospital and in the reception centre at his monastery. He has numerous contacts with families in the area, he runs a youth club, he is aware of what is happening (Enzo knows this very well, he knows that Father Damiano is an excellent observer). And what does he see? What is he talking about? He's talking about alcohol, alcohol everywhere. By now he can spot it a mile off.

> Behind so much misery there's always alcohol. In the medical wards of this hospital, one patient in every two is there because of alcohol abuse. But nobody seems to see the problem. It's normal, they say, it's just wine, everyone drinks a bit. It does you good, though of course you shouldn't overdo it. The doctors think just the same. Everyone is soaked in alcohol, even those who don't drink. Everyone treats it as entirely natural.

There are situations of suffering in local families behind the peaceful façades of their homes that he can't even begin to describe. Wives confide in him about their husbands and their drinking, husbands about their wives, misery concealed beneath affluence. People destroying themselves without knowing why, destroying their loved ones and not knowing why. It's the chronic alcoholics, outcasts without families, who come into the community, but you should look behind the normality of the normal family. And if you do, you'll see immediately...

If I can make a suggestion, says Father Damiano to Enzo, his mental health service – the best organized in the country, with all those community facilities – are too closely centred on... psychiatry. At a certain point, a psychiatric service which is too 'psychiatric', if you see what I mean, which devotes itself entirely to patients with official disorders, loses sight of reality. What lies outside goes one way, and the service goes in the other, under its own impetus. It worries about certain patients only because they have been given a label, and it passes by the others who are suffering just as much without even seeing them. In my view, the budget is lopsided: too much therapeutic investment in mental illness after it has already appeared. Not too much in absolute terms, says Father Damiano, seeing that the doctor is about to say that the resources available are anything but ample, but too much relatively to the absence of investment in fighting the alcohol that often produces the mental illness, or aggravates it, or which is any case an enormous problem in itself, which produces degradation, misery and an early death, even if these are not strictly the province of psychiatry.

As to whether anything technically appropriate can be done, why can't we just drop the technical baggage? Why can't we try something else? Because, at bottom, it's inconceivable that nothing can be done. Father Damiano doesn't know what, but that's no reason for not finding out. So psychotherapy doesn't work? Okay, let's invent something else. That is what our intelligence is for, and also a good dose of common sense. Without exaggerating the common sense, though. We must beware of being ridiculous without realizing it. We must be careful not behave like certain doctors in the medical department (he often watches them at work with alcoholics). When they discharge a drinker patient, after they've dried him out and treated his liver, they wag their fingers and admonish: 'I'm warning you, if you carry on like this, the next time we won't even admit you, so don't bother coming'. No, not like that, like a nanny with small children, not with holier-than-thou common sense. The usual hasty moralizing just to say something and then forget about it, bring on the next patient. Not like this, but there must be something that works.

At bottom – he is asking as a layman, or better as a sensible person who refuses to accept that reality is nonsensical – what exactly is meant by *helping* an alcoholic?

Helping an alcoholic means getting him to change the way he makes sense of things. For a drinker the meaning of things lies only in alcohol, so if you change that meaning you can gradually pull him round. I don't want to make a religious sermon. Of course, for me faith is the most profound meaning of life, and a mature spirituality may well be therapeutic (Bullis, 1996). Here I'm talking about any sort of 'meaning' that is acceptable, whatever hope or project or desire that is human and positive.

> This is a therapy, if we can call it a therapy, which reappropriates the human. It means humanizing everyday life, restoring value to the person, dignity to his or her family. It means making the person want to live better, more meaningfully and more fully. It means being 'on the side of man', as Fromm put it.

Damiano is a bit confused, he knows this, and he apologizes for it. He also knows that what he is saying may strike a technician (even an anti-technician, anti-psychiatrist, or whatever, like Enzo) as nonsense. It may sound 'priestly', but he *is* a priest after all. And it is as a priest that he wants to pose a challenge for the doctor: is it possible that there are no techniques in harmony with the human? If he was asking for ultra-sophisticated techniques, like transplanting parts of the brain, the sort of things that they do in high-tech clinics, then the feeling of impotence would be understandable. But in reality he is asking for something very simple: to do something that enables alcoholics to engage with their sense of life. Is it possible that nothing of this kind is contemplated by the psychiatry handbooks?

No, Enzo thinks, struck by Damiano's speech, the psychiatry handbooks have nothing to say on the matter. But the anti-psychiatry ones do. And how! Anti-psychiatry consists of the concepts just expressed by Damiano, no more and no less, though perhaps couched in less passionate terms (but Father Damiano has always been passionate, he knows him well).

Yet the chief consultant has his own personality, and his pride. That he of all people should be given lessons in anti-psychiatry! He who as a student was among the first in Italy to experiment with deinstitutionalization practices, who has corresponded with Basaglia, who even now as a member of the medical establishment had a critical view of the welfare institutions. He who sees more clearly than anyone else, and rejects, the function of social control and maintenance of the *status quo* performed by official psychiatry (and how many discussions has he had with Damiano on the matter: the friar has always been irked by 'systemic' reasoning because he places the person at the centre of everything. 'Watch out,' he says, 'by seeing only society, or the classes, you'll lapse into a paradox, because in treating the sick you support the system that produces them, and so you don't do your job, and if you don't treat them you're not doing it either'). But he's willing to accept lessons from Father Damiano, who is an instinctive anti-psychiatrist, a religious non-conformist. But he is annoyed by being wrong-footed by reality. If alcoholism can be treated by anti-psychiatry while he is an anti-psychiatrist through and through, well things do not add up. It is difficult for a chief consultant in anything to admit ignorance, but Enzo tells his friend Damiano frankly: *we don't know how to cure alcoholics.*

> Fine – says Damiano – now listen to me. Take your diary, choose one day next week – but not Thursday or Friday because I've got church business to attend to – and come with me. We're going to Trieste.

Enzo knows full well what this mention of Trieste is all about. They've already talked about it, but Enzo refused to listen. He didn't want to waste time.

I might end up with a phoney guru and I've got better things to do. I've heard positive things said about it, but it may just be a suggestion technique. I know about these things. Setting up a serious therapeutic method is a complex business. Someone comes in from outside, preaches, whips up enthusiasm, some suggestible dupe stops drinking, and it seems that the method works miracles. These things are fine for the suckers, but you won't catch me falling for them.

It was thus that Dr D. defended himself last week when Father Damiano talked to him about Vladimir Hudolin, whom he had heard about from one of the guests at his residential facility. 'Who on earth is he?', he had asked. 'Is he a psychiatrist? A colleague? And even if he were both of these, there are lots of my psychiatrist colleagues who I wouldn't trust with one of my patients.'

4.4.1. *The starting point: a dual relation... in action*

Enzo is saying the same things now as he drives to Trieste with Father Damiano sitting beside him. Damiano smiles while his doctor friend 'threatens' him that, if they are on a wild goose chase, if he discovers that the method that they are going to see is a fraud, as he thinks it is, he'll exact heavy revenge: for the next two years Father Damiano will have to open the doors of his community facility to Enzo's patients, without arguing about it as he does now ('There's no beds, we offer free accommodation. Don't the public services have their own facilities?'). Damiano objects good-naturedly that apart from the arguments – because only a few places are available – his community has always welcomed Enzo's patients. And in any case, even if it does turn out to be a wild goose chase, a trip to Trieste is always enjoyable.

Moreover, when he telephoned the Centre hosting Hudolin's week-long training course to ask if he and Enzo could watch him at work and talk to him, he had gained a good impression. He spoke to the director of the Trieste School of Social Work (Nelida Rosolen), who was the first to contact Hudolin in Zagreb and persuade him to come to Italy, first to give a course in social psychiatry at the School and then to teach his method of treating alcoholism – for years used successfully throughout Croatia – to social workers in Italy.

For a start, Father Damiano is patiently explaining, we're going to a good school for social workers. It has a creative director, well-organized training courses, a well-tried method, a celebrated lecturer, an expert in social psychiatry (which isn't anti-psychiatry but comes close to it). In short, it doesn't look like the quackery or suggestion technique that one might think ('As I did,' he admits) at first sight.

It is now eight o'clock in the evening on the same day. After saying goodbye to Hudolin and the director, Padre Damiano and Doctor D. are driving home along the motorway.

> Tomorrow – Enzo says excitedly – I shall telephone some of my doctor friends, like Fabio, Mauro and Marco, whom you know as well, young general practitioners who want to go into alternative medicine. They've already helped me with my psychiatric patients. I hope I can convince them of the enormous possibilities in the local community for non-conventional alcoholism prevention and therapy. I shall also call some doctors at the hospital – there's Roberto P. in medicine, for example, who's a good doctor. Perhaps he too is getting tired of lecturing alcoholics. Then I'll talk to our social workers, of course, as well as the trainee in our department, who can't wait to do something practical.

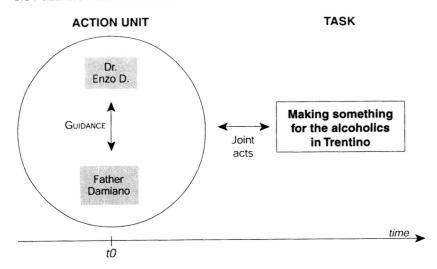

Fig. 4.5 The coping relationship at the beginning of the networking process (To).

Father Damiano listens without speaking. From time to time he murmurs agreement or nods his head, but the doctor has got the bit between his teeth and cannot be stopped. Damiano knows that the doctor's monologue is a good sign. He knows him very well: he needs to throw himself into things, be swept away by enthusiasm. If he believes in something, then he will do it. He may have to work twenty hours a day, but he will do it.

Today, Father Damiano thinks to himself, Enzo has experienced some sort of epiphany. What was he saying a moment ago? That there are enormous possibilities for the prevention and treatment of alcoholism. That's what he said: 'enormous'. Until yesterday he didn't even see these possibilities, now he says they're enormous. Jolly good!

This morning, when we walked into the room where the seminar was being held, we saw the chairs arranged in a semi-circle and Professor Hudolin listening to the discussion and occasionally intervening. I watched him the entire time. He was sitting slightly apart from the group, observing it carefully. There were doctors, psychologists, social workers, and mixed in with them, alcoholics and members of their families. When one of the professionals produced some hackneyed cliché about alcohol (alas! it happened) or some dogmatic opinion (the most frequent being that alcoholism is the symptom of an underlying psychiatric pathology), Hodulin would put questions to the alcoholics or their family members. Their ingenuous answers revealed the weakness of the experts' reasoning, like the little boy in the story who shouted out loud that the king had no clothes on. Every so often, also Hudolin spoke in his ironic way. He took the experts' premises and drew absurd conclusions from them, making everyone laugh.

It had been a 'therapeutic community' session based on principles developed by Maxwell Jones (Hudolin explained to Enzo afterwards), a social psychiatry technique that Enzo had never seen conducted so well. As a cruel way to break down the entrenched attitudes that prevent practitioners from seeing what is staring them in the face, the technique attacks the absurd sense of superiority and detachment that makes practitioners seem arrogant or inept (when perhaps they are not), as unable to separate themselves from their role which they come to confuse with their own identities. Service specialists are fixated on the idea that they are the saviours of alcoholics, who only have to trust them and wait for them to get round to curing them. It was above all this idea that Hudolin assailed, and at the beginning the experts failed to understand why he did so with such vehemence. You could see from their faces that they were asking themselves: 'What's all this? If we're practitioners, then we're therapists'.

As they continue along the motorway, Enzo keeps up his monologue. He is now explaining to Damiano all the projects that he has in mind. But the good friar is not listening. He is still thinking about the events of the day, and especially about how Enzo was so struck by Hudolin's conduct of the therapeutic community and his group of ex-alcoholics. A masterly lesson for the professionals. Astonishing. At the end of the session, Enzo went up to Hudolin and introduced himself, asking him to explain aspects of his method. Hudolin's reply (as far as Damiano could tell from a distance) was to ask Enzo to be patient until the afternoon, when a round table would present the anti-alcohol programmes set up in Friuli, after which he would explain how things were organized in Zagreb. And then another course is scheduled in three weeks' time: what Hudolin called a 'week of sensitization to alcohol-related problems'. If Enzo could attend, he would find out much more.

But it was in the afternoon that Enzo became entirely convinced that Hudolin's 'bio-psycho-social approach' (as it was then called) was to be taken seriously, and also that it opened up enormous possibilities. The organizers of the therapeutic programme began the round table by providing an interesting description of how the programme had begun and of its current development in Friuli. Hudolin then talked about self-help groups, self-managed by alcoholics and their family members under the supervision of a social worker or someone with a minimum of specific training (Hudolin called these groups 'clubs for alcoholics in treatment'). As Enzo listened, it suddenly dawned on him: *It can be done!* He was enthused by the explanation of the self-help method, which Hudolin correctly attributed to Alcoholics Anonymous, and which he had heard talk about, but always in somewhat condescending terms, as if it were something midway between the esoteric and the homespun.

Hudolin instead talked about self-help as if it were one of the greatest scientific advances of the twentieth century. He talked about Bill and Bob – the two alcoholic friends who first discovered the power of self-help and founded AA – as if they were geniuses. 'Even I, a humble friar who doesn't understand very much,' says Damiano to himself as Enzo continues to talk, 'was impressed by the method. And I was also impressed by Hudolin's variation on the Alcoholics Anonymous approach: that of including an expert practitioner in the group. This is vaguely what I had in mind: a solidarity broader than the merely technical care provided by the social services but which also includes it. Something, though, that I couldn't quite pin down.'

What exactly it was that struck the doctor so forcefully Damiano does not know. Probably some technical aspect of social psychiatry and community work. But struck he certainly was. He was bowled over, it seems. Enzo repeated over and over again: 'It can be done, why don't we do something similar?'. To which Damiano naturally replied that they had gone to Trieste for precisely that purpose.

The doctor starts speaking again. He takes his foot off the accelerator as he repeats the question. 'Will you be coming as well?' Damiano is distracted and does not understand the question. 'I'm talking,' says Enzo, 'about the Sensitization Week. Are you going to come?'.

Damiano squirms in his seat and says that they shouldn't exaggerate. Each of them has his part to play. And his part has been to prod Enzo into action. His mission is now complete. He has planted a seed. Now that seed must grow on its own. He will check every so often to see that it is still alive and healthy. He came to Trieste in order to spur a reluctant Enzo into action. He did not know how it would turn out, but, fortunately, it has turned out well. Enzo is a convert and he has a thousand projects in mind. Now he, Damiano, is probably superfluous. Instead of him Enzo should take one of his practitioner friends to the course, because he will have to rely on them from now on. And as well as the doctors, he should take Flavia, the woman that he had mentioned to Hudolin during the afternoon coffee break to see if he could include her on his treatment programme in Trieste (they had eventually decided on Udine, because the preliminary stage of the therapy was due to begin there next Monday). Flavia could be an excellent helper in the future. If Enzo agrees, he will speak to her himself.

He first met Flavia in hospital, where she had just been admitted for the third time in two months. The year before she had returned home from abroad where she had worked as a secretary in a large company for twenty-five years, and where she had become a heavy drinker. Apart from the alcohol abuse, she is a clever woman. Yesterday, for example, he had talked to her in hospital – she'd been there for ten days – and she was completely detoxified. She seemed twenty years younger than when she had been admitted. She was perfectly in command of herself and aware of her situation, except that she knows that as soon as she leaves hospital she won't be able to resist: she'll hit the bars and start drinking again. And in three days' time she'll be back in hospital. The doctors will give her the usual lecture, but it won't make any difference. She's alone at home, there's a sister who lives nearby but she is always out at work during the day, so that Flavia is left unsupervised. In the evening, when the sister comes home, she finds Flavia drunk and doesn't know what to do, and frankly she's fed up with the situation. That is why Damiano took advantage of the presence of the organizers of the Friuli programme at the round table to arrange, in Hudolin's presence, Flavia's immediate admission to the therapy. If she agrees to follow the programme in a month's time she be ready and willing to help, to apply her intelligence and sensitivity to something. Perhaps she won't be able to attend the sensitization week but she could at least make herself useful.

You can't fence Damiano in, thinks Enzo, I should have known. He's the sort of person who gets to the heart of the matter, who digs deeply and discovers things both large and small. He takes an interest in real people, in particular situations. Sometimes he spends entire days or even weeks until he has done what he feels he must do. But he never stops in one place, he gets things started and then moves on to another situation. He has always been a freewheeler as well as a freethinker.

By now it is late at night and Damiano and Enzo still have another thirty kilometres to travel. As soon as they leave the motorway they will have to drive up the hill to the Franciscan monastery. While Damiano remains silent (he is probably sleeping), Enzo reflects. He thinks about theory. Not that he likes theory very much, and he especially dislikes gobbledegook, the pompous jargon of the text books which only serves to conceal vacuity... things that, with his innate pragmatism, he can spot immediately and close the book after just a few pages. But when he sees genuine connections between reality and abstract theory, he likes to explore those principles, and then to use his imagination to understand them even better. For some time he has heard talk of relational theories, of the fundamental idea that social helping is a 'relation'. He looks over at Father Damiano (who is now definitely asleep) and sees that principle personified. The two of them at midnight in the car – they left just after five o'clock this morning

– constitute exactly the relation that the theory talks about. Their relation has produced a new reality which could also produce a further one. If other relations are grafted on to it, then, who knows, it might be an 'intervention' which truly helps alcoholics.

What does 'relation' mean? It means that if it had not been for Damiano, he, Enzo, would never have made a move. He is, or he should be, a planner and he needs someone to shake him into doing something out of the ordinary or a little risky. But conversely if it hadn't been for himself, then perhaps Damiano would never have swung into action. Damiano is an animator, he needs arms and legs to accomplish what he wants. He has an uncanny ability to sense when the time is ripe to do things, he can almost smell it. Although he does not yet know exactly what, he senses that something must be done, that it is unacceptable to hold back and do nothing. But he needs someone to see it with him and then carry things forward.

Damiano, he thinks, had intuitively sensed that what we were going to see in Trieste was worthwhile. And he was right. I instead – thinks Enzo – came to the rational conclusion that Hudolin's model is technically sound and innovative. I understood that all the pieces were in place, that Hudolin was not a humbug or something worse.

> If I'd gone on my own (although I never would have done), I would now have only my rational, technical certainty. If Damiano had gone on his own (although he never would have done), he would now have only his intuitive, emotional certainty. But together we now have complete certainty. Damiano is sure also by virtue of my technical judgement, and I am sure by virtue of his intuition.

With the friar sleeping beside me, I feel more determined, thinks Enzo. His sensations are now also to some extent my own. I feel that any investment of energy is justified, that the risk of screwing up or wasting our time is minimal. If they have got started in Friuli, then we can get started as well. Though Damiano will withdraw to a certain extent from now onwards – but Enzo is certain that he will be on hand if necessary – he will feel him always close by, spurring him on in his work.[1]

When Enzo sets about organizing things tomorrow morning (first of all by telephoning his doctor friends to tell them what he has seen, and to hear what they think about it), he is certain that he is going to feel that he has assimilated

---

[1] Which will be to act as the *guide* of the community movement that he intends to create.

a small part of the Franciscan friar. It makes him smile, but it is true. And when tomorrow Damiano contacts Flavia and her sister to tell them that Flavia can immediately begin treatment, in Udine, he's going to feel himself in small part a psychiatrist. The friar may not smile, he certainly will not take it as a compliment, but that's the way it is: the rule obviously applies to him as well.

4.4.1.2. Setting up the coping network and the birth of the first Club for Alcoholics in Treatment (CAT)

Three weeks later a meeting is in progress at Enzo's house. It is after dinner on a Friday. Present at the meeting are the three practitioners who have just returned from the sensitization course in Friuli, namely Enzo, a nurse in his department, Carla, and Dr. Fabio D., a local doctor or GP. Then there are two further doctors (Luigi D. and Flavio B.), as well as the community social worker (Angela L.) and a voluntary worker, Lino P., who is a natural helper linked with the local authority social services. None of the latter has attended the sensitization week because all the places were taken. There were applications from all over Italy and only the first three of those present at the meeting were able to participate (however, all of them have already booked for the next course scheduled for the following month, or for another to be held later in a nearby town).

Flavia is also there, accompanied by her sister. She successfully completed the preliminary short therapy stage at a hospital in Friuli. She came home two days ago, extremely motivated, and ready to begin the rehabilitation programme immediately. Father Damiano is absent, however, being taken up with his duties at the monastery.

After greeting those present, Enzo says that they have a problem as regards Flavia. The problem is that there is no Club for Alcoholics in Treatment in the town.[2] So Flavia cannot continue her treatment unless she moves to Udine. Would that make sense? Probably not, for two reasons. Firstly because the treatment must be carried forward in the community together with her family: Hudolin insisted on this during the course, and also in Enzo's view it is the core of the treatment. Secondly because it was decided at the previous meeting[3] that something was to be done here, in our area. 'So we might as well start now,' says Enzo, 'seeing that Flavia needs help immediately. What we have to decide now is how organize things, and it's not going to be easy.'

---

[2] The self-help group for alcoholics and their family members is the 'pivot' of the programme.
[3] The reference is to a meeting held at Enzo's house just before the sensitization training week.

Dr. Fabio C. now speaks to give his impressions of the course and of the therapeutic programme in general. He points out that all he knows about alcoholism is what he has learnt from the course, apart from the obvious fact that he sees a lot of alcoholics in his surgery. He is not an expert in sophisticated theories and therapies, he says, nor in specialized clinical methods. But what he has gathered from listening to Hudolin, and which strikes him as revolutionary, is that he, too, as a general practitioner who knows absolutely nothing about treating alcoholism, can nevertheless *do something.*[4] In his professional experience he has seen the process operate largely the other way round: stopping someone from doing something. 'Do you have the right specialization? Are you qualified? No? Well, stop whatever you're doing!'. The logic of corporations and professional orders – though sensible when applied to *technical* matters – is to keep out trespassers. But the strange thing is that, with such complex and serious problems, the standard reaction is to stop anyone from doing anything.

To Fabio it seems that Hudolin's approach works in reverse. Precisely because problems are complex and serious but are not technical, because in practice nobody can understand everything and resolve everything, then it's much better for everyone to take action, specialists and non-specialists alike. And in accordance with this principle (and not superficially as might seem at first sight), he and his colleagues, after a week's course and no more, are now deemed 'able to act'.

But the fact that he has obtained the training certificate only means that he is ready to start, to learn what to do together with the families, to put his intelligence to work together with that of others. It certainly does not mean that he has some sort of patent on superiority or infallibility.

It would be absurd to think that a week's attendance on a course gives you an official seal of infallibity. But a week of specific preparation so that one can begin to learn – and knowing that what one has learnt is already of great help – is more than realistic. And it is also a clear invitation and a message of encouragement for those like himself who feel inadequate but have decided to do something.

'Fine,' jokes Enzo, 'now we have the first candidate to run the first Club in our area.' Fabio has called himself 'uncertain but determined'.

> Uncertainty and determination are the necessary ingredients of a good practitioner, Hudolin had pointed out in his wry manner. If you're only uncertain, you don't know what to do. If you're only determined, even less do you know what to do.

---

4 This is the principle of empowerment.

ACTION UNIT   **TASK**

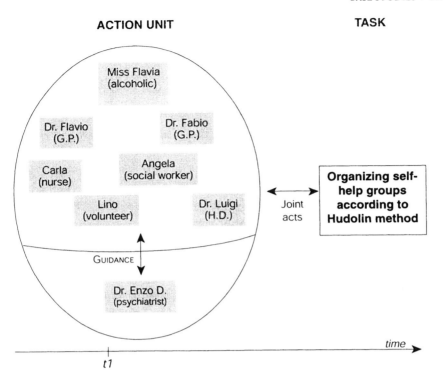

Fig. 4.6 The coping network at the time t1.

'Fabio is therefore on board. He could run the Club', Enzo says. 'The other person could be Carla, the nurse, and the third person could be myself. To run a Club you must have attended the training course, so for the moment the list consists only of us three. Bearing in mind that you've asked me to coordinate the local programmes, I'd prefer to step aside. Except that I'll obviously always be available to help out if need be. So that leaves Fabio and Carla.'

Carla says that in her opinion there is no real problem because at the moment there are only practitioners. They still haven't got the alcoholics. But it will be very different when there are large numbers of alcoholics wanting to join the Clubs, but only a few practitioners. So, whether it is herself or Fabio makes no difference at the moment, apart from the fact – she doesn't know if this is possible but it would not be so strange – that perhaps both of them could be in the group, at least for the start-up phase. 'The real problem,' she says, 'is that apart from Flavia here, who needs a Club right away, they will have to contact the other families. And then, what are we going to do about the fact that we haven't got a dispensary. Would it be possible to introduce families directly into the Club without their first passing through the community clinical service, and therefore without adequate preliminary 'instruction'? If not, then we must obviously first set up the dispensary, prepare a group of families properly, and then begin with the first Club. But if this is to be the procedure, then we won't be able to deal with Flavia's urgent problem.'

Flavia says that she has talked about the problem with Father Damiano and she believes that he has already spoken to Enzo (who nods). Father Damiano mentioned the problem when he contacted the organizers of the Friuli programme, and then spoke to Hudolin, and they indicated that a Club could start immediately with people who had not been previously prepared. This was a departure from the normal procedure, but Hudolin agreed to it, Flavia assures them, because he thought it would be an experiment to see whether the programme could work in a different way. A community clinical service should be opened at the same time, however, so that the families can receive in parallel that part of the preparatory programme which they have missed. The two things would have to be organized simultaneously, otherwise she would be forced to look for a Club somewhere in Friuli. The would not be a major problem for her, she says, because when she was in Friuli she had met some families who would be willing to let her stay with them. Consequently, there is no need to be hasty and do things badly. If it is possible, fine, if not then it doesn't matter.

'There are two problems, therefore,' says Enzo to sum up. 'The first is immediately contacting a certain number of families for the Club, which will be run by Fabio and Carla. The second is setting up the clinical service as soon as possible. Let's take the problems one at a time.'

The discussion has now continued for more than an hour, more or less in the same tones and with the same intensity, and with the participation of everyone. A summary follows for the sake of brevity.

All those present have agreed that it will not be difficult to put together a group of families willing to create the first Club in the area (five or six families would suffice to begin with). Each of them – the GPs, the hospital staff, the social worker, the voluntary worker, Flavia, as well as Father Damiano who, although absent, would certainly agree – knows people with alcohol problems and their family members. The misfortune that the area has so many alcoholics is in this case a boon. Each of them has promised to contact two or three families and to explain what the scheme involves. They must agree on who will contact whom so as not to cause confusion. The aim is to create this first nucleus as soon as possible, within a week. The first official session of the Club should take place next Friday.

As far as the clinical service is concerned, the problems have not been so straightforward, and long discussion has been necessary. In the end, it has been decided that Enzo and Dr. Roberto P. will talk to the chief medical consultant at the hospital to see if there are any beds available, and also ask him to authorize Roberto to do some work on alcoholism – not full time, obviously, but for some hours a day. Enzo and Roberto have a good relationship with the consultant and they think that he will agree. The beds are needed for alcoholics contacted externally to the hospital who require medical treatment and detoxification therapy before joining the programme. Also needed, again in the hospital, is a small room where the lessons and meetings with the families can be held. Enzo and Roberto will enquire about the availability of this room.

But, it was asked, who will run the clinical service, and how? The three people who have attended the sensitization training week – the general practitioner Fabio C., the social worker Angela D., and the consultant Dr. D. – should obviously be in the front line. During the course they had numerous lessons on the complex nature (bio-psycho-social) of alcohol-related disorders (as Hudolin calls alcoholism). They have brought photocopies and notes home with them (Angela's are the most useful because of her good handwriting) which will be of service in preparing lessons. They will meet tomorrow and again the day after tomorrow to draw up the programme together with others who want to lend a hand as 'teachers' (all the doctors present have volunteered). Dr. Enzo D. has insisted that the information provided must not be restricted to the medical aspects of alcoholism (cirrhosis, etc.) but should also cover social aspects, especially issues to do with family dynamics. This topic will evidently be covered by the social worker, although she has pointed out that she is no expert on the subject. Everyone has emphasised that everything must be kept simple and accessible, even though this will be the most difficult part, Angela the social worker has also suggested that she might ask one of her colleagues, Alessandra C., who is a talented artist, to help her prepare a set of OHP transparencies to illustrate the concepts taught during the lessons. [5]

The clinical service will not only organize information sessions on alcohol and the self-help programme. It will also set up opportunities for group dynamics during the sessions. The lessons will be supported by encounter groups designed to enhance the motivation of the alcoholics and their families, and to accustom members of the Clubs to their distinctive mutual style. Obviously, seeing that the Club will start simultaneously with the clinical service, or even before, its main function will be to work on motivation, which is a dynamic process requiring a certain amount of specialist skill. None of the doctors present

---

[5] This idea worked so well that it led to publication of an excellent guidebook.

nor the social worker feel themselves able to tackle the task. After some discussion, it has been decided that these sessions will by run by Enzo and by Dario P., who although professionally extraneous to the social services (he is, as said, a clerical worker) has long experience of voluntary work. Most importantly, he has attended several training courses on the Rogersian approach and he has run numerous growth groups. However, the two official conductors of the therapeutic communities will always be supported by Flavia, who has offered her experience of rehabilitation to the group.[6] The two Club operators (Fabio C., the doctor, and Angela D., the social worker) will also participate, as well as anyone else who may interested, so that they can receive training with a view to future schemes.

4.4.1.3. Formalizing a superordinate 'umbrella' framework: the birth of the Association of CATs

The account resumes three months after the meeting described above. Another meeting is now in progress, this time a more formal one: the first session of the board of the Association of CATs in the area.

What has happened in the meantime? As to be expected, the first Club unproblematically started up with ten families, including Flavia's. The group immediately 'meshed', driven by enthusiasm over being the first scheme of its kind in the area, and by the presence of a number of families which had unexpectedly acted as its catalysts – and also obviously through the efforts of the two operators, who immediately attuned themselves to the group and managed the first and most crucial stage well, despite their lack of experience.

At the end of the second meeting a young journalist from a local newspaper was present, having been informed about the scheme by a telephone call from Enzo. The article that subsequently appeared, with interviews and enthusiastic comments by the families, aroused great interest. Requests for treatment multiplied, also thanks to the information disseminated by each of the group's members among parents and acquaintances.

The Club grew to eighteen members. The rules of the programme, however, stipulate that a group cannot consist of more than twelve families, and this provision was reiterated by Hudolin when he made a brief supervisory visit a month ago. It was difficult to persuade the group to split, however, given that – as its members said – 'they got on so well together, it would be a pity to break up'. During a meeting at which Enzo insisted that the group had to be split, the two operators were finally convinced. They accordingly returned to the Club,

---

6 An offer which subsequently proved very useful.

and also because they had the excellent idea of not calling it a 'split' but a 'multiplication' (because there would be two groups), the group finally agreed to be divided. Of course, the two operators who had worked so well together had to say goodbye and go their separate ways.

But this was not the last of it. Shortly afterwards these two groups, too, had reached the twelve-member limit and the problem of 'multiplication' arose once again, accompanied by the problem of a lack of operators. For a while the new groups were supervised by Enzo and Dario (who was already involved in similar activities at the clinic) until two other operators (the doctor Roberto P. and the social worker Alessandra C.) could attend a sensitization course – scheduled in a few weeks time – and then take over. But enquiries were also arriving from neighbouring towns, both from families wanting to start the programme and from operators offering their services. In short, the scheme was perhaps growing too rapidly.

Advised by Hudolin, with whom he was in constant contact, doctor Enzo D. worked feverishly, with the close support of Flavia who – besides her own work in the Club as an alcoholic in treatment – attended to an enormous amount of organizational matters. Numerous meetings were held with operators and families, and in the end it seemed natural to create an Association to coordinate and promote the local Clubs. The Statute of the *Associazione Provinciale dei Club degli Alcolisti in Trattamento* (APCAT), as it is called, provides for a representative body strictly divided between professionals and family members. Hudolin insisted on this point, and in doing so aroused a certain amount of perplexity, given that everybody thought it obviously more appropriate that the professionals should occupy the most important role. One of the Association's main tasks was to handle relations with the local authorities, given that the initiative was now of evident public interest.

The Board now meeting consists of the founder-members of the Association. Flavia has just been unanimously elected President, and overcome by emotion she finds it difficult to talk coherently. Basically, this is a meeting just like any other, but Flavia feels the weight of her official position: she wants to do well, she wants things to function smoothly, she wants to live up to the expectations placed in her. She glances for help at Dr. D., who has just been elected Vice-President, but he is impassive as he waits for Flavia to present two problems that must be dealt with urgently.

'The first problem,' says Flavia, 'is that there are not enough operators for the Clubs now about to start up. There are lots of operators available, but the difficulty is that they cannot attend sensitization courses outside the province. The places are always limited, and only by lobbying Hudolin and the organizers can we get someone accepted. We should decide to organize a Course here, restricting the places to practitioners from the area who've said they want to join the programme. But setting up a week-long training course needs money, suitable premises and a great deal of organizational work.'

'The second problem is providing support and further training for operators once they have joined the programme and started working with the families. By now we've acquired substantial experience, and we know that the operators find it difficult to run the Clubs. Just as the alcoholics have the Clubs to help them with their difficulties, so the operators should be given support. I know that Dr. D. has already made inquiries: for example, he's heard from Hudolin that the local School of Social Service has suggested that it could organize a course, and he says he's willing to help. Dr. D. has already contacted a number of trainers as well. But he can tell you better than I can.'

4.4.1.4. Ten years later: a glance back

Ten years later, Enzo and Father Damiano are talking in the simple monastery cell that is the friar's home. Enzo has dropped in to say goodbye to Damiano, who has been transferred to another institution. Inevitably, they have begun reminiscing about the things that they have done together, and therefore also about the anti-alcohol programme. In ten years their initiative, which started almost by accident, has developed enormously (Enzo was right at the time to use the adjective 'enormous').

'Just yesterday,' says Enzo, 'I contacted the Centre for Studies on Alcohol-Related Problems (the Association founded jointly with the School of Social Work some years ago). I asked for the most recent figures, because I find it hard to keep up. They told me that there are now 161 CATs in the province. If you do some calculations, bearing in mind that the average Club consists of ten families (with three members each), and that new families join Clubs all the time (while others leave), then more than five thousand people affected by alcohol-related problems have been involved. Not all of them have been 'cured', obviously, but all of them have taken some sort of action: they've got involved, they've played a part in the therapy, they've talked, learned, given witness. Everyone has changed a little, so has the local community. The network that we set up has made it possible for all these people to act sensibly for their own good, while previously they were trapped in themselves and their problems.'

Father Damiano smiles and thinks that Enzo has changed a great deal in ten years. He is no longer imprisoned by the idea that his service is the centre of everything. Yet he sometimes talks as though he still thinks that it is. 'The network that we set up. You still express yourself like a chief consultant,' says

Damiano to his friend. 'Do you really think that *we* created the network?'. Enzo laughs and smacks his forehead because he realizes that he has given the friar a formidable opportunity to preach. But now it is too late.

> I personally did very little – says Father Damiano – but not even you created the community network, however much you may have done as a guide. The network created itself. Certainly, without your efforts a crucial component would have been missing, but your work wouldn't have been possible without the help of so many other people. Not only did your actions (ours, if you like) galvanize the actions of others, but at the same time their actions constantly galvanized ours.

The chief consultant, Enzo D., cheerfully admits that Father Damiano is right.

References

Adams, R. (1996a) *Social Work and Empowerment.* London: Macmillan.

Adams, R. (1996b) *The Personal Social Services.* London: Longman.

Aldwin, C. M. (1994) *Stress, Coping and Development.* New York: Guilford.

Alinsky, S. (1971) *Rules for Radicals.* New York: Vintage Books.

Amodeo, M. (1995) 'The Therapist's Role in the Drinking Stage.' In S. Brown (ed) (quoted).

Avolio, B. J. and Kahai, S. (1998) 'Inspiring Group Creativity.' *Small Group Research, 29,* 1.

Bamford, T. (1990) *The Future of Social Work.* Basingstoke: Macmillan.

Bandura, A. (1997) *Self-efficacy: The Exercise of Control.* New York, W. H. Freeman and Co.

Banks, S. (1995) *Ethics and Values in Social Work.* London: Macmillan.

Banks, S. (1999) 'The Social Professions and Social Policy: Proactive or Reactive?' *European Journal of Social Work, 2,* 3, 327-339.

Barber, J. B. (1991) *Beyond Casework.* London: Macmillan.

Barlett, W., Propper, C., Wilson, D. and Le Grand, J. (1994) (eds), *Quasi-Markets and Community Care.* Bristol: School for Advanced Urban Studies.

Barnes, M. (1996) *Care, Communities and Citizens.* London: Longman.

Barret-Lennard, G. T. (1998) *Carl Rogers' Helping System.* London: Sage.

Bartlett, H. M. (1970) *The Common Bases of Social Work Practice.* New York: NASW.

Bateman, N. (2000) *Advocacy Skills for Health and Social Care Professionals.* London: Jessica Kingsley.

Bauman, Z. (2000) 'Am I My Brother's Keeper.' *European Journal of Social Work, 3,* 5-11.

Berger, P. and Lukmann, P. (1966) *The Social Construction of Reality.* New York: Doubleday and Co.

Bernstein, G. S. and Halaszyn, J. A. (1999) *Human Services? That Must be so Rewarding.* Baltimore: Paul H. Brookes.

Bertens, H. (1996) *The idea of postmodern.* London: Routledge.

Biegel, D., Shore, B. and Gordon, E. (1984) *Building support networks for the elderly.* Beverly Hills: Sage.

Blum, P. (1998) *Surviving and Succeding in Difficult Classrooms.* London: Routledge.

Boudon, R. (1977) *Effets Pervers et Ordre Social.* Raymond Boudon: Presses universitaires de France.

Boudon, R. (1984) *La place du dèsordre. Critique des theories du changement social.* Paris: Presses Universitaire de France.

Bowdeer, P. (1997) *Caring.* London: Routledge.

Brammer, L. M. (1993) *The Helping Relationship. Process and Skill.* Boston: Allyn & Bacon.

Brooks, V. and Sikes, P. (1997) *The Good Mentor Guide.* Buckingham: Open University Press.

Brown, H. and Smith, H. (1992) (eds) *Normalisation. A Reader for the Nineties.* London: Routledge.

Brown, J. (1997) 'Can Social Work Empower?' In R. Hugman and D. Smith (quoted).

Brown, K. M., Kenny, S. and Turner, B. S. (2000) *Rhetorics of Welfare. Uncertainty, Choice and Voluntary Associations.* London: Macmillan.

Brown, S. (1995) (ed) *Treating Alcholism.* San Francisco: Jossey-Bass.

Brugha, T. S. (1996) (ed) *Social Support and Psychiatric Disorders.* Cambridge: Cambridge University Press.

Budman, S. H. and Gurman, A. S. (1988) *Theory and Practice of Brief Therapy.* New York: Guilford.

Bullis, R. (1996) *Spirituality in Social Work Practice.* New York: Taylor and Francis.

Bulmer, M. (1987) *The Social Basis of Community Care.* London: Allen and Unwin.

Butrym, Z. T. (1976) *The Nature of Social Work.* London: Macmillan.

Carkhuff, R. (1987) *The Art of Helping (6°).* Amherst, Human Resource Development Press.

Carr, E. G. et al. (1994) *Communication-Based Intervention for Problem Behaviour.* Baltimore: Paul H. Brookes.

Carrier, J. and Tomlison, D. (1996) (eds) *Asylum in the Community.* London: Routledge.

Casement, P. (1989) *On Learning from the Patient.* London: Routledge.

Ceruti, M. (1995) *Evoluzione senza fondamenti.* Bari: Laterza.

Challis, D. and Davies, B. (1986) *Case Management in Community Care.* Aldershot: Gower.

Chaskin, R. J., Joseph, M. L. and Chipenda-Dansokho, S. (1997) 'Implementing Comprehensive Community Development: Possibilities and Limitations.' *Social Work, 42,* 5.

Cherniss, C. (1980) *Staff Burnout: Job Stress in the Human Services.* Beverly Hills: California, Sage.

Clark, C. L. (1991) *Theory and Practice in Voluntary Social Action.* Aldershot: Gower Publ.

Clarke, J. (1993) (eds) *A Crisis in Care: Challenges to Social Work.* London: Sage.

Coady, N. F. (1993) 'An Argument for Generalist Social Work Practice with Families Versus Family Systems Therapy.' *Canadian Social Work Review, 10,* 1.

Collins, A. H. and Pancoast, D. L. (1976) *Natural Helping Networks.* Washington: NASW.

Corcoran, K. and Vandiver, V. (1996) *Maneuvering the Maze of Managed Care.* New York: Free Press.

Cordié, A. (1993) *Les cancres n'existent pas. Psychanalses d'enfants en échec scolaire.* Paris: Editions du Seuil.

Cotterel, J. (1996) *Social Networks: Influences in Adolescence.* London: Routledge.

Craig Clemments, M. (1997) *Getting Beyond Sobriety: Clinical Approaches to Long Term Recovery.* San Francisco: Jossey-Bass.

Craig, G. and Mayo, M. (1995) (eds) *Community Empowerment. A Reader in Participation and Development.* London: Zed Books.

Dahrendorf, R. (1988) *The Modern Social Conflict. An Essay on the Politics of Liberty.* New York: Weidenfeld & Nicolson.

Dalenberg, C. J. (2000) *Countertransference and the Treatment of the Trauma.* Washington: APA/American Psychological Association.

Dalley, G. (1996) *Ideologies of Caring.* London: Macmillan.

Davies, B. and Challis, D. (1986) *Matching Resources to Needs in Community Care.* Aldershot: Gower.

Davies, B. (1992) *Care Management: Equity and Efficiency.* Canterbury: University of Kent.

Davies, R. L. (1997) *Stress in Social Work.* London: Jessica Kingsley.

Davis, A., Ellis, K. and Rummery, K. (1997) *Access to Assessment: Disabled People's Experiences of Assessment for Community Care Services.* York: Policy Press.

Deng Ming-Dao (1996) *Everyday Tao: Living with Balance and Harmony.* San Francisco, California: Harper San Francisco.

Department of Health (1989) *Caring for People. Community Care in the Next Decade and Beyond.* London: HMSO.

Doel, M. and Sawdon, C. (1999) *The Essential Groupworker. Teaching and Learning Creative Grupwork.* London: Jessica Kingsley.

Dominelli, L. (1996) 'Deprofessionalising Social Work.' *British Journal of Social Work, 26,* 153-175.

Dominelli, L. (1997) *Sociology for Social Work.* London: Macmillan.

Dominelli, L. (1999) 'Neo Liberism, Social Exclusion and Welfare Clients in a Global Economy.' *International Journal of Social Welfare, 8,* 14-22.

Dominelli, L. (1998) 'The Changing Face of Social Work: Globalisation, Privatisation and the Technocratization of Social Work.' In B. Lesnik (eds) (quoted).

Donati, P. (1991) *Teoria relazionale della società.* Milano: Angeli.

Donati, P. and Folgheraiter, F. (1999) (eds) *Gli operatori sociali nel welfare mix.* Trento: Erickson.

Edelmann, R. J. (1993) *Interpersonal Conflicts at Work.* London, BPS Books.

Egan, G. (1990) *The Skilled Helper.* Monterey: Paul H. Brookes.

Elias, N. (1985) *Humana conditio: Beobachtung zur Entwicklung der Menschheit am 40. Jahrestag eines Kriegsendes.* Frankfurt am Main: Suhrkamp.

Elliot, J. (1991) 'A Model of Professionalism and its Implications for Teacher Education.' *British Educational Research Journal, 17,* 4.

Esping Andersen, G. (1996) *Welfare States in Transition.* London: Sage.

Eysenck, J. and Rachman, S. (1965) *The Causes and Cures of Neurosis: An Introduction to Modern Behaviour Therapy Based on Learning Theory and the Principles of Conditioning.* San Diego, California: R. R. Knapp.

Fallon, I. (1988) *Comprehensive Management of Mental Disorders.* Buckingham: Buckingham Mental Health Service.

Farber, B. A., Brink, D. C. and Raskin, P. M. (1996) (eds) *The Psychotherapy of Carl Rogers.* New York: Guilford.

Farris Kurtz, L. (1997) *Self-help and Support Groups: A Handbook for Practitioners.* London: Sage.

Feltham, L. (1997) *Time Limited Counselling.* London: Sage.

Fine, S. F. and Glasser, P. H. (1996) *The First Helping Interview: Engaging the Client and Building Trust.* London: Sage.

Folgheraiter, F. (1992) *Interventi di rete e comunità locali.* Trento: Erickson.

Folgheraiter, F. (1994) *Operatori sociali e lavoro di rete.* Trento: Erickson.

Folgheraiter, F. (1998) *Teoria e metodologia del servizio sociale. La prospettiva di rete.* Milano: Angeli.

Forder, J., Knapp, M. and Wistow, G. (1999) 'The Care Markets in England: Economical Evaluation.' In P. Donati and F. Folgheraiter (eds) (quoted).

Foxx, R. (1982) *Increasing Behaviors of Severely Retarded and Autistic Persons.* Illinois: Research Press.

Freedman, M. (1993) *The Kindness of Strangers. Adult Mentors, Urban Youth and the New Voluntarism.* San Francisco: Jossey-Bass.

Fried, M. and Cook, L. (1996) *Interactions: Collaborative Skills for School Professionals.* New York: Longman.

Froland, C. et al. (1981) *Helping Networks and Human Services.* Beverly Hills: Sage

Fromm, E. (1947) *Man for Himself, and Inquiry into the Psychology of Ethics.* New York: Rinehart.

Garrison, J. E. and Howe, J. (1976) 'Community Intervention with the Elderly: A Social Network Approach.' *Journal of American Geriatrics Society, 24.*

Gartner, R. and Riessmann, F. (1984) *The Self-help Revolution.* New York: Human Sciences Press.

Genevay, B. and Katz, R. S. (1990) (eds) *Countertransference with Older Clients.* Newbury: Sage.

Germain, C. B. and Gitterman, A. (1996) *The Life Model of Social Work Practice. Advances in Theory and Practice.* New York: Columbia University Press.

Gersuny, C. and Rosengren, W. R. (1973) *The Service Society.* Cambridge: Schenkman.

Giddens, A. (1990) *The Consequences of Modernity.* Stanford: California, Stanford University Press.

Giddens, A. (1991) *Modernity and self-identity.* Cambridge: Polity.

Goffman, E. (1967) *Interaction Ritual: Essays in Face-to-Face Behavior.* Chicago: Aldine Publ. Co.

Goldfarb, L. A., Brotherson, M. J., Summers, J. A. and Turnbull, A. P. (1986) *Meeting the Challenge of Disability or Cronic Illness: A Family Guide.* Baltimore: Paul H. Brookes.

Gouldner, A. W. (1970) *The Coming Crisis of Western Sociology.* New York: Basic Books.

Gubrium, J. F. (1991) *The Mosaic of Care: Frail Elderly and their Families in the Real World.* New York: Springer.

Haley, J. (1996) *Learning and Teaching Therapy.* New York: Guilford.

Hall, D. and Hall, P. (1996) *Practical Social Research.* London: Macmillan.

Hilgard, E. R. and Bower, G. H. (1975) *Theories of Learning.* Englewood Cliffs: Prentice Hall.

Hirshman, A. O. (1991) *The Rhetoric of Reaction, Perversity, Futility, Jeopardy.* Cambridge: Belknap Press.

Hobbs, T. (1992) (ed) *Experential Training.* Buden: Routledge.

Holmila, M. (1997) (ed) *Community Prevention of Alcohol Problems.* London: Macmillan.

Hott, L. A. (1995) *People in Crisis. Understanding and Helping.* San Francisco: Jossey-Bass.

Hough, M. (1996) *Counseling Skills.* London: Longman.

Hoyt, M. F. (1995) *Brief Therapy and Managed Care.* San Francisco: Jossey-Bass.

Hugman, R. and Smith, D. (1997) (eds) *Ethical Issues in Social Work.* London: Routledge.

Hurrelmann, K. et al. (1987) (eds) *Social Intervention: Potential and Constraint.* Berlin: de Gruyter.

Hurvitz, N. (1971) 'Similarities and Differences Between Conventional and Peer Self-Help Psychotherapy Groups.' In P. S. Rowan and H. M. Trice (quoted).

Husserl, E. (1959) *Die Krisis der europaischen Wissenschaften und die tranzendentale Phanomenologie.* L'Aja: Martinus Nijhoff's Boekhandel en Uitgeversmaatschappij.

ICF (2001) *International Classification of Functioning, Disability and Health.* WHO, Geneva.

Ignatieff, M. (1984) *The Needs of Strangers.* London: Chatto & Windus.

Illich, I. (1982) *Medical Nemesis: The Expropriation of Health.* New York: Pantheon Books.

Illich, I. (1977) *The Disabling Professions.* London: Marion Boyars.

Jackson, L. and Veeneman Panyan, M. (2002) *Positive Behavioral Support in the Classroom.* Baltimore: Paul H. Brookes.

Johnson, N. et al. (1998) 'Regulating for Quality in the Voluntary Sector.' *Journal of Social Policy, 3,* 307-328.

Jonas, H. (1974) *Philosophical Essays: From Ancient Creed to Technlogical Man.* Englewood Cliffs, N.J.: Prentice Hall.

Jonas, H. (1979) *Das Prinzip Verantwortung.* Frankfurt am Main: Insel Erlang.

Jones, K. (1988) *Experience in Mental Health: Community Care and Social Policy.* London: Sage.

Jones, M. (2000) 'Hope and Despair at the Front Line: Observations on Integrity and Change in the Human Services.' *International Social Work, 3,* 365-380.

Kahn, R. L. and Cannel, C. F. (1957) *The Dynamics of Interviewing: Theory, Technique, and Cases.* New York: Wiley.

Kahney, H. (1993) *Problem Solving: Current Issues.* Philadelphia: Open University Press.

Kapp, M. B. (1994) *Patient Self-determination in Long Term Care.* New York: Springer.

Kelly, G. A. (1955) *The Psychology of Personal Constructs.* New York: Norton.

Kerson, T. and Kerson, L. (1985) *Understanding Chronic Illness.* New York: Free Press.

Kierke, C. D. (1995) 'Teenage Peer Networks in the Community as Source of Social Problems: A Sociological Perspective.' In T. S. Brugha (ed) (quoted).

Kierkegaard, S. (1989) *Sickness into Death.* Harmondsworth: Penguin.

König, K. (1997) *Self-analysis for Analysts.* London: Jessica Kingsley.

Kramer, M. W., Kuo, C. L. and Dailey, J. (1997) 'The Impact of Brainstorming Techniques on Subsequent Groups Processes.' *Small Group Research, 28,* 2.

Krasner, B. and Joyce, A. (1995) *Truth and Trust in the Therapeutic Process.* Bristol: Brunner & Mazel.

Krishnamurti, J. (1981) *The Wholeness of Life.* San Francisco: Harper & Row.

Lalande, A. (1926) *Vocabulaire technique et critique de la philosophie.* Paris: Presses Universitarie de France.

Lehrer, P. M. and Woolfolk, R. L. (1993) *Principles and Practice of Stress Management.* New York: Guilford.

Lenoble, R. (1957) *Les origines de la pensée scientifique moderne.* Paris: Librairie Gallimard.

Lesnik, B. (1998) (eds) *Change in Social Work.* Arena: Aldershot.

Lewis, J. and Glennerster, H. (1996) *Implementing the New Community Care.* Buckingham: Open University Press.

Lewis, J. and Meredith, B. (1988) *Daughters who Care.* London: Routledge.

Litwak, E. (1985) *Helping the Elderly: The Complementary Roles of Informal Networks and Formal Systems.* New York: Guilford.

Lowman, R. L. and Resnick, R. J. (1994) (eds) *The Mental Health Professional's Guide to Managed Care.* Washington: APA/American Psychological Association.

Lyotard, J. F. (1979) *La condizion postmoderne.* Paris: Les Editions de Minuit.

McManus, M. (1995) *Troublesome Behaviour in the Classroom.* London: Routledge.

Maguire, L. (1983) *Understanding Social Networks.* New York: Sage.

Malin, N. (1995) (ed) *Services for People with Learning Disabilities.* London: Routledge.

Maluccio, A. (1979) *Learning from Clients: Interpersonal Helping as Viewed by Clients and Social Workers.* New York: The Free Press.

Mandelstam, M. and Schwehr, B. (1995) *Community Care Practice and The Law.* London: Jessica Kingsley.

Mann, T. (1993) *Die vertauschten Köpfe: eine indische Legende.* Frankfurt am Main: S. Fischer.

Maroda, K. J. (1991) *The Power of Countertransference.* New York: Wiley.

Marsland, D. (1996) *Welfare or Welfare State: Contradictions and Dilemmas in Social Policy.* London: Macmillan.

Maslach, C. and Leiter, M. P. (1997) *The Truth About Burnout: How Organisations Cause Personal Stress and What to Do About It.* San Francisco: Jossey-Bass.

Maturana, H. and Varela, F. (1983) *A Árvore do conhecimento as bases biólogicas da compreensão humana.* Palas: Athena.

McCombs, B. and Pope, J. (1994) *Motivating Hard to Reach Students.* Washington: APA/American Psychological Association.

McCrady, B. and Miller, W. (1993) (eds) *Research on Alcoholics Anonymous.* New York: Rutgers Centre of Alcohol Studies.

McDermott, F. (1975) (ed) *Self-Determination in Social Work.* London, Routledge.

McManus, M. (1995) *Troublesome Behavior in The Classroom: Meeting Individual Needs.* London: Routledge.

McNamee, S. and Gergen, K. (1992) *Therapy as Social Construction.* London: Sage.

Meichenbaum D. (1985) *Stress Inoculation Training.* Oxford: Pergamon.

Miller, W. and Rollnick, S. (1991) *Motivational Interviewing.* New York: Guilford.

Morin, E. (1986) *La méthode.* Paris: Editions du Seuil.

Morrison, J. D., Howard, J., Johnson, C., Navarro, F. J., Plachetka, B. and Bell, T. (1997) 'Strengthening neighborhood by developing community networks.' *Social Work, 42,* 5.

Moxley, D. P. (1989) *The Practice of Case Management.* Newbury Park: Sage.

Mucchielli, R. (1983) *L'entretien de face to face dans la relation d'aide.* Paris: Editions ESF.

Neill, J. R. and Krisken D. P. (1989) *From Psyche to System.* New York: Guilford.

Neimeyer, G. (1993) *Constructivist Assessment.* London: Sage.

Netting, F. E., Kettner, P. M. and McMurtry, S. L. (1998) *Social Work Macro Practice.* New York: Longman.

Nitsun, M. (1996) *The Anti-Group: Destructive Forces in the Group and Their Creative Potential.* London: Routledge.

O'Hagan, K. (1987) *Crisis Intervention in Social Services.* London: Macmillan.

Orme, J. and Glastonbury, B. (1993) *Care Management.* London: Macmillan.

Parsloe, P. (1996) *Pathways to Empowerment.* Birmingham: Venture Press.

Parton, N. (1996) *Social Theory, Social Change and Social Work.* London: Routledge.

Parton, N. and O'Byrne, P. (2000) *Constructive Social Work: Toward a New Practice.* London: Macmillan.

Payne, M. (1993) *Linkages: Effective Networking in Social Care.* London: Whiting and Birch.

Payne, M. (1995a) *Social Work and Community Care.* London: Macmillan.

Payne, M. (1995b) 'The end of British Social Work.' *Professional Social Work,* 5.

Payne, M. (1997) *Modern Social Work Theory.* London: Macmillan.

Payne, M. (1999) Case Management and Social Work: Evaluation of British Experience. In P. Donati and F. Folgheraiter (eds), *Gli operatori sociali nel welfare mix,* Trento (Italy), Erickson.

Payne, M. (2000) *Teamwork in Multiprofessional Care.* London: Macmillan.

Perlman, H. H. (1957) *Social Casework. A Problem Solving Process.* Chicago: University Press.

Pierce, G. R., Sarason, B. R. and Sarason I. G. (1996) (eds) *Handbook of Social Support and the Family.* New York: Plenum Press.

Piercy, F. P., Sprenkle, D. H. and Wethler, J. L. (1996) *Family Therapy Sourcebook.* New York: Guilford.

Popper, K. R. (1972) *Objective Knowledge: An Evolutionary Approach.* Oxford: Clarendon Press.

Popper, K. R. (1994) 'Knowledge and the Body-Mind Problem: In Defence of Interaction.' In M.A. Notturno (ed), London, New York, Routledge.

Prior, L. (1993) *The Social Organization of Mental Illness.* London: Sage.

Quinn, J. (1993) *Successful Case Management in Long Term Care.* New York: Springer.

Reder, P. and Lucey, C. (1995) (eds) *Assessment of Parenting: Psychiatric and Psychological Contributions.* London: Routledge.

Riessman, F. and Carroll, D. (1995) *Redefining Self-help: Policy and Practice.* San Francisco: Jossey-Bass.

Rikards, T. (1974) *Problem Solving Through Creative Analysis.* Epping: Gower Press.

Roberts, A.R. (1995) (ed) *Crisis Intervention and Time-Limited Treatment.* London: Sage.

Rogers, C. and Kinget, M. (1969) *Psychotérapie et relations humaines: théorie et pratique de la thérapie nonédirective.* Louvain, Publications universitaires, Paris: B. Nauwelaerts.

Rose, S. M. (1992) *Case Management and Social Work Practice.* London: Wiley.

Rowan, P. S. and Trice, H. M. (1974) *The Sociology of Psychotherapy.* New York: Armanson.

Roy, M. C., Gauvin, S. and Limayern, W. (1996) 'Electronic Group Brainstorming.' *Small Group Research, 27,* 2.

Rubin, I. M. and Campbell, T. J. (1998) *The ABC of Effective Feedback: A Guide for Caring Professionals.* San Francisco: Jossey-Bass.

Sacks, H. (1992) *Lectures on Conversations, Vol. 1/2,* Oxford: Blackwell.

Santroch, J. W., Minnett, A. M., Campbell, B. D. (1994) *The Authoritative Guide to Self-Help Books.* New York: Guilford.

Sharp, S. and Smith, P. K. (1994) *Tackling Bulling in your School.* London: Routledge.

Schön, D. (1991) *Educating the Reflecting Practitioner.* San Francisco: Jossey-Bass.

Schopler, E. (1995) (ed) *Parent Survival Manual. A Guide to Crisis Resolution in Autism.* New York: Plenum.

Schütz, A. (1972) *The Phenomenology of the Social World.* London: Heinemann Educational.

Seed, P. (1990) *Introducing Network Analysis in Social Work.* London: Jessica Kingsley.

Selener, D. (1997) *Participatory Action Research and Social Change.* New York: Cornell University Participatory Action Research Network.

Severino, E. (1994) *La filosofia antica.* Milano: Rizzoli.

Sharkey, S. and Barna, S. (1990) *Community Care: People Leaving Long Stay Hospitals.* London: Routledge.

Shaw Anstrad, C. S. (1996) *Is Long-Term Psychotherapy Unethical?* San Francisco: Jossey-Bass.

Sherman, S. G. (1999) *Total Customer Satisfaction: A Comprehensive Approach to Health Care Providers.* San Francisco: Jossey-Bass.

Siegal, H. A. and Rapp, R. C. (1995) *Care Management in the Treatment of Drug and Alcohol Abuse.* New York: Springer.

Simmel, G. (1908) *Soziologie, Untersuchungen uber die Formen der Vergesellschaftung.* Duncker und Humblot: Leipzing.

Silverman, P. (1980) *Mutual Help Groups.* New York: Sage.

Simpson, R. L. and Zionts, P. (1992) *Autism. Information and Resources for Parents, Families and Professionals.* Austin: Pro-Ed.

Skovolt, T. M. (1974) 'The Client as a Helper.' *Counseling Psychologist, 4,* 3.

Sluzky, C. E. and Ramson, D. C. (1976) *Double Bind: The Foundation of the Communicational Approach to the Family.* New York, Grune & Stratton, London: Academic Press.

Smart, B. (1999) *Facing modernity: ambivalence, reflexivity and morality.* London: Sage.

Smith G. (1995) 'Assessing Protectiveness in Cases of Child Sexual Abuse.' In P. Reder and C. Lucy (quoted).

Stainback, W. and Stainback, S. (1993) *Support Network for Inclusive Schooling.* Baltimore: Paul H. Brookes.

Steinberg, D. M. (1997) *The Mutual Aid Approach to Working With Groups: Helping People to Help Each Others.* Northvale: J. Aronson.

Stratton, P. and Hanks, H. (1995) 'Assessing Family Functioning in Parenting Breakdown.' In P. Reder and C. Lucey (quoted).

Talmon, M. (1990) *Single-session Therapy.* San Francisco: Jossey-Bass.

Thane, P. (1996) *Foundations of the Welfare State.* Essex: Longman.

Thomas, G. (1992) *Effective Classroom Teamwork.* London: Routledge.

Thompson, N. (1993) *Anti Discriminatory Practice.* London: Macmillan.

Thorne, B. (1992) *Carl Rogers.* London: Sage.

Topping, K. (1988) *The Peer Tutoring Handbook.* Beckenham: Croom Helm.

Tornow, W. W. and London M. (1998) *Maximizing the Value of 360-Degree Feedback.* San Francisco: Jossey-Bass.

Valacich, J. S., Dennis, A. R. and Connolly, T. (1994) 'Group Versus Individual Brainstorming.' *Organisational Behaviour and Human Decision Processes, 57.*

Vattimo, G. (1988) *The End of Modernity: Nihilism and Hermeneutics in Post-Modern Culture.* Cambridge: Polity Press.

Venkatesh, S. A. (1997) 'The Three-Tier Model: How Helping Occurs in Urban, Poor Communities.' *Social Service Review, 71,* 4.

Warr, M. (1995) *Building Social Capital: Self-help in a Twenty First Century Welfare State.* London: Institute for Public Policy.

Warren, I. D. (1981) *Helping Networks: How People Cope with Problems in the Urban Community.* Indiana: Notre Dame Press.

Watzlawick, P. (1988) *Ultra-Solution, or, how to Fail Most Succesfully.* New York: Norton.

Weil, M., Karls, J. M., et al. (1985) *Case Management in Human Service Practice.* San Francisco: Jossey-Bass.

Werger, G. C. (1994) *Understanding Support Networks and Community Care.* Aldershot: Avebury.

West, M. A. (1994) *Effective Team Work*. Leicester: BPS Books.

White, P. A. (1995) *The Understanding of Causation and Production of Action*. Exeter: Lawrence Erlbaum Associates.

Whittaker, J. K. and Gambarino, J. (1983) *Social Support Network: Informal Helping in the Human Services*. New York: Aldine.

Wilke, H. (1987) 'Observations, Diagnosis, Guidance: A System Theoretical View of Interventions.' In K. Hurrelmann et al. (eds) *Social Intervention: Potential and Constraints,* Berlin: de Gruyter.

Winegar, N. and Bistline, J. L. (1994) *Marketing Mental Health Services to Managed Care*. New York: Haworth.

Winert, F. E. and Kluwe, R. H. (1987) (eds) *Metacognition, Motivation and Understanding*. Hillsdale: Erlbaum.

Wistow, G., Knapp, M., Hardy, B. and Allen, C. (1994) *Social Care in a Mixed Economy.* Buckingham: Open University Press.

Wistow, G., Knapp, M., Hardy, B., Forder, J., Kendall, J. and Manning, R. (1996) *Social Care Markets: Progress and Prospect*. Buckingham: Open University Press.

Wolfensberger, W. (1972) *The Principle of Normalisation in Human Services.* Toronto: National Institute of Mental Retardation.

Woods, S.K. and Ploof, W.H. (1997) *Understanding ADHD: Attention Deficit Hyperactivity Disorder and the Feeling Brain*. London: Sage.

Yenney, S.L. (1994) *Business Strategies for a Caring Profession.* Washington: APA/American Psychological Association.

Subject index

Author index

Printed in the United Kingdom
by Lightning Source UK Ltd.
135581UK00001B/163-174/A

9 781843 101918